PROFESSIONAL HADOOP®

PROFESSIONAL

Hadoop®

PROFESSIONAL

Hadoop®

Benoy Antony
Konstantin Boudnik
Cheryl Adams
Branky Shao
Cazen Lee
Kai Sasaki

Professional Hadoop®

Published by
John Wiley & Sons, Inc.
10475 Crosspoint Boulevard
Indianapolis, IN 46256
www.wiley.com

Published simultaneously in Canada

ISBN: 978-1-119-26717-1
ISBN: 978-1-119-26718-8 (ebk)
ISBN: 978-1-119-26720-1 (ebk)

Manufactured in the United States of America

10 9 8 7 6 5 4 3 2 1

Library of Congress Control Number: 2016934264

ABOUT THE AUTHORS

BENOY ANTONY is an Apache Hadoop committer and has contributed features related to security and HDFS. He is the founder of DataApps (http://dataApps.io), a company that specializes in creating applications for big data. He maintains a Hadoop Security wiki at http://HadoopSecurity.org. Benoy is a Hadoop architect at eBay where he focuses on enhancing security and availability on eBay's Hadoop clusters without limiting user productivity. He regularly speaks at conferences like Hadoop Summit.

DR. KONSTANTIN BOUDNIK, co-founder and CEO of Memcore.io, is one of the early developers of Hadoop and a co-author of Apache Bigtop, the open source framework and the community around creation of software stacks for data processing projects. With more than 20 years of experience in software development, big- and fast-data analytic, Git, distributed systems and more, Dr. Boudnik has authored 15 US patents in distributed computing. Dr. Boudnik contributed to a dozen of open source projects in the area of distributed computing and data processing. He has helped and championed a number of successful Apache projects in the area.

CHERYL ADAMS is a senior cloud data and infrastructure architect. Her work includes supporting healthcare data for large government contracts; deploying production-based changes through scripting, monitoring, and troubleshooting; and monitoring environments using the latest tools for databases, web servers, web API, and storage.

BRANKY SHAO is a software engineer at eBay where he is building real time applications with Elasticsearch, Cassandra, Kafka, and Storm. He has been working with the Hadoop ecosystem technologies since 2010. He has extensive experience designing and implementing various software including distributed systems, data integration, framework/APIs, and web applications. He is passionate about open source and is a contributor to the Cascading project.

CAZEN LEE is a software architect at Samsung SDS. He is currently in charge of the Hadoop module for Samsung's big data platform. Prior to joining Samsung, Cazen served as a developer and architect for the integrated data warehouse layer in the financial industry, including work with Samsung Life Insurance and Korea Securities Finance Corp. He is also interested in both machine learning and neural network models.

KAI SASAKI is a Japanese software engineer who is interested in distributed computing and machine learning. Currently he is working at Treasure Data Inc., launched by Japanese entrepreneurs based in Silicon Valley. Although the beginning of his career didn't start with Hadoop or Spark, his interest in middleware and the fundamental technologies that support a lot of these types of big data services and the Internet drove him toward this field. He has been a Spark contributor, developing mainly MLlib and ML libraries. Nowadays, he is trying to research the great potential of combining deep learning and big data. He believes that Spark can play a significant role even in artificial intelligence within the big data era. You can find him on GitHub at https://github.com/Lewuathe.

ABOUT THE TECHNICAL EDITORS

SNEHAL NAGMOTE is a staff software engineer for the search infrastructure team at Walmart Labs. Some of his responsibilities include building data platform applications using the big data stack, and using tools such as Hadoop, Hive, Kafka, Flume, and Spark. Currently, he is focusing on building a near real time indexing data pipeline using Spark Streaming and Kafka.

RENAN PINZON is a software architect at NeoGrid and has been working with Hadoop there for more than three years. He has a lot of experience with mission-critical software and data processing/analysis. He started using Hadoop for real-time processing (HBase + HDFS) and then started to use it in data analysis with RHadoop, Pig, Crunch, and is now moving to Spark. He also has been working with search engines using Apache Solr for real-time indexing and search as well as using Elasticsearch outside of Hadoop. Despite his professional experience being more in software development, he has a strong background in infrastructure, mainly in regard to Hadoop where he has been working tuning applications.

MICHAEL CUTLER has deep experience with the Hadoop ecosystem since building one of the UK's earliest Hadoop Clusters for BSkyB in 2008 after successfully pitching CXO management for innovation funding to explore the tools and techniques, which have now become known as big data. He has real world experience in training predictive models from huge multi-terabyte datasets across diverse business use cases as: automated fraud detection, fault prediction and classification, recommendations, click-stream analysis, large scale business simulations and modeling. Michael was an invited speaker on machine learning at Hadoop World in New York. He is well connected in the open source ecosystem and is a regular speaker at data science and big data events in London.

CREDITS

PROJECT EDITOR
Charlotte Kughen

TECHNICAL EDITORS
Snehal Nagmote
Renan Pinzon
Michael Cutler

PRODUCTION EDITOR
Barath Kumar Rajasekaran

COPY EDITOR
Troy Mott

MANAGER OF CONTENT DEVELOPMENT & ASSEMBLY
Mary Beth Wakefield

PRODUCTION MANAGER
Kathleen Wisor

MARKETING MANAGER
David Mayhew

PROFESSIONAL TECHNOLOGY & STRATEGY DIRECTOR
Barry Pruett

BUSINESS MANAGER
Amy Knies

EXECUTIVE EDITOR
Jim Minatel

PROJECT COORDINATOR, COVER
Brent Savage

PROOFREADER
Nancy Bell

INDEXER
Nancy Guenther

COVER DESIGNER
Wiley

COVER IMAGE
silvrock/Shutterstock

ACKNOWLEDGMENTS

Special thanks to the massive contributions to the Hadoop project by all the volunteers who spent their time to move the Apache Bigtop project forward, helping it to become a true integration hub of the 100% open source Apache data processing stack!

A special thanks also to the volunteers who spent their time to move the Apache Ignite project forward and helping it to become a real core of open source in-memory computing.

And a special thanks goes to Gridgain for their donation of the production grade software to the Apache Software Foundation. It was both a challenge and an honor to transform this project into the Apache TLP.

CONTENTS

INTRODUCTION

Hadoop is an open source project available under the Apache License 2.0. It has the ability to manage and store very large data sets across a distributed cluster of servers. One of the most beneficial features is its fault tolerance, which enables big data applications to continue to operate properly in the event of a failure. Another benefit of using Hadoop is its scalability. This programming logic has the potential to expand from a single server to numerous servers, each with the ability to have local computation and storage options.

WHO IS THIS BOOK FOR?

This book is for anyone using Hadoop to perform a job that is data related, or if you have an interest in redefining how you can obtain meaningful information about any of your data stores. This includes big data solution architects, Linux system and big data engineers, big data platform engineers, Java programmers, and database administrators.

If you have an interest in learning more about Hadoop and how to extract specific elements for further analysis or review, then this book is for you.

WHAT YOU NEED TO USE THIS BOOK

You should have development experience and understand the basics of Hadoop, and should now be interested in employing it in real-world settings.

The source code for the samples is available for download at `www.wrox.com/go/professionalhadoop` or `https://github.com/backstopmedia/hadoopbook`.

HOW THIS BOOK IS STRUCTURED

This book was written in eight chapters as follows:

Chapter 1: Hadoop Introduction

Chapter 2: Storage

Chapter 3: Computation

Chapter 4: User Experience

Chapter 5: Integration with Other Systems

Chapter 6: Hadoop Security

Chapter 7: Ecosystem at Large: Hadoop Stack with Apache Bigtop

Chapter 8: In-Memory Computing in Hadoop Stack

CONVENTIONS

To help you get the most from the text and keep track of what's happening, we've used a number of conventions throughout the book.

As for styles in the text:

- We *highlight* new terms and important words when we introduce them.
- We show code within the text like so: `persistence.properties`.
- We show all code snippets in the book using this style:

```
FileSystem fs = FileSystem.get(URI.create(uri), conf);
InputStream in = null;
try {
```

- We show URLs in text like this:

```
http://<Slave Hostname>:50075
```

SOURCE CODE

As you work through the examples in this book, you may choose either to type in all the code manually, or to use the source code files that accompany the book. All the source code used in this book is available for download at `www.wrox.com`. Specifically for this book, the code download is on the Download Code tab at:

`www.wrox.com/go/professionalhadoop`

You can also search for the book at `www.wrox.com` by ISBN (the ISBN for this book is 9781119267171) to find the code. And a complete list of code downloads for all current Wrox books is available at `www.wrox.com/dynamic/books/download.aspx`.

> **NOTE** *Because many books have similar titles, you may find it easiest to search by ISBN; this book's ISBN is 978-1-119-26717-1.*

Once you download the code, just decompress it with your favorite compression tool. Alternately, you can go to the main Wrox code download page at `www.wrox.com/dynamic/books/download.aspx` to see the code available for this book and all other Wrox books.

ERRATA

We make every effort to ensure that there are no errors in the text or in the code. However, no one is perfect, and mistakes do occur. If you find an error in one of our books, like a spelling mistake or faulty piece of code, we would be very grateful for your feedback. By sending in errata, you may save another reader hours of frustration, and at the same time, you will be helping us provide even higher quality information.

To find the errata page for this book, go to

`www.wrox.com/go/professionalhadoop`

and click the Errata link. On this page you can view all errata that have been submitted for this book and posted by Wrox editors.

If you don't spot "your" error on the Book Errata page, go to `www.wrox.com/contact/techsupport.shtml` and complete the form there to send us the error you have found. We'll check the information and, if appropriate, post a message to the book's errata page and fix the problem in subsequent editions of the book.

P2P.WROX.COM

For author and peer discussion, join the P2P forums at `http://p2p.wrox.com`. The forums are a web-based system for you to post messages relating to Wrox books and related technologies and interact with other readers and technology users. The forums offer a subscription feature to e-mail you topics of interest of your choosing when new posts are made to the forums. Wrox authors, editors, other industry experts, and your fellow readers are present on these forums.

At `http://p2p.wrox.com`, you will find a number of different forums that will help you, not only as you read this book, but also as you develop your own applications. To join the forums, just follow these steps:

1. Go to `http://p2p.wrox.com` and click the Register link.
2. Read the terms of use and click Agree.
3. Complete the required information to join, as well as any optional information you wish to provide, and click Submit.
4. You will receive an e-mail with information describing how to verify your account and complete the joining process.

> **NOTE** *You can read messages in the forums without joining P2P, but in order to post your own messages, you must join.*

Once you join, you can post new messages and respond to messages other users post. You can read messages at any time on the Web. If you would like to have new messages from a particular forum e-mailed to you, click the Subscribe to This Forum icon by the forum name in the forum listing.

For more information about how to use the Wrox P2P, be sure to read the P2P FAQs for answers to questions about how the forum software works, as well as many common questions specific to P2P and Wrox books. To read the FAQs, click the FAQ link on any P2P page.

1

Hadoop Introduction

WHAT'S IN THIS CHAPTER?

- The components of Hadoop
- The roles of HDFS, MapReduce, YARN, ZooKeeper, and Hive
- Hadoop's integration with other systems
- Data integration and Hadoop

Hadoop is an essential tool for managing big data. This tool fills a rising need for businesses managing large data stores, or data lakes as Hadoop refers to them. The biggest need in business, when it comes to data, is the ability to scale. Technology and business are driving organizations to gather more and more data, which increases the need to manage it efficiently. This chapter examines the Hadoop Stack, as well as all of the associated components that can be used with Hadoop.

In building the Hadoop Stack, each component plays an important role in the platform. The stack starts with the essential requirements contained in the Hadoop Common, which is a collection of common utilities and libraries that support other Hadoop modules. Like any stack, these supportive files are a necessary requirement for a successful implementation. The well-known file system, the Hadoop Distributed File System or HDFS, is at the heart of Hadoop, but it won't threaten your budget. To narrow your perspective on a set of data, you can use the programming logic contained within MapReduce, which provides massive scalability across many servers in a Hadoop cluster. For resource management, you can consider adding Hadoop YARN, the distributed operating system for your big data apps, to your stack.

ZooKeeper, another Hadoop Stack component, enables distributed processes to coordinate with each other through a shared hierarchical name space of data registers, known as znodes. Every znode is identified by a path, with path elements separated by a slash (/).

There are other systems that can integrate with Hadoop and benefit from its infrastructure. Although Hadoop is not considered a Relational Database Management System (RDBMS), it can be used along with systems like Oracle, MySQL, and SQL Server. Each of these systems has developed connector-type components that are processed using Hadoop's framework. We will review a few of these components in this chapter and illustrate how they interact with Hadoop.

Business Analytics and Big Data

Business Analytics is the study of data through statistical and operational analysis. Hadoop allows you to conduct operational analysis on its data stores. These results allow organizations and companies to make better business decisions that are beneficial to the organization.

To understand this further, let's build a big data profile. Because of the amount of data involved, the data can be distributed across storage and compute nodes, which benefits from using Hadoop. Because it is distributed and not centralized, it lacks the characteristics of an RDBMS. This allows you to use large data stores and an assortment of data types with Hadoop.

For example, let's consider a large data store like Google, Bing, or Twitter. All of these data stores can grow exponentially based on activity, such as queries and a large user base. Hadoop's components can help you process these large data stores.

A business, such as Google, can use Hadoop to manipulate, manage, and produce meaningful results from their data stores. The traditional tools commonly used for Business Analytics are not designed to work with or analyze extremely large datasets, but Hadoop is a solution that fits these business models.

The Components of Hadoop

The Hadoop Common is the foundation of Hadoop, because it contains the primary services and basic processes, such as the abstraction of the underlying operating system and its filesystem. Hadoop Common also contains the necessary Java Archive (JAR) files and scripts required to start Hadoop. The Hadoop Common package even provides source code and documentation, as well as a contribution section. You can't run Hadoop without Hadoop Common.

As with any stack, there are requirements that Apache provides for configuring the Hadoop Common. Having a general understanding as a Linux or Unix administrator is helpful in setting this up. Hadoop Common, also referred to as the Hadoop Stack, is not designed for a beginner, so the pace of your implementation rests on your experience. In fact, Apache clearly states on their site that using Hadoop is not the task you want to tackle while trying to learn how to administer a Linux environment. It is recommended that you are comfortable in this environment before attempting to install Hadoop.

The Distributed File System (HDFS)

With Hadoop Common now installed, it is time to examine the rest of the Hadoop Stack. HDFS delivers a distributed filesystem that is designed to run on basic hardware components. Most businesses find these minimal system requirements appealing. This environment can be set up in a Virtual Machine (VM) or a laptop for the initial walkthrough and advancement to server deployment. It is highly fault-tolerant and is designed to be deployed on low-cost hardware. It provides high throughput access to application data and is suitable for applications having large datasets.

Hardware failures are unavoidable in any environment. With HDFS, your data can span across thousands of servers, with each server containing an essential piece of data. This is where the fault tolerance feature comes into play. The reality is that with this many servers there is always the risk that one or more may become nonfunctional. HDFS has the ability to detect faults and quickly perform an automatic recovery.

HDFS is optimally designed for batch processing, which provides a high throughput of data access, rather than a low latency of data access. Applications that run on HDFS have large datasets. A typical file in HDFS can be hundreds of gigabytes or more in size, and so HDFS of course supports large files. It provides high aggregate data bandwidth and scales to hundreds of nodes in a single cluster.

Hadoop is a single functional distributed system that works directly with clustered machines in order to read the dataset in parallel and provide a much higher throughput. Consider Hadoop as a power house single CPU running across clustered and low cost machines. Now that we've described the tools that read the data, the next step is to process it by using MapReduce.

What Is MapReduce?

MapReduce is a programming component of Hadoop used for processing and reading large data sets. The MapReduce algorithm gives Hadoop the ability to process data in parallel. In short, MapReduce is used to compress large amounts of data into meaningful results for statistical analysis. MapReduce can do batch job processing, which is the ability to read large amounts of data numerous times during processing to produce the requested results.

For businesses and organizations with large data stores or data lakes, this is an essential component in getting your data down to a manageable size to analyze or query.

The MapReduce workflow, as shown in Figure 1-1, works like a grandfather clock with a number of gears. Each gear performs a particular task before it moves on to the next. It shows the transitional states of data as it is chunked into smaller sizes for processing.

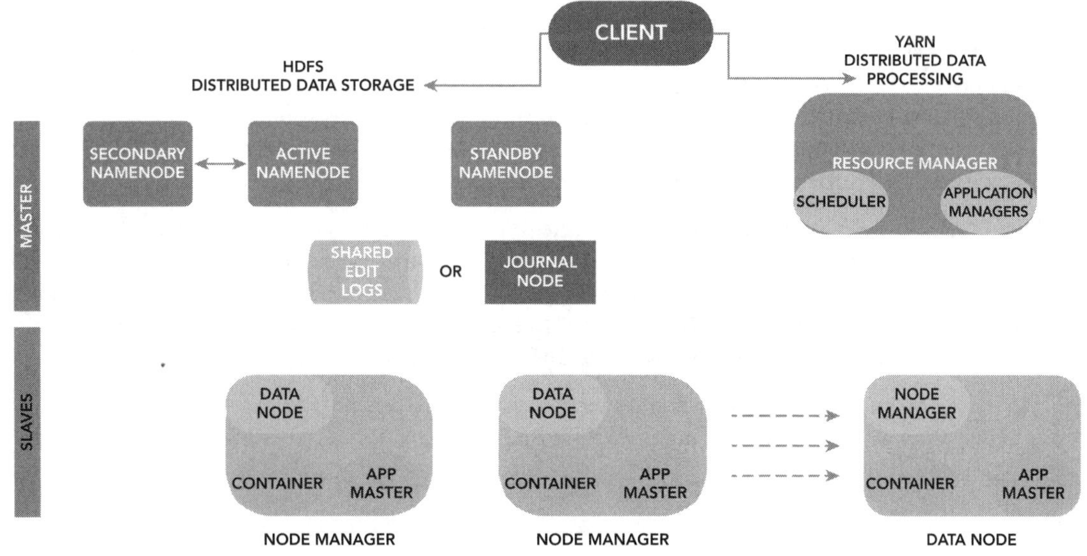

FIGURE 1-1

The capabilities of MapReduce make it one of the most used batch-processing tools. The flexibility of this processor opens the door to use its leverage against existing systems. MapReduce will allow its users to process unlimited amounts of data of any type that's stored in HDFS by dividing workloads into multiple tasks across servers that are run in parallel. MapReduce thus makes Hadoop a powerhouse tool.

With the recent developments in Hadoop, another component, called YARN, is now available that can be used to further leverage your Hadoop Ecosystem.

What Is YARN?

The YARN Infrastructure (Yet Another Resource Negotiator) is the framework responsible for providing the computational resources (memory, CPUs, etc.) needed for executing applications.

What features or characteristics are appealing about YARN? Two important ones are Resource Manager and Node Manager. Let's build the profile of YARN. First consider a two level cluster where Resource Manager is in the top tier (one per cluster). The Resource Manager is the master. It knows where the slaves are located (lower tier) and how many resources they have. It runs several services, and the most important is the Resource Scheduler, which decides how to assign the resources. The Node Manager (many per cluster) is the slave of the infrastructure. When it starts, it announces itself to the Resource Manager. The node has the ability to distribute resources to the cluster, and its resource capacity is the amount of memory and other resources. At run-time, the Resource Scheduler will decide how to use this capacity. The YARN framework in Hadoop 2 allows workloads to share cluster resources dynamically between a variety of processing frameworks, including MapReduce, Impala, and Spark. YARN currently handles memory and CPU and will coordinate additional resources like disk and network I/O in the future.

WHAT IS ZOOKEEPER?

ZooKeeper is another Hadoop service—a keeper of information in a distributed system environment. ZooKeeper's centralized management solution is used to maintain the configuration of a distributed system. Because ZooKeeper is maintaining the information, any new nodes joining will acquire the up-to-date centralized configuration from ZooKeeper as soon as they join the system. This also allows you to centrally change the state of your distributed system just by changing the centralized configuration through one of the ZooKeeper clients.

The Name service is a service that maps a name to some information associated with that name. It is similar to Active Directory being a name service that maps the user id (name) of a person to certain access or rights within an environment. In the same way, a DNS service is a name service that maps a domain name to an IP address. By using ZooKeeper in a distributed system you can keep track of which servers or services are up and running and look up their status by name.

If there is a problem with nodes going down, ZooKeeper has an automatic fail-over strategy via leader election as an off-the-shelf support solution (see Figure 1-2). Leader election is a service that can be installed on several machines for redundancy, but only one is active at any given moment. If the active service goes down for some reason, another service rises to do its work.

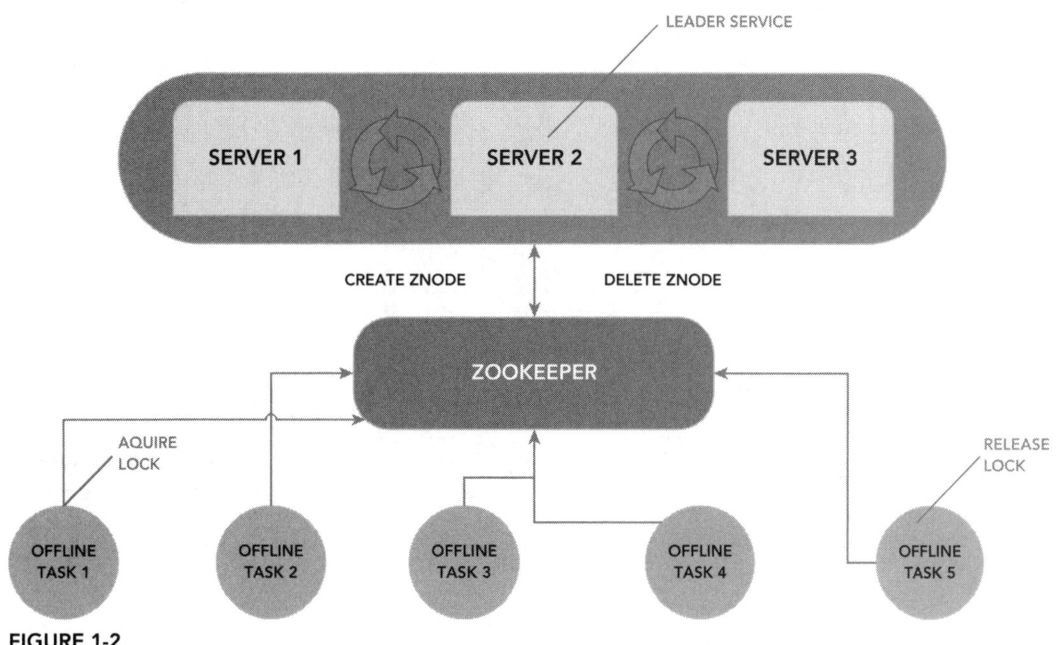

FIGURE 1-2

ZooKeeper allows you to process more data, more reliably and in less time. ZooKeeper can help you build more robust systems. A managed database cluster can benefit from centralized management services in terms of *name services*, *group services*, *leader election*, *configuration management*, and more. All of these coordination services can be managed with ZooKeeper.

WHAT IS HIVE?

Hive was originally designed to be a part of Hadoop, but now it is a standalone component. It is being mentioned briefly here, because some users find it beneficial to use it in addition to the standard Hadoop Stack.

We can briefly summarize Hive in this way: It is a data warehouse infrastructure built on top of Hadoop for providing data summarization, query, and analysis. If you are longing for the database experience and missing the structure (see Figure 1-3) of a relational environment when working with Hadoop, this might be your solution. Keep in mind this is not to be compared to a traditional database or data structure. Nor can it replace your existing RDBMS environment. Hive provides a conduit to project structure onto this data, and queries the data using a SQL-like language called HiveQL.

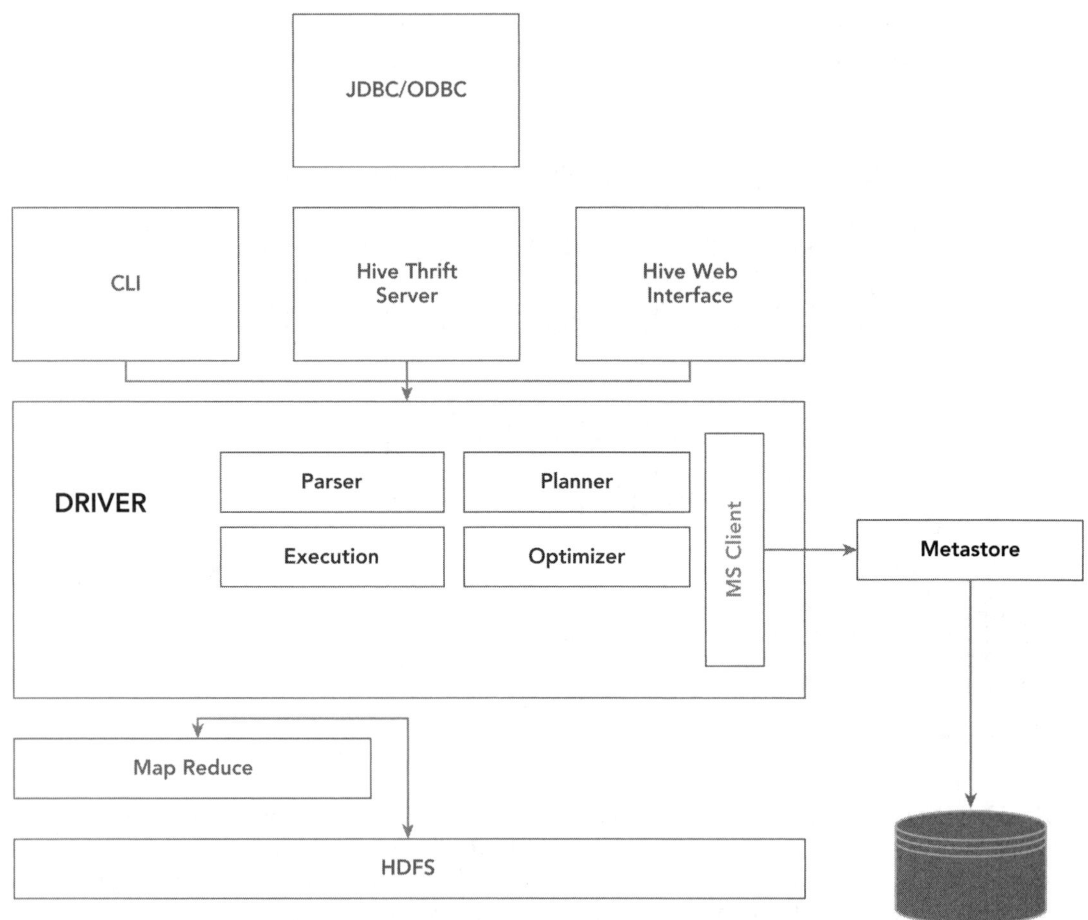

FIGURE 1-3

INTEGRATION WITH OTHER SYSTEMS

If you work in the technical field, you are well aware that integration is an essential part of any successful implementation. Generally, through some discovery process or planning session, organizations can pinpoint a need to manage big data more effectively. Subsequent steps involve making the determination as to how you will be implementing Hadoop into your existing environments.

Organizations implementing or considering Hadoop are likely introducing it into an existing environment. To gain the most benefit it is important to understand how Hadoop and your existing environment can work together, and what opportunities are available to leverage your existing environment.

To illustrate, consider a well-known building toy that allows you to create new toys based on connecting bricks together. There are endless possibilities of what you can create by simply connecting bricks together. The key component is the connector dots that exist on every brick. Similar to the toy bricks, vendors have developed connectors to allow other enterprise systems to connect to Hadoop. By using the connectors, you will be able to leverage your existing environments by bringing Hadoop into the fold.

Let's review some of the components that have been developed to integrate Hadoop with other systems. You should consider any leverage that you may gain by using these connectors within your environment. Clearly when it comes to integration, you must be your own SME (Subject Matter Expert) regarding the systems within your environment.

These connectors for Hadoop will likely be available for the latest release of the system within your environment. If the systems you would like to leverage with Hadoop are not on the latest release for your application or database engine, you need to factor in an upgrade in order to use the full features of this enhancement. To avoid disappointment, we recommend a complete review of your system requirements to avoid frustration and disappointment. The ecosystem of Hadoop brings everything together under one technical roof.

The Hadoop Ecosystem

Apache calls their integration an ecosystem. The dictionary defines an ecosystem as a community of living organisms in conjunction with the nonliving components of their environment (things like air, water, and mineral soil) interacting as a system. The technology-based ecosystem has similar attributes. It is a combination of product platforms defined by core components made by the platform owner and complemented by applications made by autonomous (machines that act independently from humans) companies in the periphery (surrounding a space).

Hadoop's open source and enterprise ecosystem continues to grow based on the wide variety of products available from Apache, and a large number of vendors providing solutions for integrating Hadoop with enterprise tools. HDFS is a primary component of the ecosystem. Because Hadoop has a low commodity cost, it is easy to explore the features of Hadoop either through a VM or setting up a hybrid ecosystem within your existing environment. It is an excellent way to review your current data methodologies with Hadoop solutions and its growing vendor pool. By leveraging these services and tools, Hadoop's ecosystem will continue to evolve and eliminate some of the road blocks associated with the analytics processing and managing of large data lakes. Hadoop integrates into the architectural layers of the data ecosystem by using some of the tools and services discussed in this chapter.

One ecosystem is the Horton Data Platform (HDP). HDP helps you get started with Hadoop by using a single-node cluster in a virtual machine, as illustrated in Figure 1-4. Because Hadoop is a commodity (little to no additional cost) solution, HDP gives you the ability to deploy to the cloud or within your own data center.

HDP gives you the data platform foundation to build your Hadoop infrastructure, including a long list of Business Intelligence (BI) and other related vendors. The platform is designed to deal with data from many sources and formats, allowing you to design your own custom solution. The list of resources is too large to define here, but it is highly recommended that you obtain this information directly from the vendor. The beauty of selecting a product like HDP is that they are one of the leading committers with Hadoop. This opens more doors for using Hadoop with multiple database resources.

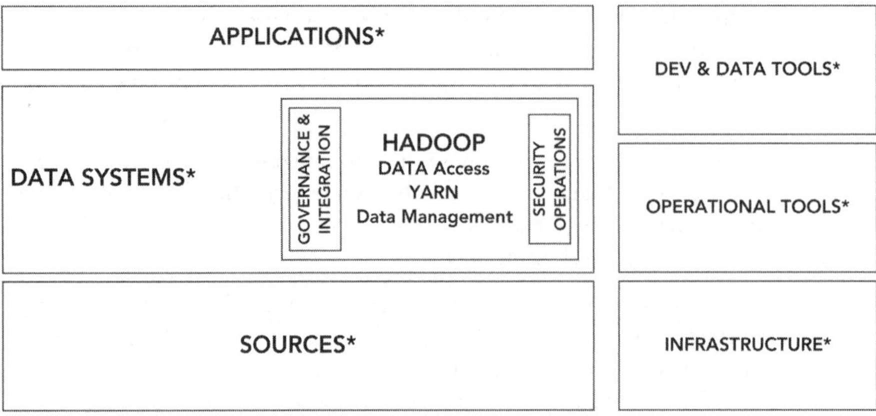

FIGURE 1-4

HDP is considered an ecosystem because it creates a community of data, bringing Hadoop and additional tools together.

Cloudera (CDH) creates a similar ecosystem for its data platform. Cloudera sets the stage with the ability to integrate structured and unstructured data. Using the platform-delivered unified services, Cloudera opens the doors to process and analyze several different data types (see Figure 1-5).

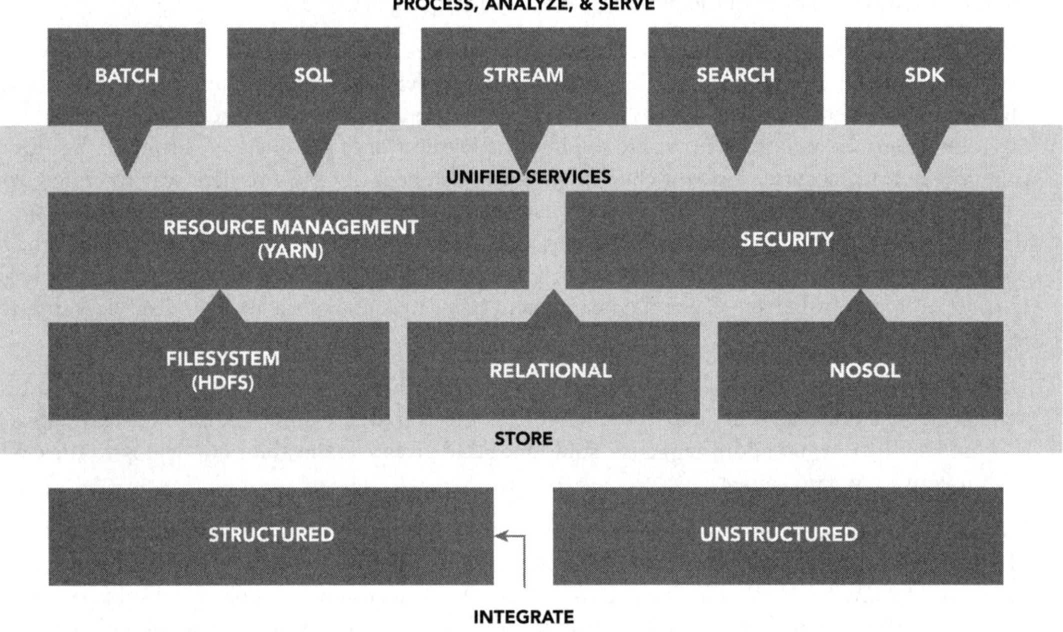

FIGURE 1-5

Data Integration and Hadoop

Data Integration is a key step in the Hadoop solution architecture. A number of vendors use open source integration tools to easily connect Apache Hadoop to hundreds of data systems without having to write code. This is a definite plus if you are not a programmer or developer by trade. Most of these vendors use a variety of open source solutions for big data integration that natively supports Apache Hadoop, including connectors for HDFS, HBase, Pig, Sqoop, and Hive (see Figure 1-6).

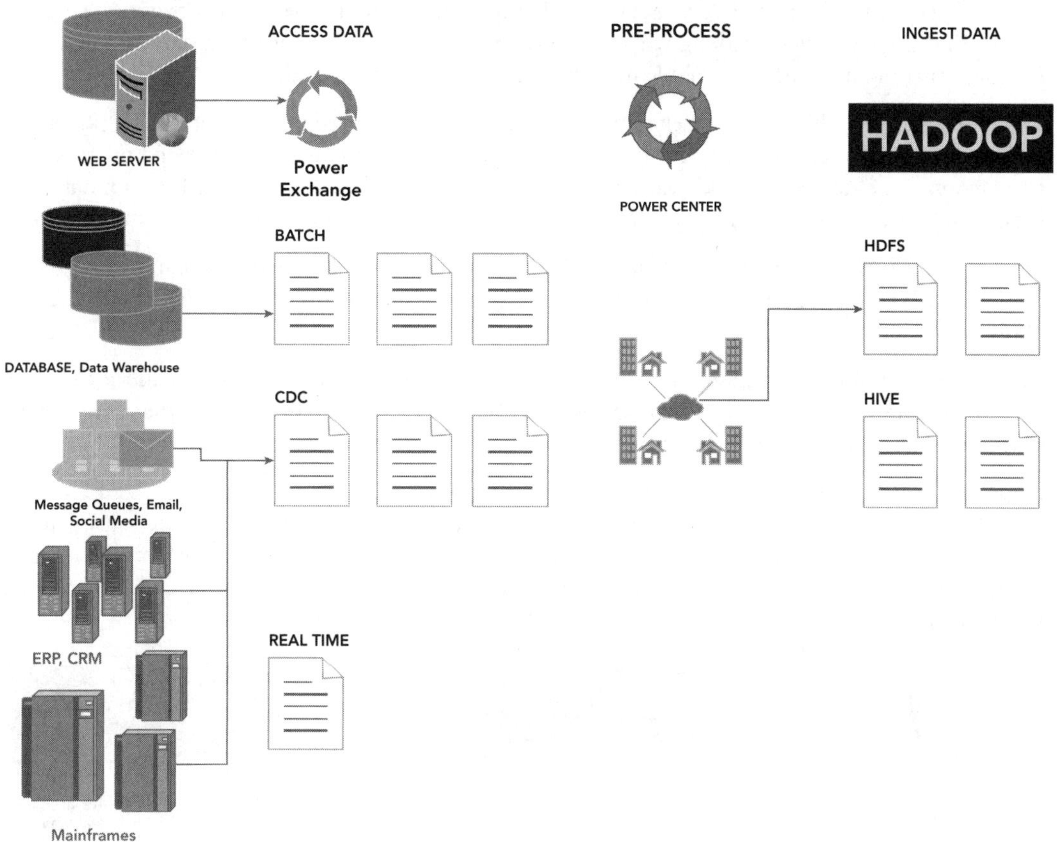

FIGURE 1-6

Hadoop-based applications are well balanced and have the ability to focus on the Windows platform and integrate well with the Microsoft BI tools such as Excel, Power View, and PowerPivot, creating unique ways for the easy analysis of massive amounts of business information.

This does not mean that Hadoop or the other data platform solutions do not run in a non–Windows based environment. It would be prudent to review your current or planned environment to determine the best solution. A data platform or data management platform is just what it says it is. It is a centralized computing system for collecting, integrating, and managing large sets of structured and unstructured data.

In theory, either HortonWorks or Cloudera could be the platform you have selected along with the RDBMS connector that works with your current data environment and Hadoop. Most vendors have highly detailed information regarding system requirements. In general, a significant number of tools will mention a Windows operating system or a Windows-based component, because of the breadth of Windows-based BI tools available. Microsoft SQL Server is the leading Windows tool for database services. Organizations using this enterprise tool are no longer limited by big data. Microsoft has the ability to work and integrate with Hadoop by providing flexibility and enhanced connectivity for Hadoop, Windows Server, and Windows Azure. Informatica software, using the *Power Exchange Connector* along with Hortonworks, optimizes the entire big data supply chain on Hadoop, turning data into actionable information to drive business value.

The modern data architecture, for example, is increasingly being used to build large data pools. By combining data management services into a larger data pool, companies can store and process massive amounts of data across a wide variety of channels including social media, clickstream data, server logs, customer transactions and interactions, videos, and sensor data from equipment in the field.

Hortonworks or Cloudera Data Platforms, along with Informatica, allows companies to optimize their ETL (Extract, Transform, Load) workloads with long-term storage and processing at scale in Hadoop.

The integration of Hadoop along with enterprise tools allows organizations to use all of the data internally and externally for an organization to achieve the full analytical power that drives the success of modern data-driven businesses.

Hadoop Applier, another example, provides real-time connectivity between MySQL and Hadoop's Distributed File System, which can be used for big data analytics—for purposes like sentiment analysis, marketing campaign analysis, customer churn modeling, fraud detection, risk modeling, and many others. Many widely used systems, such as Apache Hive, also use HDFS as a data store (see Figure 1-7).

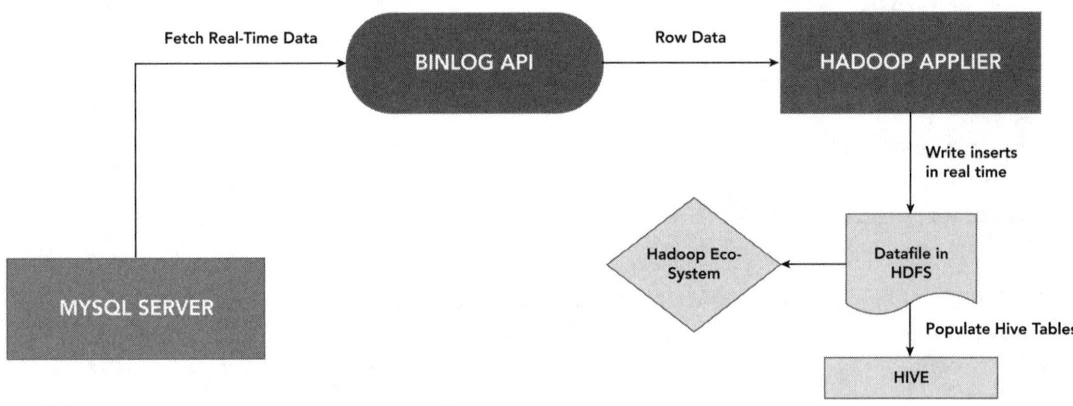

FIGURE 1-7

Oracle has developed an offering for its flagship database engine and Hadoop. It is a collection of useful tools to assist with integrating Oracle's services with the Hadoop stack. The Big Data

Connectors Suite is a collection of tools that have the ability to provide a deep dive into the information discovery waters of analytics and a fast integration of all the data stored within your infrastructure. All tools are considered scalable, which fits nicely into your environment if you are a current or future Oracle customer. Oracle has several tools in their suite, but we will only feature a few of them in this chapter.

Oracle XQuery for Hadoop (see Figure 1-8) runs a process, based on transformations expressed in the XQuery language, by translating them into a series of MapReduce jobs, which are executed in parallel on the Apache Hadoop cluster. The input data can be located in a filesystem accessible through the Hadoop Distributed File System (HDFS), or stored in Oracle's NoSQL Database. Oracle XQuery for Hadoop can write the transformation results to Hadoop files, to the Oracle NoSQL Database, or to the Oracle Database.

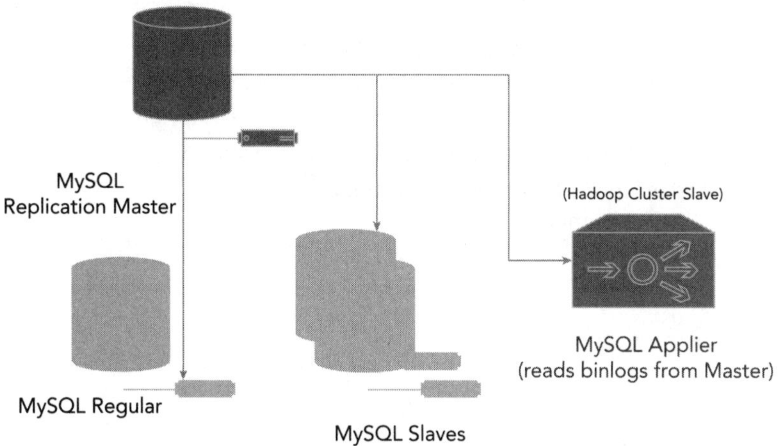

FIGURE 1-8

Oracle SQL Connector for the Hadoop Distributed File System (HDFS) is a high speed connector for loading or querying data in Hadoop with the Oracle Database (see Figure 1-9). Oracle SQL Connector for HDFS pulls data into the database; the data movement is initiated by selecting data via SQL in the Oracle Database. Users can load data into the database, or query the data in place in Hadoop, with Oracle SQL via external tables. Oracle SQL Connector for HDFS can query or load data in text files or Hive tables over text files. Partitions can also be pruned while querying or loading from Hive-partitioned tables.

Another Oracle solution, the Oracle Loader for Hadoop, is a high performance and efficient connector to load data from Hadoop into the Oracle Database. Oracle Loader for Hadoop pushes data into the database as data transfers are initiated in Hadoop (see Figure 1-10). Oracle Loader for Hadoop takes advantage of Hadoop compute resources to sort, partition, and convert data into Oracle-ready data types before loading. Pre-processing data on Hadoop reduces database CPU usage when loading data. This minimizes the impact on database applications and alleviates competition for resources, which is a common issue when ingesting large data volumes. It makes the connector particularly useful for continuous and frequent loads.

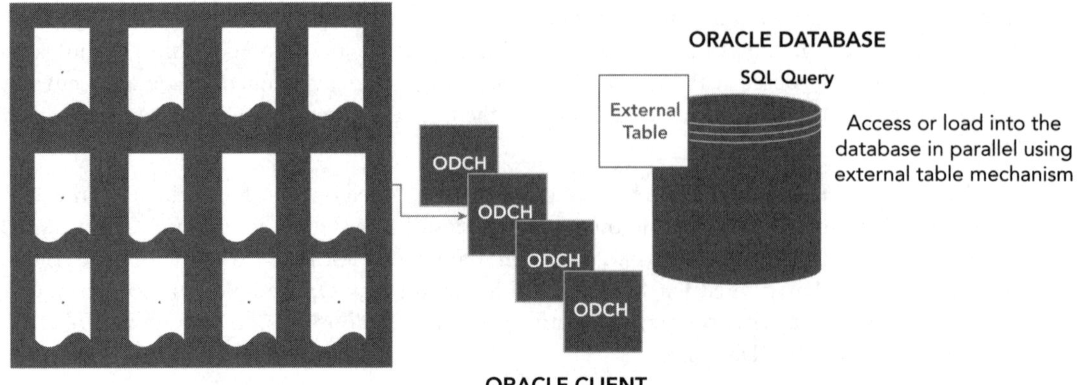
ORACLE DATABASE
SQL Query
External Table
Access or load into the database in parallel using external table mechanism
ODCH
ODCH
ODCH
ODCH
ORACLE CLIENT
HDFS
• Access and analyze data in place on HDFS
• Query and join data on HDFS database resident data
• Load into the database using SQL if required
• Automatic load balancing to maximize performance

FIGURE 1-9

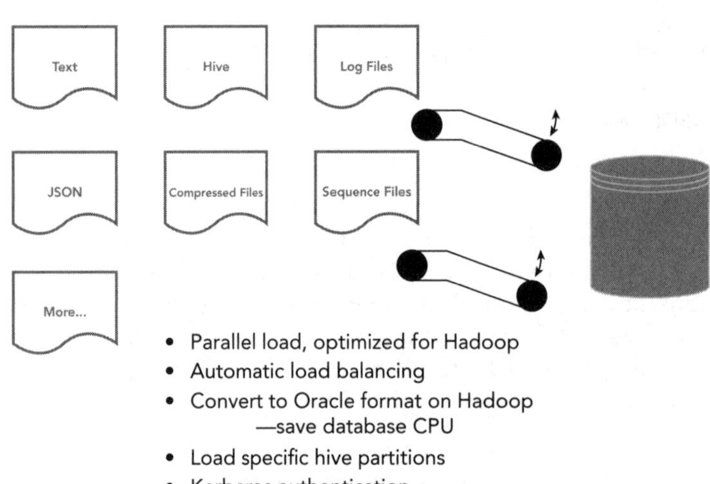
Text
Hive
Log Files
JSON
Compressed Files
Sequence Files
More...
• Parallel load, optimized for Hadoop
• Automatic load balancing
• Convert to Oracle format on Hadoop —save database CPU
• Load specific hive partitions
• Kerberos authentication
• Load directly into in-memory table

FIGURE 1-10

Oracle R Connector for Hadoop enables rapid development with R-style debugging capabilities of parallel R code on user desktops, supported by simulating parallelism (see Figure 1-11). The connector enables analysts to combine data from several environments—client desktop, HDFS, Hive, Oracle Database, and in-memory R data structures—all in the context of a single analytic task execution, thus simplifying data assembly and preparation. Oracle R Connector for Hadoop also provides a general computation framework for the execution of R code in parallel.

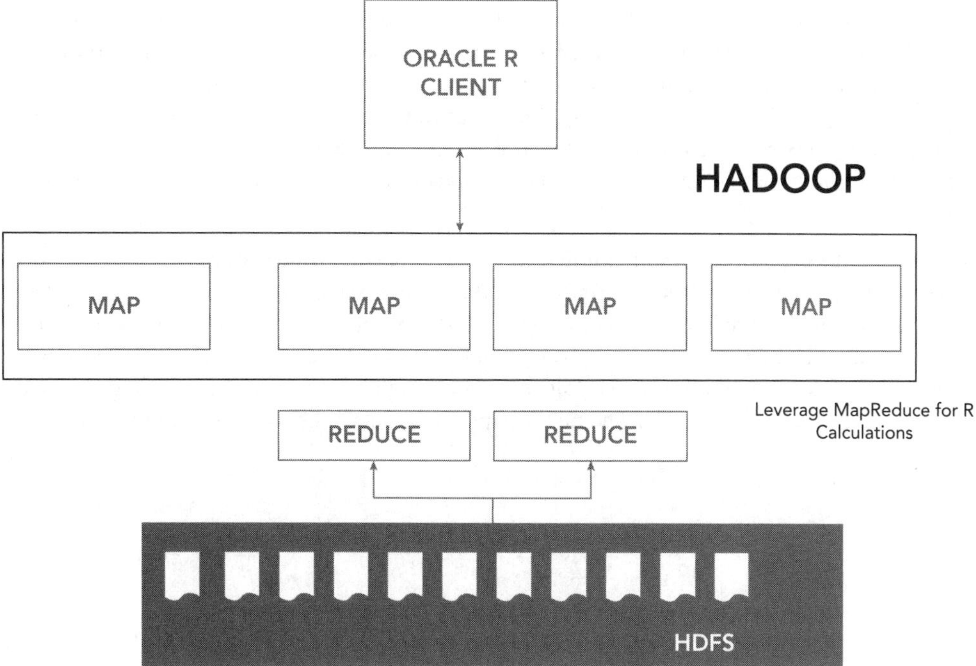

FIGURE 1-11

If Oracle is your organization's tool of choice, you have a suite of tools to choose from, as described in this section. They have partnered with Hadoop, and the Oracle site is well documented and allows you to download any of the previously mentioned connectors as well as configure them to work with the Hadoop ecosystem.

SUMMARY

By using the Hadoop Stack, you leverage the best practices in enterprise Hadoop, combined with a mix of programming and high-level tools. Most clusters are on your premises today, but service providers are giving even more options for data to exist in the Cloud. SQL, relational, and non-relational data stores can now leverage functionality using Hadoop.

Hadoop has established itself for the long haul when it comes to data. This is very fitting, because data continues to grow over time. It uses pre-existing enterprise systems that can expand into Hadoop's data platform. Companies and developers within the open source community are designing and defining the best practices for Hadoop-based large scale enterprise data. The businesses, as well as the IT community, are deeply concerned with scalability for all data types. With Hadoop, companies are no longer confined to expensive enterprise solutions or pricey warehouse appliances.

Hadoop is not a replacement for the existing data rich environments that populate most organizations. When you consider Hadoop, it is important to consider aspects like MapReduce or YARN, which are making huge strides in deep data analysis and advanced analytics. Hadoop provides real-time processing of big data, which can provide an immediate impact on decisions that can affect your bottom line. Various industries, from finance to healthcare, can get immediate benefits from using the Hadoop Stack, or any of its related components. It pushes the limit of what was previously thought to only be achieved with a data mining tool. It literally makes you look at data differently. Hadoop has provided the bridge that does not replace but improves how organizations look at data. Hadoop removes limitations and continues to cover new ground in all aspects of development.

Understanding Hadoop's storage system allows you to leverage data integration and business analytics to consolidate large data lakes and analyze all data types, which are not dependent on their current source. Having a complete understanding of Hadoop's platform allows its users to process a vast amount of scalable data in real time delivering optimum analytics. The beauty of Hadoop's storage process is that there is no additional storage or computing expense. There are only gains, such as increased data accuracy and analytics. The next chapter will detail the aspects of Hadoop's storage.

2

Storage

WHAT'S IN THIS CHAPTER?

- Providing the basic concept and architecture of HDFS
- Usage of HDFS CLI for operation
- Showing how to set up HDFS clusters and the default of configurations
- Advanced features of HDFS including future releases
- Popular file formats used by HDFS

Hadoop is not only a data analysis platform but it also handles storage, because you need a place to store data before you can analyze it. Hadoop is a distributed system, and the workload requirements on a distributed system are often different from web applications or consumer applications. The popular Hadoop-implemented specific storage system is called HDFS (Hadoop Distributed File System). As the name suggests, HDFS is a filesystem. The data on HDFS can be a file or a directory, like the ordinal filesystems that you use every day. You might be familiar with the usage and interface of HDFS, but it is built on a totally different architecture for achieving high availability and scalability.

In this chapter, we will introduce the basic concept and the usage of HDFS. In most cases, the Hadoop MapReduce application accesses the data on HDFS. So, improving the HDFS cluster often immediately improves the MapReduce performance. In addition, other external frameworks, such as Apache HBase and Apache Spark, can also access HDFS data for their workload. Therefore, HDFS provides fundamental functionality for the Hadoop ecosystem, and although HDFS was developed during the initial Hadoop era, it continues to be a crucial component. In this chapter we cover important and advanced features of HDFS. This advanced functionality makes HDFS data more reliable and more efficient to access. One of these functions is Erasure Coding, which drastically saves storage capacity in comparison with ordinal replication HDFS. Although this function has not yet been released, it is actively being developed, and is important to examine.

BASICS OF HADOOP HDFS

One challenge with implementing HDFS is achieving availability and scalability at the same time. You may have a large amount of data that can't fit on a single physical machine disk, so it's necessary to distribute the data among multiple machines. HDFS can do this automatically and transparently while providing a user-friendly interface to developers. HDFS achieves these two main points:

- High scalability
- High availability

Some of the machines in the HDFS cluster can be broken at any time due to a broken disk or a power shutdown. HDFS will continue providing its service and the required data, even if some of the nodes are unavailable. HDFS efficiently provides all required data to an application. This is a requirement because there are many types of applications running on Hadoop processes, and also because there is a huge amount of data stored on HDFS. This may require the full use of the network bandwidth or disk I/O operations. HDFS must even provide this same performance when the data stored on HDFS is growing.

Let's examine the basic concepts and architecture of HDFS that provide these requirements for its distributed storage system.

Concept

HDFS is a storage system that stores large amounts of data to be sequentially accessed. HDFS data doesn't fit into a random-access pattern. Here are three important points about HDFS characteristics:

- **Huge file:** In the HDFS context, *huge* means hundreds of megabytes, or even gigabytes, and more. HDFS is specialized for huge data files. Therefore, a lot of small files hinder HDFS performance because its metadata consumes a lot of memory space on the master component called NameNode, which is explained in the next section.
- **Sequential access:** Both read and write operations in HDFS should be handled sequentially. Random access hurts HDFS performance because of network latency. But reading the data once and writing it many times is a suitable situation for an HDFS use case. MapReduce and other execution engines can efficiently read HDFS files any number of times as long as files are read sequentially. HDFS puts an emphasis on the throughput of total access, rather than low latency. It is more important to achieve high throughput than to achieve low latency, because the total time for reading all data relies on throughput metrics.
- **Commodity hardware:** Hadoop HDFS does not require specialized hardware made for big data processing or storage because many IT vendors already provide this. If Hadoop requires a specific type of hardware, the cost of using Hadoop will increase, and scalability will perish due to the difficulty of always buying the same hardware.

HDFS manages the stored data with block units similar to a standard filesystem. Each block has a limited, maximum size configured by HDFS, which defines how files that would span multiple blocks are divided. The default block size is 128MB. Each file is separated into 128MB blocks when written on the HDFS (see Figure 2-1). A file that's smaller than the block size does not occupy the total block. A 100MB file keeps only 100MB on one HDFS block. The block is an important abstraction of HDFS. The blocks are distributed across multiple nodes, so that you can create a file larger than the disk size of a single node. Thus, you can create any size of file thanks to the abstraction of the blocks that are used to store the file.

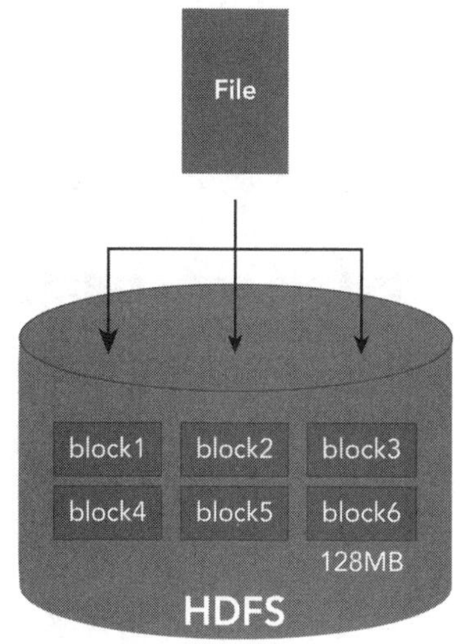

FIGURE 2-1

In addition to this abstraction, one other thing HDFS does that is different from typical filesystems is to simplify the overall structure. The abstraction of the block's organization also simplifies the disk management. Because blocks are a fixed size, calculating the number of blocks that fit into a single physical disk is easy (divide the disk size by the block size). This means the overall capacity of each node is also easily calculated (by adding the block capacity of each disk). So, the capacity of the entire cluster is also easy to determine. To manage the combination of the blocks and metadata, HDFS is divided into two subsystems. One system manages the metadata, including the name of the file, directory, and other metadata. The other system is used to manage the underlying block organization as blocks are spread across the nodes, and the other is for managing blocks and the corresponding node list. The two systems can be separated by the block abstraction.

The key to the power and flexibility of HDFS is the efficient use of commodity hardware. Rather than relying on expensive, specialized hardware, you can use low-cost commodity hardware instead. Although this low-cost hardware is more likely to fail, HDFS works around this by providing an abstraction layer that overcomes the potential for failure. In a normal system where all of the day's data is stored on a single disk, a failure of that disk creates a loss of this data. In a distributed system, where there are multiple nodes using the same commodity hardware, it's also possible that the entire node would fail, perhaps due to power supply, CPU, or network failure.

Most systems that support High Availability (HA) of the data do so by replicating the entire data structure, usually across two nodes. This ensures that if one node, or data source, fails, the other node or copy of the data can be used in its place. HDFS expands on this by making use of the data block abstraction. Instead of replicating the data once, by default in HDFS, data is replicated twice, making a total of three copies of each block. To improve upon this even further, rather than replicating all of the blocks on, for example, node A to node B, HDFS distributes the blocks across multiple nodes (see Figure 2-2).

For example, imagine a large file that would normally occupy three blocks on an HDFS filesystem, and we have 5 nodes in the Hadoop cluster. Copy 1 of block 1 might be stored physically on nodes A, B and C; block 2 on nodes B, C and D, and block 3 on nodes D, E and A.

This distribution of the data is made possible by the block abstraction, and also ensures that the data will remain available even if two nodes in the system fail, because the additional copies of the data blocks are spread across multiple nodes. The file can still be recreated by using the copies on the other nodes that are still running. For example, if nodes B and C failed, we can still recover the three blocks from nodes A and D. Of course these replicas must be distributed among different nodes, as described in Figure 2-2.

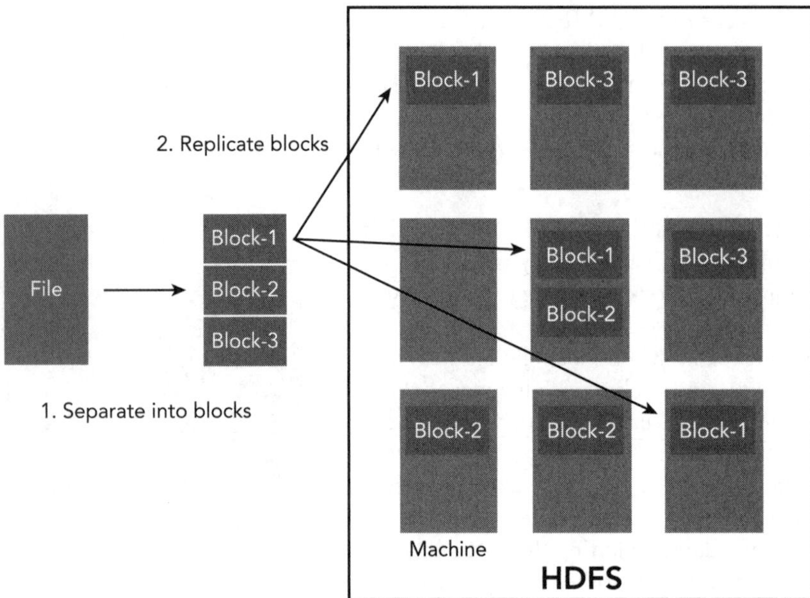

FIGURE 2-2

If more than two replicas are lost, then the failure of one machine can cause the total loss of data. Hadoop controls this by putting each replica on a different machine, and by enabling the number of replicas of each block to be configurable. You can change the replication factor with the `dfs.replication` configuration, but when you increase the replication factor you decrease available disk capacity (because you have to store N copies of each block). An application accessing the data uses only one of the blocks, since the other blocks are merely copies to be used in the event of a failure. The distribution of data is not used to improve performance (see Figure 2-3).

To improve fault tolerance further, HDFS can be configured to take into account the physical topology of the data and how it is stored, and the location of each machine within the racks used to house modern server hardware. The machines in the data center are usually put in a rack or some type of container for storing server machines. One rack can store dozens of machines. The machines are usually close in proximity and also close in network context. The connection between the machines in the same rack is more efficient than the connection between the machines across racks. By providing HDFS with the physical architecture, the performance and resilience of the distributed file system is improved. Blocks can be distributed across multiple nodes in the same rack, and better, across multiple racks, so that if an entire rack of servers fails, the blocks have been distributed in such a way that the data is not lost.

This process also takes into account the improved connectivity available within a single rack. Consequently, putting all replicas on one rack is very efficient because there is no restriction of network bandwidth between the racks. For example, the first replica (replica1) is put on the same node where the client is running. The second replica (replica2) is put on another machine in a different rack. The third replica is put on a different machine in the same rack where the second replica is located.

The result is that HDFS provides a good balance between maximizing network performance within racks and supporting fault tolerance across the racks.

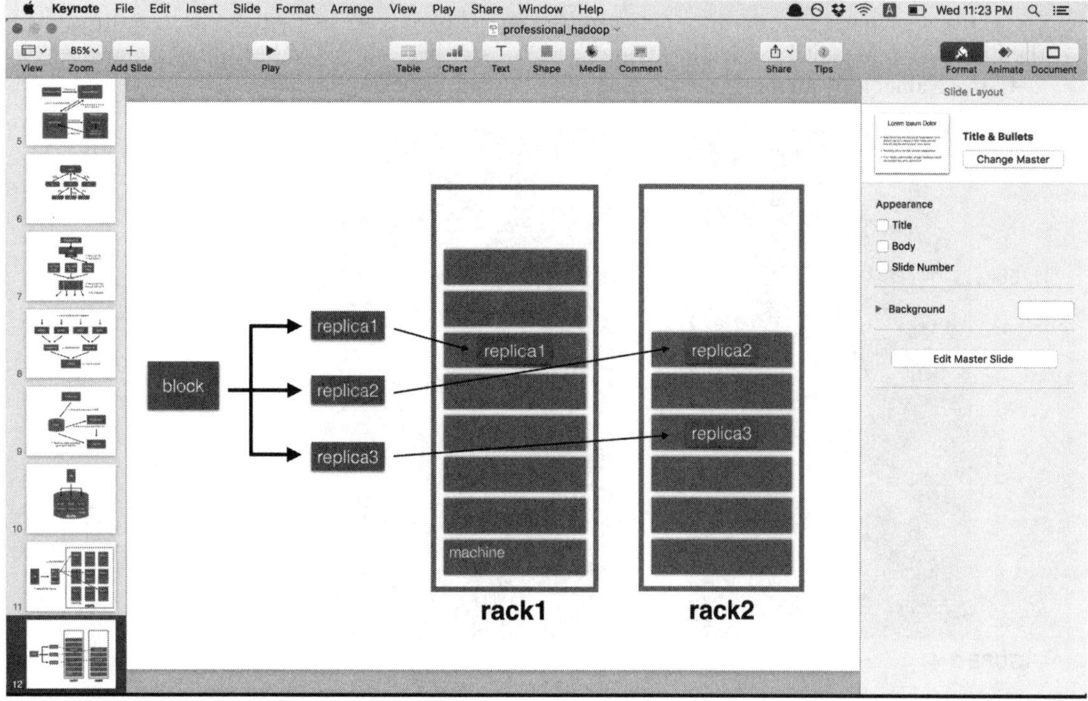

FIGURE 2-3

Architecture

Hadoop HDFS uses a master-slave architecture. The master server is called the NameNode, and it is responsible for managing the metadata of the filesystem, such as filename, permission, and creation time. All HDFS operations—such as write, read, and create—are first submitted to NameNode. NameNode does not store the actual data. Instead, slave servers called DataNodes store the individual blocks that make up a file. By default, there is only one Active NameNode in an HDFS cluster. Losing the NameNode can lead to the loss of your data because it stores the only copy of the block allocation.

To improve the fault-tolerance, HDFS can use a high-availability architecture and support one or more backup NameNodes that contain copies of the metadata and block allocation information. Any number of machines can be DataNodes in one HDFS cluster, and in most Hadoop clusters the majority of nodes will be DataNodes, often numbering in the thousands of servers in the larger clusters. The overview of the relationship between NameNode and DataNodes is covered next.

NameNode has a class that retains the information to manage the relationship between file and blocks: FSNamesystem. This class keeps information that is necessary to manage the mapping from file to blocks. Each file is represented as an INode, which is the term used by all filesystems including HDFS to refer to the key filesystem structure. INodes are put under FSDirectory in a tree structure. INode can represent both file, directory, and other entities on the filesystem. The concrete correspondence relationships between INode and blocks are delegated to a structure called the BlocksMap included in the BlockManager. As described in the architecture overview (see Figure 2-4), the NameNode manages the relationship between INode and blocks.

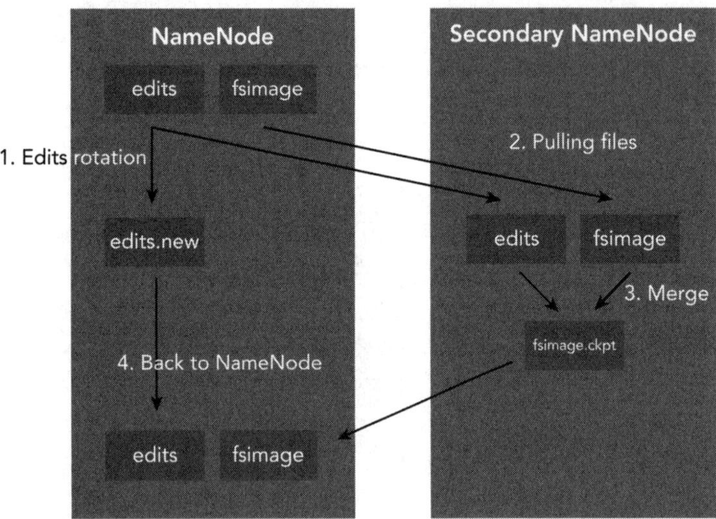

FIGURE 2-4

All metadata is managed in memory while the NameNode is running normally. But, in order for the metadata to remain persistent, the NameNode must write the metadata to a physical disk. Without this operation, the metadata and block structure will be lost if the NameNode crashes. A periodic checkpoint is used to write metadata, and the edit log (a record of all of the individual changes) on disk and is usually handled by a new node called a secondary NameNode. A secondary NameNode is almost the same as the normal NameNode except that the secondary NameNode can't behave as a NameNode. The only task the secondary NameNode is expected to handle is to periodically merge metadata changes and the current snapshot of the information stored on disk.

The merging task is often heavy and time consuming. It is not efficient for the NameNode to merge this information by itself, since it has to handle the general requests for metadata and file information for the running cluster. So, the Secondary NameNode handles the merging for NameNode using the periodic checkpoint process. If the NameNode experiences a failure, you need to run the checkpoint manually, but the process often takes a lot of time. HDFS will remain unavailable until the merging process is complete. Therefore, the regular checkpoint process is indispensable for a healthy HDFS cluster.

One thing to note here is that HDFS can now support a high-availability (HA) structure. The Hadoop cluster can operate with two NameNodes operating in an HA architecture. One is the active NameNode and the other is the standby NameNode. They share the in-memorying block and log files through the quorum journal manager. Thanks to sharing metadata between the active NameNode and the standby NameNode, the standby NameNode can become active immediately when failover happens. NameNode is not a Single Point of Failure (SPOF) anymore. In addition, the standby NameNode can play a role as a Secondary NameNode, performing the required periodic checkpoint process. It is not necessary to configure a Secondary NameNode and a Standby NameNode. The recommended configuration is to use the HA Standby NameNode, which automatically provides the Secondary NameNode functionality.

The sync process with journal nodes and active NameNode is shown in Figure 2-5. You need to avoid the so-called "split brain" situation in this architecture. A split brain occurs when the standby NameNode becomes active, but the old failed NameNode is technically still available within the cluster. This can be a really serious problem, because the metadata of the HDFS name system can be corrupted by inconsistent updating operations issued by the active NameNode and standby NameNode.

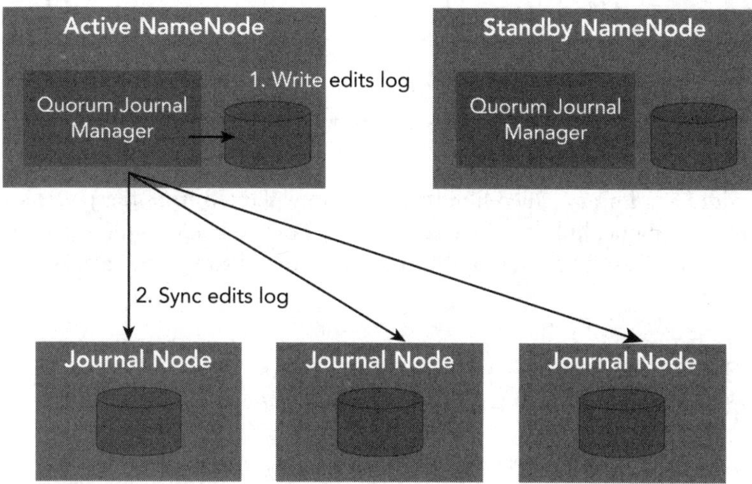

FIGURE 2-5

To help prevent this situation, the quorum manager uses an epoch number. When the standby node tries to become active, it increments the epoch number for all of the journal nodes. The number of successes of the increment operation needs to be more than a fixed number that is usually a majority number of journal nodes. If both active NameNode and standby NameNode try to increment the number, both can succeed. But, the writing (authoritative) NameNode includes the NameNode's epoch number with the metadata. The receiver of the journal node accepts the operation and the epoch number; if the epoch number receives the NameNode, the epoch number of the NameNode that matches the journal nodes is the one used as the valid operation. The entire negotiation process and validation with the epoch number and each operation are taken care of automatically by Hadoop, and it is not up to either the developers or administrators to control the operation.

The detail of configuration for setting up HA NameNode is described here: (`http://hadoop.apache.org/docs/current/hadoop-project-dist/hadoop-hdfs/HDFSHighAvailabilityWithQJM.html`). It is necessary to prepare two machines for active and standby NameNodes, and at least three journal node machines. Since edit log modification has to be written on the majority of journal nodes, the number of journal nodes is recommended to be an odd number (3, 5, 7, etc.). When you are running N journal nodes in your HDFS cluster, your HDFS system tolerates at most (N – 1) / 2 failures in order to operate normally.

Interface

HDFS provides several types of interfaces for filesystem users. The most basic one is the command-line tool included in Hadoop HDFS. Command-line tools can be separated into two categories: the filesystem shell interface and the admin tool for HDFS.

- **File system shell:** This tool provides various types of shell-like commands that directly interact with HDFS data. You can read or write file data with the shell tool. Also, you can access the data stored in other storage systems such as HFTP, S3, and FS that HDFS is now supporting.
- **Java API:** This is the most basic API. File system shells and most other interfaces use the Java API internally. In addition, the API is also used by many applications running on HDFS. When you write an application that accesses HDFS data, you should use the Java API.
- **WebHDFS:** WebHDFS provides an HTTP REST API through NameNode. WebHDFS supports all filesystem operations, including Kerberos authentication. You can enable WebHDFS with `dfs.webhdfs.enabled=true`.
- **libhdfs:** Hadoop provides a C library called libhdfs that is transplanted from the Java filesystem interface. In spite of its name, libhdfs can access any type of the Hadoop filesystem, not only HDFS. `libhdfs` calls a filesystem client implemented in Java through the Java Native Interface (JNI).

> **NOTE** *Some APIs provided by the Java client are not fully implemented in libhdfs because of a development delay. A pre-built binary distributed by the Apache project is 32-bit binary. If you use libhdfs on another platform, you have to build it yourself.*

Let's examine the basic usage of the command-line interface and the Java API. The command-line interface is provided by the bin/hdfs script, and it's deprecated. A current command-line tool is used through `bin/hadoop fs <args>`. The filesystem shell provides a POSIX-like interface, and the full commands are listed in Tables 2-1, 2-2 and 2-3. (`http://hadoop.apache.org/docs/current/hadoop-project-dist/hadoop-common/FileSystemShell.html`).

TABLE 2-1: Read Operations

COMMAND	USAGE	DESCRIPTION
cat	`hadoop fs -cat <URI>`	Copies the content of source paths to stdout
copyToLocal	`hadoop fs -copyToLocal <Source URI> <Local URI>`	Copies a file onto the local filesystem

COMMAND	USAGE	DESCRIPTION
cp	hadoop fs -cp <Source URI> <Dest URI>	Copies a file from the source path to the dest path and is the same as the cp command
ls	hadoop fs -ls <URI>	Returns the stat of the file or directory
find	hadoop fs -find <URI>	Returns all files that match a given specified expression
get	hadoop fs -get <Source URI> <Dest URI>	Copies a file from the source path to the dest path in a local file system
tail	hadoop fs -tail <URI>	Displays the last kilobytes of the file to output

TABLE 2-2: Write Operations

COMMAND	USAGE	DESCRIPTION
appendToFile	hadoop fs -appendToFile <Local URI> <dest URI>	Append some local file data to the dest URI file
copyFromLocal	hadoop fs -copyFromLocal <Local URI> <Remote URI>	Copies a file from the remote filesystem to the local filesystem
put	hadoop fs -put <Local URI> ...<Remote URI>	Copies files from the local filesystem to the remote filesystem
touch	hadoop fs -touchz <URI>	Create a file that has zero length

TABLE 2-3: Other Operations

COMMAND	USAGE	DESCRIPTION
chmod	hadoop fs -chmod <URI>	Change the permission of files
chown	hadoop fs -chown <URI>	Change the owner of files
df	hadoop fs -df <URI>	Display free space under a specified URI
du	hadoop fs -du <URI>	Display the size of files contained in a given directory

continues

TABLE 2-3: *(continued)*

COMMAND	USAGE	DESCRIPTION
mv	`hadoop fs -mv <Source URI> ... <Dest URI>`	Move files from source to destination
rm	`hadoop fs -rm <URI>`	Remove files of a given URI
rmdir	`hadoop fs -rmdir <URI>`	Remove directories of a given URI
stat	`hadoop fs -stat <URI>`	Display statistics of a given URI

You might be familiar with most of the CLI commands. They are for filesystem users, and many of the commands can manipulate a stored file or directory. In addition, HDFS provides the commands for administrators of the HDFS cluster, called `dfsadmin`. You can use it with `bin/hdfs dfsadmin <sub command>`. The full list of admin commands is written here: (`http://hadoop.apache.org/docs/current/hadoop-project-dist/hadoop-hdfs/HDFSCommands.html#dfsadmin`).

The Java filesystem API is helpful if you want to do programming or access HDFS data from your application. The filesystem API also encapsulates the authentication process and the interpretation of a given configuration. Let's create a tool that reads file data and outputs it to stdout. You need to know how to write a Java program and how to use Maven in order to build the tool. We assume that you have this knowledge. The dependency should be written as follows:

```
<dependency>
    <groupId>org.apache.hadoop</groupId>
    <artifactId>hadoop-client</artifactId>
    <version>2.6.0</version>
</dependency>
```

Of course, the version of Hadoop can change according to your Hadoop cluster. Our tool is named `MyHDFSCat`. The concrete implementation is shown here:

```
import org.apache.hadoop.conf.Configuration;
       import org.apache.hadoop.conf.Configured;
       import org.apache.hadoop.fs.FileSystem;
       import org.apache.hadoop.fs.Path;
       import org.apache.hadoop.io.IOUtils;
       import org.apache.hadoop.util.Tool;
       import org.apache.hadoop.util.ToolRunner;
       import java.io.InputStream;
       import java.net.URI;

public class MyHDFSCat extends Configured implements Tool {
    public int run(String[] args) throws Exception {
        String uri = null;
        // Target URI is given as first argument
               if (args.length > 0) {
                 uri = args[0];
               }
        // Get the default configuration put on your HDFS cluster
```

```
                Configuration conf = this.getConf();
        FileSystem fs = FileSystem.get(URI.create(uri), conf);
        InputStream in = null;
        try {
                  in = fs.open(new Path(uri));
                  IOUtils.copyBytes(in, System.out, 4096, false);
                } finally {
                  IOUtils.closeStream(in);
                }
                return 0;
    }


    public static void main(String[] args) throws Exception {
        int exitCode = ToolRunner.run(new MyHDFSCat(), args);
                System.exit(exitCode);
    }
}
```

You can compile the implementation with `mvn package -DskipTests`. The next thing to do is to upload the JAR file to your cluster. You can see the JAR file under the `target` directory of the project root. Just before running `MyHDFSCat`, upload the target file to HDFS.

```
$ echo "This is for MyHDFSCat" > test.txt
$ bin/hadoop fs -put test.txt /test.txt
```

You can use the `jar` subcommand of the `hadoop` command to run your Java class included in the JAR file. The JAR file is `myhdfscat-0.0.1-SNAPSHOT.jar`. (The way of constructing the HDFS cluster will be described in the next section.) Running the command of `MyHDFSCat` can look like this:

```
$ bin/hadoop jar myhdfscat-0.0.1-SNAPSHOT.jar MyHDFSCat hdfs:///test.txt
This is for MyHDFSCat
```

You can do other operations, not only reading file data, but also writing, deleting, and referring status info from the HDFS file. Here you can see that the example tool for referring the `FileStatus` is the same as `MyHDFSCat`.

```
Import org.apache.hadoop.conf.Configuration;
       import org.apache.hadoop.conf.Configured;
       import org.apache.hadoop.fs.FileStatus;
       import org.apache.hadoop.fs.FileSystem;
      import org.apache.hadoop.fs.Path;
       import org.apache.hadoop.util.Tool;
       import org.apache.hadoop.util.ToolRunner;
       import java.net.URI;
public class MyHDFSStat extends Configured implements Tool {
    public int run(String[] args) throws Exception {
        String uri = null;
        if (args.length > 0) {
                   uri = args[0];
               }
        Configuration conf = this.getConf();
               FileSystem fs = FileSystem.get(URI.create(uri), conf);
               FileStatus status = fs.getFileStatus(new Path(uri));
        System.out.printf("path: %s\n", status.getPath());
```

```
            System.out.printf("length: %d\n", status.getLen());
            System.out.printf("access: %d\n", status.getAccessTime());
            System.out.printf("modified: %d\n", status.getModificationTime());
            System.out.printf("owner: %s\n", status.getOwner());
            System.out.printf("group: %s\n", status.getGroup());
            System.out.printf("permission: %s\n", status.getPermission());
            System.out.printf("replication: %d\n", status.getReplication());

            return 0;
        }

        public static void main(String[] args) throws Exception {
                int exitCode = ToolRunner.run(new MyHDFSStat(), args);
                System.exit(exitCode);
            }
    }
```

You can run `MyHDFSStat` in the same way as `MyHDFSCat`. The output will look like this:

```
$ bin/hadoop jar myhdfsstat-SNAPSHOT.jar \
                    com.lewuathe.MyHDFSStat hdfs:///test.txt
path: hdfs://master:9000/test.txt
length: 18
access: 1452334391191
modified: 1452334391769
owner: root
group: supergroup
permission: rw-r--r--
replication: 1
```

You can write a program to manipulate HDFS data. If you have no HDFS cluster yet, you should launch your HDFS cluster. We will explain how to set up a distributed HDFS cluster next.

SETTING UP THE HDFS CLUSTER IN DISTRIBUTED MODE

Now that you understand the overview architecture and interface of HDFS, it is time to learn about launching your HDFS cluster. To do this, it is necessary to procure several machines prepared for each component role in an HDFS cluster. One machine should be created for the master machine where NameNode and ResourceManager are installed. The other machines should be created for slave machines where DataNode and NodeManager are installed. The total number of servers is 1 + N machines, where N is dependent on the scale of your workloads. The HDFS cluster can be set up in secure mode. We will omit the detail of a secure Hadoop cluster because it is explained in Chapter 6. So, this time we will set up a normal HDFS cluster. As a prerequisite, please make sure all servers are installed with Java 1.6+ before starting the Hadoop installation. The tested JDK versions of the Hadoop project are listed on this page: (`http://wiki.apache.org/hadoop/HadoopJavaVersions`).

Install

To start, go ahead and download the Hadoop package from the mirror site (`http://hadoop.apache.org/releases.html`). Use BUILDING.txt included in the Hadoop source directory if you want to build the Hadoop package from the source file. The Hadoop project provides a Docker image for building the Hadoop package: `start-build-env.sh` is used for that purpose. If you have already installed Docker on your machine, you can build an environment, including all dependencies for building the Hadoop package:

```
$ ./start-build.env.sh
$ mvn package -Pdist,native,docs -DskipTests -Dtar
```

The built package is put under `hadoop-dist/target/hadoop-<VERSION>-SNAPSHOT.tar.gz`, if you install the package under `/usr/local`:

```
$ tar -xz -C /usr/local
$ cd /usr/local
$ ln -s hadoop-<VERSION>-SNAPSHOT hadoop
```

HDFS configurations are put in `core-default.xml` and `etc/hadoop/core-site.xml`, `hdfs-default.xml`, and `etc/hadoop/hdfs-site.xml`. The former is the default value for HDFS, and the latter is for specific configurations for your cluster. You should not change `hdfs-default.xml`, but you can modify `hdfs-site.xml` if necessary. In addition, there are several environmental variables that must be set.

```
export JAVA_HOME=/usr/java/default
export HADOOP_COMMON_PREFIX=/usr/local/hadoop
export HADOOP_PREFIX=/usr/local/hadoop
export HADOOP_HDFS_HOME=/usr/local/hadoop
export HADOOP_CONF_DIR=/usr/local/hadoop/etc/hadoop
```

These variables are used in the `hadoop` or `hdfs` script to launch daemons where you find the exec script or configuration files. The actual configurations for each daemon are written in `core-site.xml` and `hdfs-site.xml`. As the name specifies, `core-site.xml` is for the Hadoop Common package, and `hdfs-site.xml` is for the HDFS package. First, `fs.defaultFS` is necessary in order to specify the HDFS cluster used in the `hadoop` script.

```
<configuration>
  <property>
    <name>fs.defaultFS</name>
    <value>hdfs://<Master hostname>:9000</value>
  </property>
</configuration>
```

The `hadoop` script is used for launching MapReduce jobs and the `dfsadmin` command. Thanks to the `fs.defaultFS` configuration, the system can detect where the HDFS cluster is, only you should write in `core-site.xml`. The next step is adding `hdfs-site.xml`.

```
<configuration>
    <property>
        <name>dfs.replication</name>
        <value>1</value>
    </property>
</configuration>
```

`dfs.replication` specifies the minimum replication factor for each block on HDFS. Since the default value is set to three, it is not necessary to set it again here. The configurations that are related to the NameNode daemon are listed in Table 2-4.

TABLE 2-4: NameNode Daemon Configurations

PARAMETER	NOTES
dfs.namenode.name.dir	Meta data such as fsimage or edits logs are stored in this directory of the NameNode machine
df.hosts / dfs.hosts.excluded	List of permitted/excluded DataNodes
dfs.blocksize	Specifies the block size of the HDFS file
dfs.namenode.handler.count	The number of threads that it handles

Since the same configuration files are distributed among HDFS clusters to both NameNode and DataNodes in many cases, the configurations for DataNodes can be written in `hdfs-site.xml` (see Table 2-5).

TABLE 2-5: DataNode Daemon Configurations

PARAMETER	NOTES
dfs.datanode.data.dir	DataNode stores actual block data under the specified directory. Multiple directories can be set with a comma separated list of directories.

After writing configurations for the HDFS cluster, it is necessary to format it if it's the first time to launch the HDFS cluster on that machine.

```
$ bin/hdfs namenode -format
```

Once NameNode is formatted, you can start the HDFS daemons. The launch commands are included in the `hdfs` script for both NameNode and DataNodes.

```
# On NameNode machine
      $ bin/hdfs namenode
# On DataNode machine
      $ bin/hdfs datanode
```

You can launch these processes as a daemon by using upstart (`http://upstart.ubuntu.com/`) and daemontools (`https://cr.yp.to/daemontools.html`). If you want to launch NameNode and DataNodes (see Figure 2-6) as a daemon, there are utility scripts in the Hadoop source code.

```
# On NameNode machine
      $ sbin/hadoop-daemon.sh --config $HADOOP_CONF_DIR --script hdfs start namenode
# On DataNode machine
      $ sbin/hadoop-daemon.sh --config $HADOOP_CONF_DIR --script hdfs start datanode
```

After launching the HDFS cluster, you can see the NameNode UI at http://<Master Hostname>:50070.

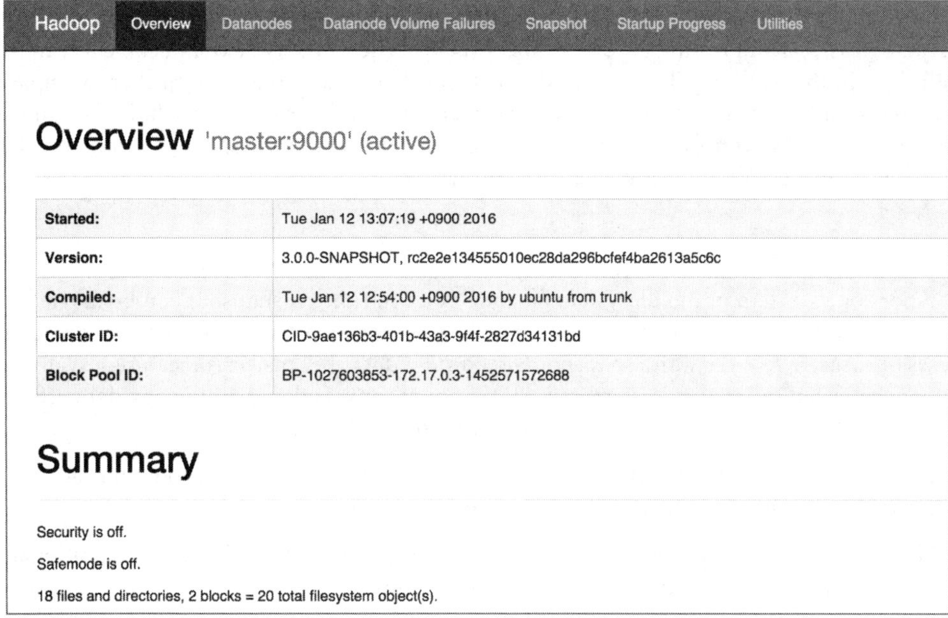

FIGURE 2-6

NameNode also has a metric API provided by JMX. You can see the metrics that show configuration parameters of the HDFS cluster and information of resource usage. This is shown in http://<Master Hostname>:50070/jmx. The JMX metrics will be useful for cluster monitoring and profiling cluster performance. When it is necessary to shut down the HDFS cluster, you can do that in the same way.

```
# On NameNode machine
        $ sbin/hadoop-daemon.sh --config $HADOOP_CONF_DIR --script hdfs stop namenode
# On DataNode machine
        $ sbin/hadoop-daemon.sh --config $HADOOP_CONF_DIR --script hdfs stop datanode
```

DataNode also has a web UI at the port number 50075. You can see http://<Slave Hostname>:50075. This is the basic way to set up the HDFS cluster. But, it might be reasonable to use some Hadoop distribution such as CDH from Cloudera or HDP from Hortonworks in many cases on an enterprise usage. These packages include a set up manager called Cloudera Manager or Ambari. These are reasonable options for setting up your HDFS cluster. The details are here:

- **Cloudera Manager:** https://www.cloudera.com/content/www/en-us/products/cloudera-manager.html
- **Apache Ambari:** http://ambari.apache.org/

ADVANCED FEATURES OF HDFS

The content shown so far is basically enough to set up and try HDFS. But, there are several features you should know in order to reliably perform operations on HDFS. HDFS often stores business critical data. So, it is very important to run a stable HDFS cluster. We will explain some advanced features of HDFS in this section. The list includes features that are not released yet. For example, Erasure Coding is under active development, yet it is merged into the master branch. Although we cannot use it with a release version, it stores your data more efficiently and saves you money. HDFS is progressing even now so we will show you some of that here.

Snapshots

HDFS snapshot copies a data in the filesystem at some point in time. A snapshot can be taken for a subtree or the entire filesystem. Snapshot can usually be used for data backup for protection against some failures or disaster recovery, and snapshot is read-only data, because it is meaningless if you can modify the snapshot data after it is created. HDFS snapshot was designed to copy data efficiently, and the main effectiveness of making HDFS snapshot includes:

- Creating a snapshot takes constant time order O(1), excluding the inode lookup time, because it does not copy actual data but only makes a reference.
- Additional memory is used only when the original data is modified. The size of additional memory is proportional to the number of modifications.
- The modifications are recorded as the collection in reverse chronological order. The current data is not modified any more, and the snapshot data is computed by subtracting the modifications from the current data.

Any directory can create its own snapshot once it is set as snapshottable. There is no limitation of the number of snapshottable directories in one filesystem, and a snapshottable directory can have at most 65536 snapshots at the same time. Administrators can set any directory to snapshottable, and any user can create a snapshot once it's set as snapshottable by the administrator. One thing to note is that a nested snapshottable directory is not currently allowed. So, a child whose parent is already snapshottable can't be set as snapshottable. Let's explain how to create a snapshot on HDFS along with some administrator operations.

A snapshot directory is created under its own directory. Snapshot is also an HDFS directory, including all data that exists when the snapshot is created. One snapshottable directory can keep multiple snapshots, and they can be identified with a unique name defined at the time they are created. So, let's look at how to use snapshot in your HDFS directory. There are two types of commands in a snapshot operation. One is for users and the other is for administrators.

```
$ bin/hadoop fs -mkdir /snapshottable
$ bin/hdfs dfsadmin -allowSnapshot /snapshottable
```

An administrator command will allow snapshots. Although it seems like there is no change with an `-allowSnapshot` command, it allows users to create snapshots at any time. The creation of a snapshot can be done by using the `fs -createSnapshot` command.

```
$ bin/hadoop fs -put fileA /snapshottable
$ bin/hadoop fs -put fileB /snapshottable
```

```
$ bin/hadoop fs -createSnapshot /snapshottable
$ bin/hadoop fs -ls /snapshottable/
Found 2 items
-rw-r--r--   1 root supergroup       1366 2016-01-14 07:46 /snapshottable/fileA
-rw-r--r--   1 root supergroup       1366 2016-01-14 08:27 /snapshottable/fileB
```

fileA and fileB are normally stored under /snapshottable. But, where is snapshot? We cannot see the snapshot directory, only the ls command, but we can find it by specifying the full path to a snapshot directory called .snapshot.

```
$ bin/hadoop fs -ls /snapshottable/.snapshot
Found 1 items
drwxr-xr-x   - root supergroup          0 2016-01-14 07:47 /snapshottable/.snapshot/↵
s20160114-074722.738
```

All files stored when snapshot is taken are stored under the directory.

```
$ bin/hadoop fs -ls /snapshottable/.snapshot/s20160114-074722.738
Found 2 items
-rw-r--r--   1 root supergroup       1366 2016-01-14 07:46 /snapshottable/.snapshot/↵
s20160114-074722.738/fileA
-rw-r--r--   1 root supergroup       1366 2016-01-14 07:46 /snapshottable/.snapshot/↵
s20160114-074722.738/fileB
```

These files will no longer be modified. So if the files/directories once snapshotted are needed, all you have to do is to move or copy the data to a normal directory. The big advantage of using the HDFS snapshot is that you don't need to know any new commands or operations, because they are only HDFS files. Any operations you can do to normal HDFS files/directories can also be done to snapshot files/directories.

Next, let's take another snapshot and see the difference of modification after a first snapshot.

```
$ bin/hadoop fs -put fileC /snapshottable
$ bin/hadoop fs -ls /snapshottable
Found 3 items
-rw-r--r--   1 root supergroup       1366 2016-01-14 07:46 /snapshottable/fileA
-rw-r--r--   1 root supergroup       1366 2016-01-14 08:27 /snapshottable/fileB
-rw-r--r--   1 root supergroup       1366 2016-01-14 08:27 /snapshottable/fileC
$ bin/hdfs -createSnapshot /snapshottable
```

You can see the second snapshot under the /snapshottable directory.

```
$ bin/hadoop fs -ls /snapshottable/.snapshot
Found 2 items
drwxr-xr-x   - root supergroup          0 2016-01-14 07:47 /snapshottable/.snapshot/↵
s20160114-074722.738
drwxr-xr-x   - root supergroup          0 2016-01-14 08:30 /snapshottable/.snapshot/↵
s20160114-083038.580
```

The snapshotDiff command can be used to check the total modification that is done to the snapshottable directory. It does not show the actual contents that are modified, but it is enough to check the overview of modifications.

```
$ bin/hdfs snapshotDiff /snapshottable s20160114-074722.738 s20160114-083038.580
Difference between snapshot s20160114-074722.738 and snapshot s20160114-083038.580 ↵
under↵
 directory /snapshottable:
M       .
+       ./fileC
```

The first characters of each line represent the modification types, which are listed in Table 2-6.

TABLE 2-6: snapshotDiff Modification Types

CHARACTER	MODIFICATION TYPE
+	The file/directory has been created
–	The file/directory has been deleted
M	The file/directory has been modified
R	The file/directory has been renamed

Note the difference between deletion and rename. It is regarded as a deletion if the result file after renamed goes to the outside of a snapshottable directory. It is regarded as a rename only if the file is kept on a snapshottable directory. HDFS snapshot provides a simple way to keep copies of file/directory at a time. Although it is useful, HDFS snapshot is not recommended to be used as a full backup. As you know, HDFS snapshot is only an HDFS file/directory. Snapshot data has the same fault tolerance and availability to the file/directory of HDFS. So, the full backup must be provided with more safe and secure storage.

The full instruction of the HDFS snapshot is described at: `http://hadoop.apache.org/docs/current/hadoop-project-dist/hadoop-hdfs/HdfsSnapshots.html`.

Offline Viewer

The offline edit viewer and image viewer provide a way to see the current state of the filesystem by only checking the edits log and fsimage files. All you need is two files. It does not stop the HDFS service to check the name system state. In addition, the offline viewer only depends on files. It is not necessary to operate the HDFS service to check with offline viewers. As described earlier, there are two types of files managed by the HDFS service: the edits log and fsimage. So there are also two types of offline viewers corresponding to these files: the offline edits viewer and offline image viewer. In this section, you learn how to use these offline viewers and their command usage.

First, let's explain the offline edits viewer, which is included as a subcommand of the hdfs command:

```
$  bin/hdfs oev
Usage: bin/hdfs oev [OPTIONS] -i INPUT_FILE -o OUTPUT_FILE
Offline edits viewer
Parse a Hadoop edits log file INPUT_FILE and save results
in OUTPUT_FILE.
```

```
Required command line arguments:
-i,--inputFile <arg>   edits file to process, xml (case
                       insensitive) extension means XML format,
                       any other filename means binary format
-o,--outputFile <arg>  Name of output file. If the specified
                       file exists, it will be overwritten,
                       format of the file is determined
                       by -p option

Optional command line arguments:
-p,--processor <arg>   Select which type of processor to apply
                       against image file, currently supported
                       processors are: binary (native binary format
                       that Hadoop uses), xml (default, XML
                       format), stats (prints statistics about
                       edits file)
-h,--help              Display usage information and exit
-f,--fix-txids         Renumber the transaction IDs in the input,
                       so that there are no gaps or invalid
                       transaction IDs.
-r,--recover           When reading binary edit logs, use recovery
                       mode.  This will give you the chance to skip
                       corrupt parts of the edit log.
-v,--verbose           More verbose output, prints the input and
                       output filenames, for processors that write
                       to a file, also output to screen. On large
                       image files this will dramatically increase
                       processing time (default is false).


Generic options supported are
-conf <configuration file>     specify an application configuration file
-D <property=value>            use value for given property
-fs <local|namenode:port>      specify a namenode
-jt <local|resourcemanager:port>    specify a ResourceManager
-files <comma separated list of files>    specify comma separated files to be copied to↵
 the map reduce cluster
-libjars <comma separated list of jars>    specify comma separated jar files to include↵
 in the classpath.
-archives <comma separated list of archives>    specify comma separated archives to be↵
 unarchived on the compute machines.

The general command line syntax is
command [genericOptions] [commandOptions]
```

The offline edits viewer is a converter that can convert unreadable binary edits log files into readable files, such as XML. Let's assume you have a filesystem like the one shown in Figure 2-7.

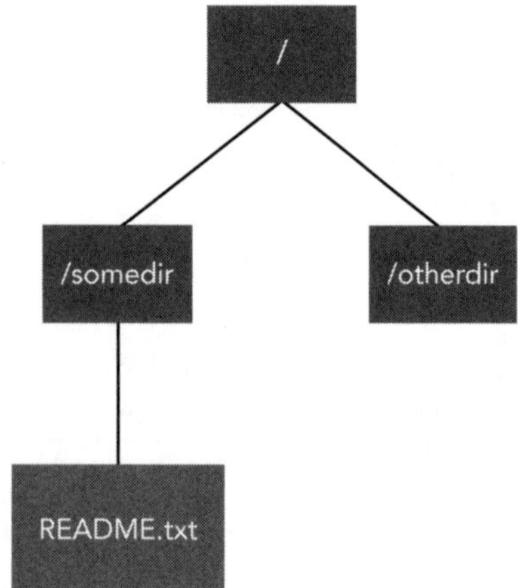

FIGURE 2-7

You can see the results here using this filesystem.

```
$ bin/hdfs oev -i ~/edits_inprogress_0000000000000000001 -o edits.xml
$ cat edits.xml
<?xml version="1.0" encoding="UTF-8"?>
<EDITS>
  <EDITS_VERSION>-64</EDITS_VERSION>
  <RECORD>
    <OPCODE>OP_START_LOG_SEGMENT</OPCODE>
    <DATA>
      <TXID>1</TXID>
    </DATA>
  </RECORD>
  <RECORD>
    <OPCODE>OP_MKDIR</OPCODE>
    <DATA>
      <TXID>2</TXID>
      <LENGTH>0</LENGTH>
      <INODEID>16386</INODEID>
      <PATH>/tmp</PATH>
      <TIMESTAMP>1453857409206</TIMESTAMP>
      <PERMISSION_STATUS>
        <USERNAME>root</USERNAME>
        <GROUPNAME>supergroup</GROUPNAME>
        <MODE>504</MODE>
      </PERMISSION_STATUS>
    </DATA>
  </RECORD>
  <RECORD>
    <OPCODE>OP_MKDIR</OPCODE>
    <DATA>
      <TXID>3</TXID>
      <LENGTH>0</LENGTH>
      <INODEID>16387</INODEID>
      <PATH>/tmp/hadoop-yarn</PATH>
```

```
        <TIMESTAMP>1453857409411</TIMESTAMP>
        <PERMISSION_STATUS>
          <USERNAME>root</USERNAME>
          <GROUPNAME>supergroup</GROUPNAME>
          <MODE>504</MODE>
        </PERMISSION_STATUS>
      </DATA>
    </RECORD>
    <RECORD>
...
```

Although this is only part of the output, you can see how each operation performed on HDFS is recorded in the file. It is useful to investigate the current HDFS state at the binary level. In addition, the offline edits viewer can convert back to binary with the XML file.

```
$ bin/hdfs oev -p binary -i edits.xml -o edit
```

You can specify the conversion algorithm with -p (processor) option. You can use binary when you want to go back to binary format. The candidates of the option are binary, XML, and stats, but XML is the default. You can see the statistics of each operation with the `stats` option:

```
$ bin/hdfs oev -p stats -i edits.xml -o edit_stats
$ cat edits_stats
    VERSION                            : -64
    OP_ADD                        (  0): 1
    OP_RENAME_OLD                 (  1): 1
    OP_DELETE                     (  2): null
    OP_MKDIR                      (  3): 8
    OP_SET_REPLICATION            (  4): null
    OP_DATANODE_ADD               (  5): null
    OP_DATANODE_REMOVE            (  6): null
    OP_SET_PERMISSIONS            (  7): 1
    OP_SET_OWNER                  (  8): null
    OP_CLOSE                      (  9): 1
    OP_SET_GENSTAMP_V1            ( 10): null
    OP_SET_NS_QUOTA               ( 11): null
    OP_CLEAR_NS_QUOTA             ( 12): null
    OP_TIMES                      ( 13): null
    OP_SET_QUOTA                  ( 14): null
    OP_RENAME                     ( 15): null
    OP_CONCAT_DELETE              ( 16): null
    OP_SYMLINK                    ( 17): null
      ...
```

Keep in mind that you can't change the stats file back to an XML or binary file, because it loses some information. So, when should you use the offline edits viewer? If you can read edits log then you can also edit it. If the edits log file has been broken by accident, but remains partially intact, you can restore the original file by manually rewriting the edits log. In that case, first you need to convert the edits log into XML, and then you can edit the XML file as you like if you have a true operation sequence, making it back to binary format. After getting back to binary format, HDFS can read it once it's restarted. But in some cases, the manual editing of the edits log can cause further serious problems, such as a typo or invalid operation types. Please pay attention to the manual operation if you have to do this.

There is one more very similar tool called the offline image viewer. The offline edits viewer is for viewing the edits log in a readable format. In the same way, the offline image viewer is for viewing fsimage in a readable format. The offline image viewer enables you to not only view image file contents, but also to access through the WebHDFS API to analyze and examine it deeply. It is usually necessary to run a checkpoint to create an fsimage file. But, you can do it manually too. If you have fsimage on your cluster, you do not need to do run the checkpoint. Saving a current HDFS namespace into fsimage can be done via the `savesNamespace` command.

```
$ bin/hdfs dfsadmin -safemode enter
Safe mode is ON
$ bin/hdfs dfsadmin -saveNamespace
Save namespace successful
$ bin/hdfs dfsadmin -safemode leave
Safe mode is OFF
```

Although we won't explain the detail of safe mode here, it is a command to make the HDFS read-only mode do maintenance. Otherwise write operations can occur using HDFS while saving the namespace in the fsimage file. After leaving safe mode, you can see the new fsimage file under the HDFS NameNode root directory.

```
$ ls -l /tmp/hadoop-root/dfs/name/current
-rw-r--r-- 1 root root     214 Jan 27 04:41 VERSION
-rw-r--r-- 1 root root 1048576 Jan 27 04:41 edits_inprogress_0000000000000000018
-rw-r--r-- 1 root root     362 Jan 27 01:16 fsimage_0000000000000000000
-rw-r--r-- 1 root root      62 Jan 27 01:16 fsimage_0000000000000000000.md5
-rw-r--r-- 1 root root     970 Jan 27 04:41 fsimage_0000000000000000017
```

The latest fsimage file is fsimage_0000000000000000017. Launch the WebHDFS server with the offline image viewer using the oiv command.

```
$ bin/hdfs oivl -i fsimage_0000000000000000017
16/01/27 05:03:30 WARN channel.DefaultChannelId: Failed to find a usable hardware↵
 address from the network interfaces; using random bytes: a4:3d:28:d3:a7:e5:60:94
16/01/27 05:03:30 INFO offlineImageViewer.WebImageViewer: WebImageViewer started. ↵
 Listening on /127.0.0.1:5978. Press Ctrl+C to stop the viewer.
```

You can simply access the server by specifying the webhdfs schema.

```
$ bin/hadoop fs -ls webhdfs://127.0.0.1:5978
bin/hadoop fs -ls webhdfs://127.0.0.1:5978/
Found 3 items
drwxr-xr-x   - root supergroup          0 2016-01-27 01:20 webhdfs://127.0.0.1:5978/↵
otherdir
drwxr-xr-x   - root supergroup          0 2016-01-27 01:20 webhdfs://127.0.0.1:5978/↵
somedir
drwxrwx---   - root supergroup          0 2016-01-27 01:16 webhdfs://127.0.0.1:5978/tmp
```

This is similar to the directory structure shown in Figure 2-7. WebHDFS provides the REST API through HTTP. So, you can access the offline image viewer through wget, curl, and other tools.

```
curl -i http://127.0.0.1:5978/webhdfs/v1/?op=liststatus
HTTP/1.1 200 OK
content-type: application/json; charset=utf-8
content-length: 690
connection: close
```

```
{"FileStatuses":{"FileStatus":[
{"fileId":16394,"accessTime":0,"replication":0,"owner":"root","length":0,
"permission":"755","blockSize":0,"modificationTime":1453857650965,"type":
"DIRECTORY","group":"supergroup","childrenNum":0,"pathSuffix":"otherdir"},
{"fileId":16392,"accessTime":0,"replication":0,"owner":"root","length":0,
"permission":"755","blockSize":0,"modificationTime":1453857643759,"type":
"DIRECTORY","group":"supergroup","childrenNum":1,"pathSuffix":"somedir"},
{"fileId":16386,"accessTime":0,"replication":0,"owner":"root","length":0,
"permission":"770","blockSize":0,"modificationTime":1453857409411,"type":
"DIRECTORY","group":"supergroup","childrenNum":1,"pathSuffix":"tmp"}
]}}
```


There is one more offline image viewer command due to the internal layout change of fsimage. The offline image viewer uses a lot of memory and loses some functions. If you want to avoid this problem, use the offline image viewer legacy (`oiv_legacy`), which is the same as the `oiv` command in Hadoop 2.3.

Tiered Storage

The storage capacity required for enterprise usage is rapidly increasing, whereas the data stored in Hadoop HDFS is growing exponentially. The cost of data storage is also increasing. While making use of data earns a lot of money and grows businesses, data management costs a lot of time and money. Tiered storage is an idea designed to use storage capacity more efficiently. According to HDFS-6584 (`https://issues.apache.org/jira/browse/HDFS-6584`), this feature is called Archival Storage in HDFS. Keep in mind that the data frequency usage is not always the same. Some data is frequently used from the workload, such as MapReduce jobs, and others are rarely used because they become old. Archival storage defines a new metric called temperature in terms of the frequency of accessing the data. The frequently accessed data is categorized as HOT. It is better to put HOT data on memory or SSD in order to increase the total throughput of workloads. The data is rarely accessed and categorized into COLD data, which can be put on slow disk or archive storage. You can achieve a reasonable amount of cost savings, because using a slow disk provides more benefits than using a low latency disk. So, archival storage provides you an option for easily managing this type of heterogeneous storage system.

There are two concepts that should be known in advance: storage types and storage policies.

- **Storage types:** Storage types represent a physical storage system. This is originally introduced by HDFS-2832, aiming to use various types of a storage system under HDFS. Currently `ARCHIVE`, `DISK`, `SSD` and `RAM_DISK` are supported. ARCHIVE is a type of machine that has high density storage, but little compute power. `RAM_DISK` is supported for putting a single replica in memory. Their names do not necessarily represent the actual physical storage, even if you can configure their types arbitrarily according to your hardware.
- **Storage policies:** Blocks can be stored on multiple heterogeneous storages, according to the storage policy. Embedded policies are as follows.
    - **Hot:** The data that is frequently used should stay on the Hot policy. When a block is Hot, all replicas are stored in `DISK`.
    - **Cold:** The data that is no longer used on a daily basis should stay on Cold policy. Moving Hot data to Cold data is the usual case. When a block is Cold, all blocks are stored in `ARCHIVE`.

- **Warm:** This policy is between the Hot and Cold policy. When a block is Warm, some of its replicas are stored in `DISK` and the remaining replicas are stored in `ARCHIVE`.
- **All_SSD:** When a block is All_SSD, all blocks are stored in `SSD`.
- **One_SSD:** When a block is One_SSD, one replica is stored in `SSD`. The remaining replicas are on `DISK`.
- **Lazy_Persist:** When a block is Lazy_Persist, the single replica is stored in memory. The replica is first written on `RAM_DISK` and then persisted in `DISK`.

The preceding list is summarized in Table 2-7.

TABLE 2-7: Policy Details

POLICY ID	POLICY NAME	BLOCK PLACEMENT (N REPLICAS)
15	Lazy_Persist	`RAM_DISK: 1, DISK: n - 1`
12	All_SSD	`SSD: n`
10	One_SSD	`SSD: 1, DISK: n - 1`
7	Hot (default policy)	`DISK: n`
5	Warm	`DISK: 1, ARCHIVE: n - 1`
2	Cold	`ARCHIVE: n`

The file policy can be specified with the command `dfsadmin -setStoragePolicy`. The list in Table 2-7 can be seen with `bin/hdfs storagepolicies -listPolicies`:

```
$ bin/hdfs storagepolicies -listPolicies
Block Storage Policies:
BlockStoragePolicy{COLD:2, storageTypes=[ARCHIVE], \
        creationFallbacks=[], replicationFallbacks=[]}
BlockStoragePolicy{WARM:5, storageTypes=[DISK, ARCHIVE], \
        creationFallbacks=[DISK, ARCHIVE], replicationFallbacks=[DISK, ARCHIVE]}
BlockStoragePolicy{HOT:7, storageTypes=[DISK], \
        creationFallbacks=[], replicationFallbacks=[ARCHIVE]}
BlockStoragePolicy{ONE_SSD:10, storageTypes=[SSD, DISK], \
        creationFallbacks=[SSD, DISK], replicationFallbacks=[SSD, DISK]}
BlockStoragePolicy{ALL_SSD:12, storageTypes=[SSD], \
        creationFallbacks=[DISK], replicationFallbacks=[DISK]}
BlockStoragePolicy{LAZY_PERSIST:15, storageTypes=[RAM_DISK, DISK], \
        creationFallbacks=[DISK], replicationFallbacks=[DISK]}
```

In addition, you need to write some type of configuration for HDFS cluster.

- `dfs.storage.policy.enabled`: Enabling/Disabling the archival storage feature on your cluster. The default value is true.
- `dfs.datanode.data.dir`: This is a comma separated storage location. It specifies which directory corresponds to which policy. For example, you can specify the `/tmp/dn/disk0` as `DISK` policy with `[DISK]file:///tmp/dn/disk0`.

Archival storage is a solution to reduce the unnecessary usage of storage capacity. Using storage efficiently has a huge impact on cost savings, and eventually even on business performance. So, the HDFS project is now progressing with development to solve the problem.

Erasure Coding

HDFS Erasure Coding has not been released yet. This project is under active development. The purpose of Erasure Coding is the same as Archival storage; it enables you to more efficiently use storage capacity. Erasure coding takes an approach similar to a RAID parity drive system. So, Erasure coding achieves fault tolerance by creating parity blocks instead of replication. This means original data can be reconstructed with other blocks. Reconstructing original data takes time, and can be costly, due to the computing cost of decoding. Erasure coding can achieve a relatively higher fault tolerance than an ordinal replication system on HDFS. The basic architecture of Erasure coding is described next.

In a replication context, a block is replicated and distributed across the cluster. Since a block is usually copied to three replicas, the overhead of storage capacity is 2x, and the redundancy of each block is 3x. This is usually good for the workload itself, because it is necessary to fetch only one replica to obtain a block data. You cannot use only one third of the storage capacity of a whole cluster because of the overhead of storage capacity. On the other hand, Erasure coding divides a block into 9 blocks that have different data than the original block. 6 blocks are called data blocks and 3 blocks are called parity blocks. The total number of data blocks is the same as the original data. So, any 6 blocks out of 9 blocks can reconstruct any other blocks. This means that you can lose at most 3 corresponding blocks, because you can generate the whole data if 6 blocks remain on the storage system. The overhead of storage capacity is 1.5x (= all 9 blocks / 6 data blocks). The redundancy of each block is 3x, because you can lose any 3 blocks. The coding algorithm used in this case is called Reed-Solomon (see Table 2-8), which is the default algorithm used in Erasure coding.

TABLE 2-8: Reed-Solomon in Erasure Coding

	3 REPLICATION	(6,3) REED-SOLOMON
Maximum Toleration	2	3
Disk space usage	3x	1.5x
Client-DataNode connection (write)	1	9
Client-DataNode connection (read)	1	6

As you can see in Table 2-8, the connections that are necessary for reading and writing in the Reed-Solomon case are larger than the replication cases, because Reed-Solomon always requires you to create all 9 blocks when writing, and to read at least 6 blocks to reconstruct original data (see Figure 2-8). This is the cost of using Erasure coding in your cluster. Therefore, Erasure coding should be used infrequently with Cold data. Since Cold data is not used on a daily basis, you might consider reducing the storage cost of keeping cold data, even if it sacrifices some throughput or latency, which can be done using. Erasure coding.

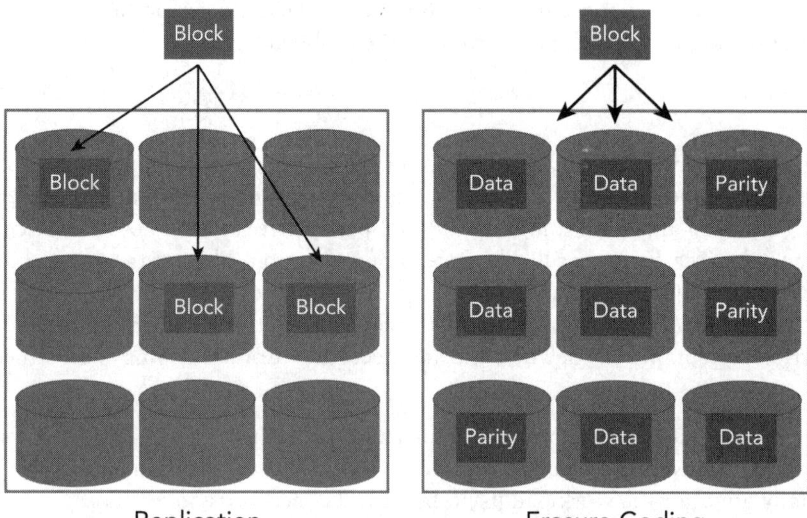

FIGURE 2-8

Let's briefly examine some Erasure coding. The Erasure coding feature was merged into the `trunk` branch of the HDFS source code repository. If you can build it, you can also try Erasure coding in the same way. Since the explanation about how to build HDFS is written in `BUILDING.txt` in the source tree, we will omit that detail here.

First, you need to specify which directory is for Erasure coding. The `hdfs` command provides the `erasurecode` subcommand for this purpose:

```
$ bin/hdfs erasurecode
Usage: hdfs erasurecode [generic options]
       [-getPolicy <path>]
       [-help [cmd ...]]
       [-listPolicies]
       [-setPolicy [-p <policyName>] <path>]
       [-usage [cmd ...]]
```

The policy in the Erasure coding context indicates the algorithm used for calculating data blocks and parity blocks. You can confirm what types of policies are supported using the `-listPolicies` option.

```
$ bin/hdfs erasurecode -listPolicies
RS-6-3-64k
```

RS-6-3-64k specifies the algorithm using Reed-Solomon that has 6 data blocks and 3 parity blocks with a 64KB coding unit. You can set the Erasure coding directory using the -setPolicy option:

```
$ bin/hadoop fs -mkdir  /ecdir
$ bin/hdfs erasure code -setPolicy
$ bin/hdfs erasurecode -setPolicy -p RS-6-3-64k /ecdir
EC policy set successfully at hdfs://master:9000/ecdir
```

All new data put on /ecdir is automatically created according to the Erasure coding algorithm.

```
$ bin/hadoop fs -put README.txt /ecdir
$ bin/hdfs erasurecode -getPolicy /ecdir
ErasureCodingPolicy=[Name=RS-6-3-64k, Schema=[ECSchema=[Codec=rs, numDataUnits=6, ↲
 numParityUnits=3]], CellSize=65536 ]
```

You can check that the blocks are separated into nine blocks from the web UI of NameNode (see Figure 2-9).

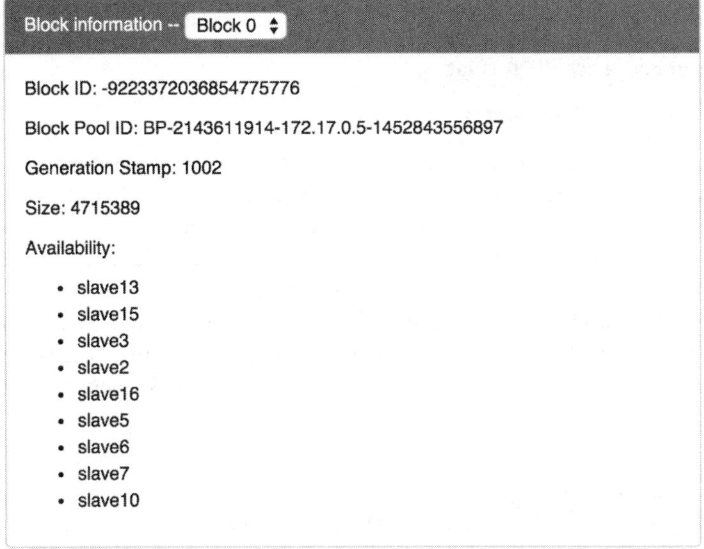

FIGURE 2-9

The interface of the Erasure coding file is not changed. You can do any operations with Erasure coded files, as well as ordinal replication files. Thus, Erasure coding provides a new way to more efficiently manage storage capacity. We look forward to seeing the release of the Erasure coding feature in future HDFS versions.

FILE FORMAT

HDFS can store any type of data, including text data in binary format, including even image or audio files. HDFS was initially and currently developed to be used by MapReduce. So, the file format that fits to the MapReduce or Hive workload is usually used. You can achieve better performance by using the appropriate file format for your workload. The detail on how to use these file formats will be described in the following chapters. In this section, we briefly introduce some types of file formats that are usually used by HDFS and MapReduce. It is necessary, however, to know the purpose of the workload and to specify the necessity. For example, the necessity may be to finish the job in 10 minutes or finish processing the job with 10TBs of input data. The purpose and necessity decide not only the job execution engine, such as MapReduce, but also the storage file format. In addition, it is also important to specify the frequency of updating the data in HDFS, or the size of input data in order to choose the compression algorithm. Let's look at some points here before choosing the file format.

- **SequenceFile:** SequenceFile is a binary format that contains key/value pairs, and it is the format included in the Hadoop project. SequenceFile supports a custom compression codec that can be specified by `CompressionCodec`. There are three different formats for SequenceFile. All of these types share the common header that contains the metadata of actual data, such as version, key/value class name, compression codec, etc. The three data formats are:
    - Uncompressed SequenceFile format
    - Record-compressed SequenceFile format
    - Block-compressed SequenceFile format
- The uncompressed format is the most simple and easy to understand. Each record is represented as a key/value pair. The record-compressed format compresses the record data, where each record is represented as a key and a compressed value pair (see Figure 2-10). The block-compressed format compresses many records at once. SequenceFile retains a synchronization marker between some of the records. It is essential to use SequenceFile in a MapReduce job, because MapReduce requires a splittable file format to distribute each task. Since SequenceFile is supported by Hive by default, it is not necessary to write a specific setting. SequenceFile is a row-oriented format, and the API documentation of SequenceFile is written here: (`https://hadoop.apache.org/docs/stable/api/org/apache/hadoop/io/SequenceFile.html`).

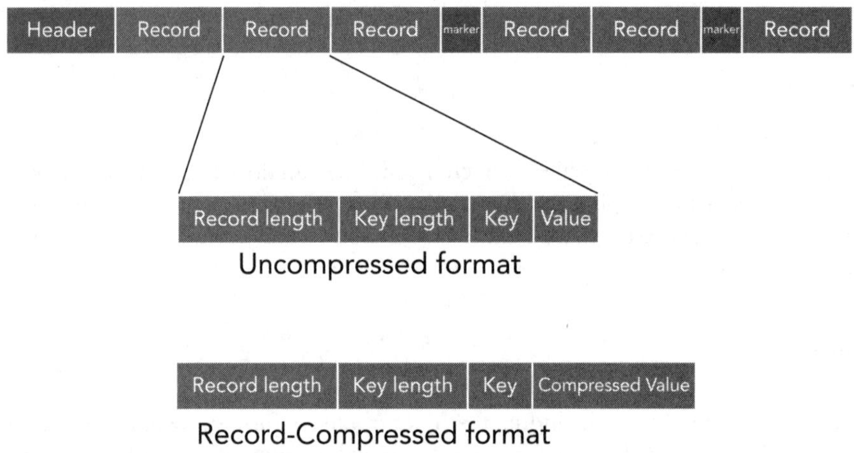

FIGURE 2-10

- **Avro:** Avro is very similar to SequenceFile. Avro was started in order to achieve portability that can't be obtained by SequenceFile. Avro can be used by various types of programming languages: C/C++, C#, Java, Python, and more. Avro is a self-described data format, and it has a metadata that includes a schema of contained records. In addition, Avro supports the compression of contained data just as well as SequenceFile can. So Avro is also a row-oriented storage format. In addition, the Avro file also retains a splittable synchronization marker. The Avro schema is usually written in a `*.avsc` file. If the file is put on a class path, you can load any custom schema. Though the API of using the `*.avsc` file directly is a generic method, you can also generate the specific API code by using the Avro Maven plugin (`avro-maven-plugin`). The latest getting started guide for Avro is here: (`https://avro.apache.org/docs/1.7.7/gettingstartedjava.html`).
- **Parquet:** Parquet is a columnar storage format for Hadoop frameworks. Parquet is a format for achieving nested name space in a columnar format, and is inspired by the Dremel paper: (`http://research.google.com/pubs/pub36632.html`). This nested space feature is the main advantage of using Parquet, compared to using XML/JSON. In addition, it can efficiently store sparse data that contains a lot of null fields. The encoding/decoding specification is described here: (`https://github.com/Parquet/parquet-mr/wiki/The-striping-and-assembly-algorithms-from-the-Dremel-paper`). Parquet uses Thrift as its serialization format. Ordinary columnar-oriented databases require you to often read columnars from multiple machines. It increases the cost of I/O due to its network accessing requirement. Parquet defines row groups and column chunks. A row group is a logical collection of rows that also consists of some column chunks, which are chunks for a specific column. Since they are guaranteed to be contiguous in a file, it is possible to reduce the cost of a multiple reading I/O. A file contains some columns for each record, so it might not be necessary to read another file in order to fetch another column if a current Parquet file already contains it. There are several implementations of Parquet. They are listed on `https://github.com/apache/parquet-mr`. You can use Parquet in MapReduce, Hive, or Pig without writing new code. Adapting Parquet can help you achieve good performance and reduce the development cost at the same time.
- **ORCFile:** ORCFile is an optimized version of RCFile. ORCFile is also a columnar storage file format. Though ORCFile initially was developed inside the Hive project, it doesn't currently depend on the Hive metastore. The original RCFile has limitations, because it does not retain its semantics and type information. ORCFile is a completely self-describing file format that also supports nested type data. It makes use of type information for a reader and writer that provides compression techniques such as dictionary encoding, bit packing, and delta encoding. One characteristic of the ORCFile is that it keeps minimum and maximum values for each column of a set of rows, although a query doesn't need to access actual column data by using this statistical data. ORCFile is mainly stored in HDFS and read by Hive queries. So, the index of data is written at the end of the file because HDFS does not support changing the data after it is written. If your main workload is through Hive, then ORCFile is the best candidate for your storage.

These file formats that we have explored are primarily used by HDFS. Since they are also actively developed, you will see more of them implemented in the future. Of course, the storage file format should fit your workload, meaning you have to choose the storage file format used in your HDFS. Now let's cover some of the important points for choosing storage file formats.

- **Query engine:** If your SQL engine does not support ORCFile, you cannot use ORCFile. You have to choose the storage file format supported by your query engine or application framework such as MapReduce.
- **Updating frequency:** Columnar storage format does not fit into high frequency updated data, because it requires the use of a whole file. It is necessary to take into consideration the requirements of data updating.
- **Splittability:** The data must be splittable in order to be distributed for each task. This is a critical problem if you are considering using a distributed framework such as MapReduce.
- **Compression:** You may want to reduce the storage cost rather than the throughput or latency of the workload. It is necessary to investigate the compression supported by each file format further in this case.

This list should be helpful when choosing the storage file format for use in your HDFS. Make sure you run the benchmark and also measure the performance of each candidate with your actual use cases.

CLOUD STORAGE

In this last section, we will introduce some cloud services that provide storage on HDFS. We covered how to use HDFS and how to construct an HDFS cluster. But it is not always the best option to use HDFS, because of the cost of maintenance and hardware used in HDFS. Therefore, using a cloud service to fit your enterprise requirements can be a good idea. You may be able to reduce not only the money to buy hardware and network equipment, but also the time to set up a cluster and maintain it. Here is a list of major services that are providing cloud storage on HDFS.

- **Amazon EMR:** Amazon Elastic MapReduce is a cloud service for Hadoop. It provides an easy way to create Hadoop clusters on EC2 instances and to access HDFS or S3. You can use major distributions on Amazon EMR such as Hortonworks Data Platform, and MapR distributions. The launching process is automated and simplified by Amazon EMR, and HDFS can be used to store intermediate data generated while running a job on an Amazon EMR cluster. Only input and final output are put on S3, which is the best practice for using EMR storage: (`http://aws.amazon.com/documentation/elastic-mapreduce/`).
- **Treasure Data Service:** Treasure Data is a fully managed cloud data platform. You can easily import any type of data on a storage system managed by Treasure Data, which uses HDFS and S3 internally, but encapsulates their detail. You do not have to pay attention to these storage systems. Treasure Data mainly uses Hive and Presto as its analytics platform. You can write SQL to analyze what is imported on a Treasure Data storage service. Treasure Data is using HDFS and S3 as its backend and makes use of their advantages respectively. If you do not want to do any operation on HDFS, Treasure Data can be a best choice: (`http://www.treasuredata.com`).

- **Azure Blob Storage:** Azure Blob Storage is a cloud storage service provided by Microsoft. The combination of Azure Blob Storage and HDInsight provides a full-featured HDFS compatible storage system. A user who is used to HDFS can seamlessly use Azure Blob Storage. A lot of Hadoop ecosystems can operate directly on the data that Azure Blob Storage manages. Azure Blob Storage is optimized to be used by a computation layer such as HDInsight, and it provides various types of interfaces, such as PowerShell and of course Hadoop HDFS commands. The developers who are already comfortable using Hadoop can get started easily with Azure Blob Storage: (`https://azure.microsoft.com/en-us/documentation/services/storage/`).

SUMMARY

This chapter covered the HDFS basic architecture and the role it plays among all Hadoop ecosystems, including Spark, Tez, Hive, and Pig. In short, HDFS is a basic system of all big data infrastructures. Operating HDFS can be hard work and requires a skillful DevOps engineer to make the system reliable in your company. This chapter should help you during your daily operational work on the HDFS cluster. In addition, this chapter covered some descriptions about advanced features of HDFS. Of course we didn't cover all of the HDFS features. For a full list of features, see the official documentation: (`http://hadoop.apache.org/docs/current/hadoop-project-dist/hadoop-hdfs/HdfsUserGuide.html`). You won't find more about Erasure coding in this guide because Erasure coding hasn't been released yet. We strongly recommend that you don't currently use Erasure coding in production, but trying usage and bug reports are always welcome. Please wait for this coming release for one of the biggest features in HDFS!

3

Computation

WHAT'S IN THIS CHAPTER?

- Explaining the architecture of Hadoop MapReduce components
- Setting up a MapReduce job
- Details of MapReduce operations
- Spark job and MapReduce differences

In the previous chapter we set up a Hadoop integrated storage system, where we stored huge amounts of data to be used by a distributed computation engine. Hadoop MapReduce is the major distributed computation framework that has been used for a long time. Hadoop MapReduce is an actual open source implementation of MapReduce, supported by various types of companies and individuals. The reliability and results of Hadoop MapReduce for enterprise usage is outstanding among many of the distributed computation frameworks.

In this chapter, we will introduce the basic concept of MapReduce, and the details of implementing Hadoop MapReduce. Hadoop MapReduce is easily understood by engineers who are familiar with distributed computation or high performance computing. If you have sufficient knowledge in that area, please skip this first section about the basics of MapReduce.

BASICS OF HADOOP MAPREDUCE

Hadoop MapReduce is an open source version of a distributed computational framework originally introduced by Google. MapReduce enables you to easily write general distributed applications on Hadoop, and the MapReduce computational model is so general that you can write almost any type of process logic used in enterprise. Here we will explain the basic concepts and purposes of the MapReduce framework needed to write a MapReduce application. We will then introduce the concrete architecture of Hadoop MapReduce.

Concept

There are three primary features that MapReduce is trying to solve:

- High scalability
- High fault tolerance
- High level interface to achieve these two points

MapReduce does not achieve high scalability with distributed processing and high fault tolerance at the same time. Distributed computation is often a messy thing, so it is difficult to write a reliable distributed application by yourself. There are various kinds of failures that are introduced when distributed applications are running: Some servers might fail abruptly, whereas some disks may get out of order. Keep in mind that writing code to handle failures by yourself is very time consuming and can also cause new bugs in your application.

Hadoop MapReduce, however, can take care of fault tolerance. When your application fails, the framework can handle the cause of failure and retry it or abort. Thanks to this feature, the application can complete its tasks while overcoming failures.

Hadoop MapReduce is integrated with HDFS, which was introduced in Chapter 2. The MapReduce framework handles the input and output between your application and HDFS. You don't have to write I/O code between these two frameworks. HDFS can also handle block failure, and as long as you use HDFS with MapReduce, you don't have to pay attention to storage layer failure. On the contrary, you should not use a storage system that doesn't take disk failure or node failure into consideration with the MapReduce framework. Otherwise, the reliability and scalability of your application will worsen.

The MapReduce application is divided into several phases, which are described in the following list and illustrated in Figure 3-1. The tasks you must write are map and reduce, but the other tasks are managed by the MapReduce framework.

- **map:** Read the data from a storage system such as HDFS.
- **sort:** Sort the input data from the map task according to their keys.
- **shuffle:** Divide the sorted data and repartitioning among cluster nodes.
- **merge:** Merge the input data sent from mapper on each node.
- **reduce:** Read the merged data and integrate them into one result.

Hadoop MapReduce defines all sort, shuffle, and merge operations in advance. You must write the map and reduce operations, which are defined by `Mapper` and `Reducer`. Hadoop MapReduce prepares a sufficient abstraction for the distributed programming model. Basically, the data type MapReduce can manipulate is a tuple that contains a key and a value. You can use any type of key or value as long as they are serializable, but you must pass the data between `Mapper` and `Reducer` in the tuple format. `Mapper` converts an input record into a tuple that has a key and a value, and you can define which part needs to be extracted from the input data by `Mapper`. `Mapper` has a method named `map` for converting input data. Keep in mind that the output tuple data type from the `Mapper` class is not necessarily the same as the input data type.

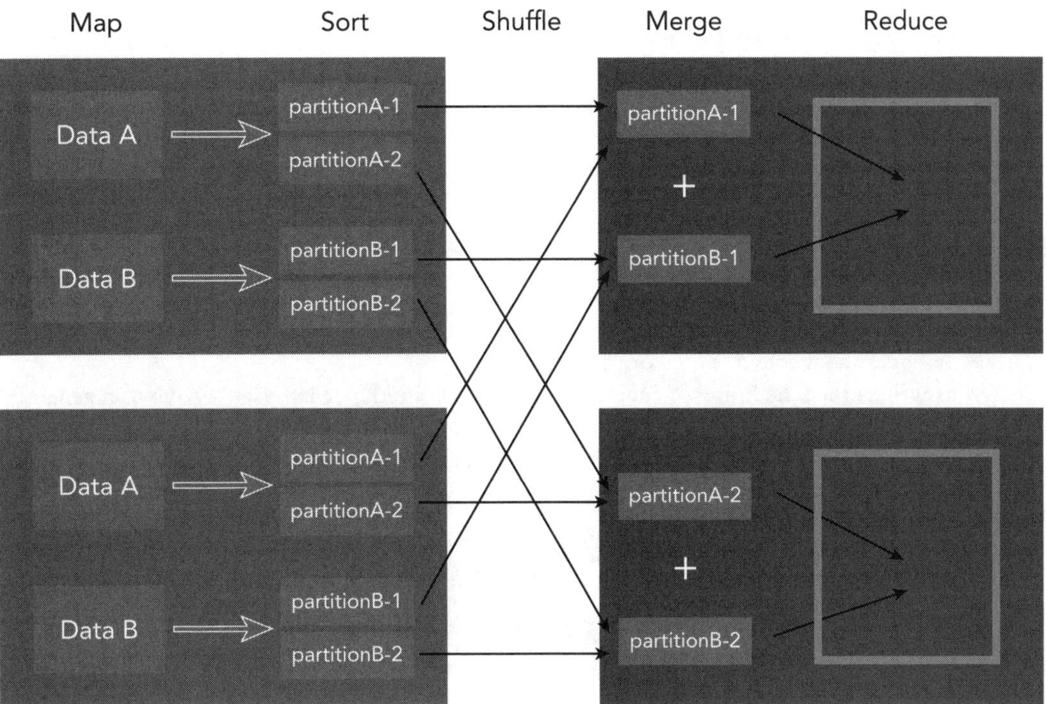

FIGURE 3-1

The outputs from the `Mapper` class are transferred to `Reducers`. Tuples that have the same key are all transferred to the same `Reducer`. Therefore, if a tuple has a "Dog" text as a key and is transferred to reducer1, the next tuple that has a "Dog" as its key must be transferred to reducer1 (see Figure 3-2). If it is necessary to aggregate some type of value, you should set the same key in the `Mapper` class. For example, if you want to count the number of appearances of each word in text, a key should be the word itself in the `Mapper` class. The same words are transferred to the same `Reducer`, and the `Reducer` can take the sum of the total tuples transferred from `Mappers`.

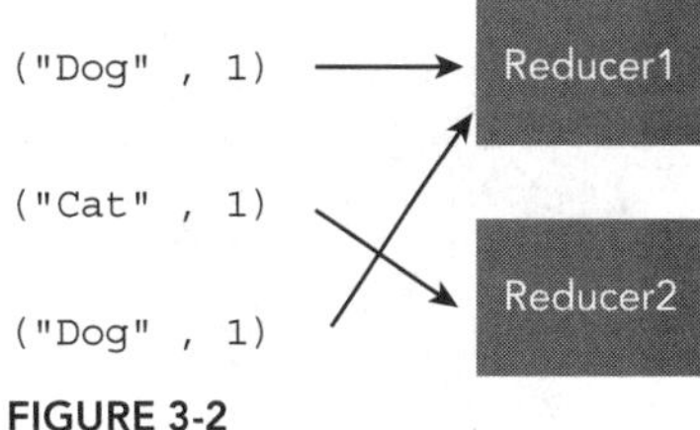

FIGURE 3-2

Figure 3-3 shows the overall abstraction of data flow in MapReduce. As you can see, the important notion in the MapReduce data flow is a key-value tuple. Once a record in the storage system is converted into a key-value tuple by `Mapper`, the MapReduce system manipulates the data according to the key-value tuple abstraction as described in Figure 3-3.

You may think that this programming model is not powerful and flexible, given that the only things you can define are how to convert input data into key-value tuples, and how to get results from aggregated tuples. But, you can write many types of applications that are needed for daily data analysis. This has certainly been proven by Hadoop use cases in many companies. A concrete MapReduce application will be written later in this chapter.

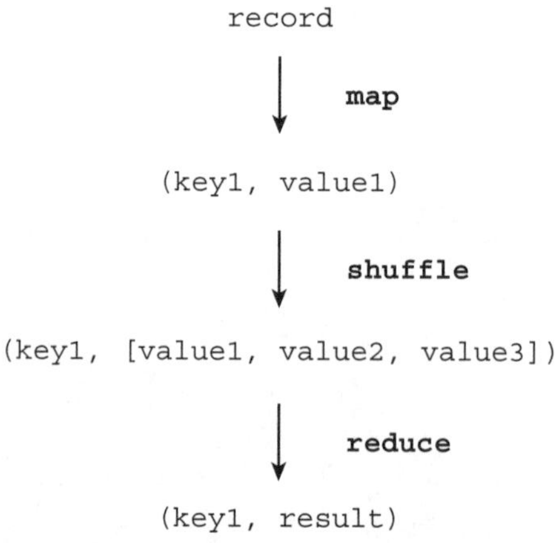

FIGURE 3-3

Architecture

Hadoop MapReduce currently runs on YARN, which is a resource manager developed by the Hadoop project. YARN manages the whole resource of your Hadoop cluster, as well as the scheduling of each application submitted by each user. YARN is a general resource management framework, which is not specific to the MapReduce application. Recently, a lot of framework applications such as Spark, Storm, and HBase are able to run on YARN. An overview of YARN and the MapReduce application is shown in Figure 3-4.

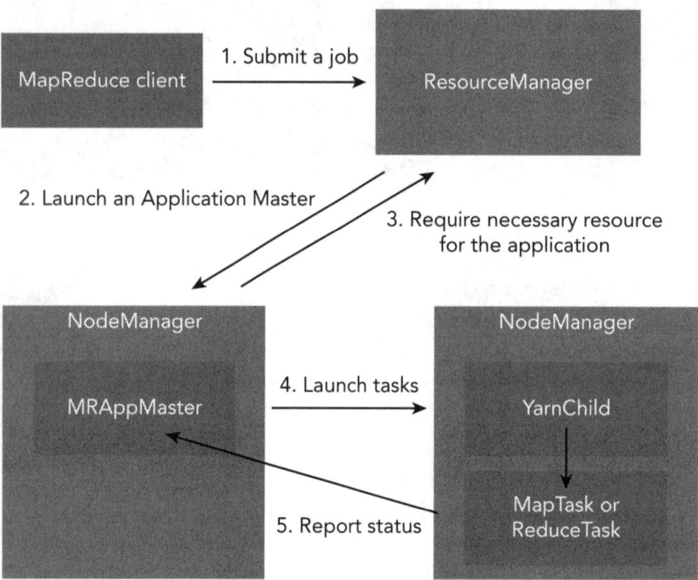

FIGURE 3-4

Figure 3-4 illustrates the use of both YARN and the MapReduce framework. YARN components are permanent daemons that keep running after applications have finished. Let's examine ResourceManager and NodeManager:

- **ResourceManager:** ResourceManager manages whole memory and CPU cores of the YARN cluster. ResourceManager decides how much memory and how many CPU cores can be given to each application. After finishing the application, ResourceManager collects log files generated through each task so that you can find the cause of any failures in your application. ResourceManager is a master server of the YARN cluster, and there is usually one ResourceManager in one YARN cluster.

- **NodeManager:** NodeManager manages concrete tasks. After requesting to launch a process called a container for each task from the application master, NodeManager will do this same thing on each node. NodeManager is a slave server in a YARN cluster. Increasing servers in a YARN cluster often means increasing servers managed by NodeManager. The total capacity of YARN clusters in terms of memory and CPU cores is determined by the number of slaves managed by NodeManagers.

Components shown in Figure 3-4 are temporary, and are necessary only when an application is running. They are diminished after an application has successfully finished. The flow of submitting a MapReduce application on YARN is also described in Figure 3-4.

1. Requesting to submit an application using ResourceManager. When the request finishes successfully, the job client uploads resource files such as any JARs and configurations on HDFS.
2. ResourceManager submits a request to a NodeManager to launch a container for the application master that manages the whole progress of this application. In the case of the MapReduce framework, MRAppMaster plays a role as an application master.
3. MRAppMaster requests the ResourceManager to provide the necessary resources. ResourceManager replies with the number of containers and the list of available NodeManagers.
4. According to the given resource from ResourceManager, MRAppMaster launches containers on NodeManagers. NodeManagers launch a process called YarnChild in a MapReduce application, and YarnChild runs a concrete task such as Mapper or Reducer.
5. While the application is running, MapTask and ReduceTask report the progress to MRAppMaster. MRAppMaster knows the whole progress of the application thanks to the given status report from each task. The progress can be seen with the ResourceManager web UI, because ResourceManager knows where MRAppMaster is running.

After the application finishes, MRAppMaster, and each task process, will clean up temporary data generated from the running application. The log files are collected by the YARN framework or the history server (which will be explained in the following section) and archived on HDFS. It is necessary to investigate the cause of any failures introduced by your application, which is the overview of the whole process of the MapReduce application on YARN. You know the importance of resource management in distributed applications such as MapReduce. The number of memory and CPU cores must be shared successfully among applications running on one YARN cluster. This resource distribution is managed by the scheduler in ResourceManager. Currently there are two implementations of scheduler on YARN:

- **Fair scheduler**: Fair scheduler tries to distribute the same resource to each user in a fixed span. It does not mean that a user who submits more jobs than other users can obtain more resources than other average users. Each user has a resource pool for their own jobs, which are put in the resource pool. If a resource pool can't receive sufficient resources, the

Fair scheduler can kill a task that uses too many resources and gives the resources to the resource pool that cannot receive enough resources in a span.

- **Capacity scheduler**: Capacity scheduler prepares job queues for all users. Each queue is a priority FIFO (First In First Out). The queues have a hierarchical structure, so a queue might be a child of another queue. Thanks to assigning each queue to an organization, you can make the utilization of a maximum cluster guarantee sufficient capacity for each organization's SLA. Users or organizations can regard a queue as a separated cluster for their own workload. In addition to this, Capacity scheduler can also provide free resources to any queue beyond its capacity. Applications can be assigned to a queue running below capacity at the future time by the scheduler. You write `capacity-scheduler.xml` to configure the scheduler settings. The `root` queue is a pre-defined queue, and all queues are children of the `root` queue.

The `root` queue has a full capacity for your cluster. The children of the root queue divide the capacity according to each assignment set by `capacify-scheduler.xml`. You can make queues under the root like the following:

```
<property>
       <name>yarn.scheduler.capacity.root.queues</name>
       <value>a,b,c</value>
     </property>
<property>
       <name>yarn.scheduler.capacity.root.b.queues</name>
       <value>b1,b2,b3</value>
     </property>
```

As you know, when you want to make a queue `a` under `root` queue, you have to set `yarn.scheduler.capacity.root.queues=a`. The name of queues can be set hierarchically, so you can set the child of queue `a` like `yarn.scheduler.capacity.root.a.queues=a1,a2`. The resource capacity of a queue can also be set with `yarn.scheduler.capacity.<queue-path>.capacity`. The total capacity of the same layer queues must be 100% as shown in Figure 3-5. In this description, queue `b2` can be assigned `0.4(40%) * 0.7(70%) = 0.28(28%)` resources of the whole cluster. You can set the maximum and minimum resource for each queue. Capacity scheduler can guarantee minimum resources for each organization to satisfy their SLA (Service Level Agreement).

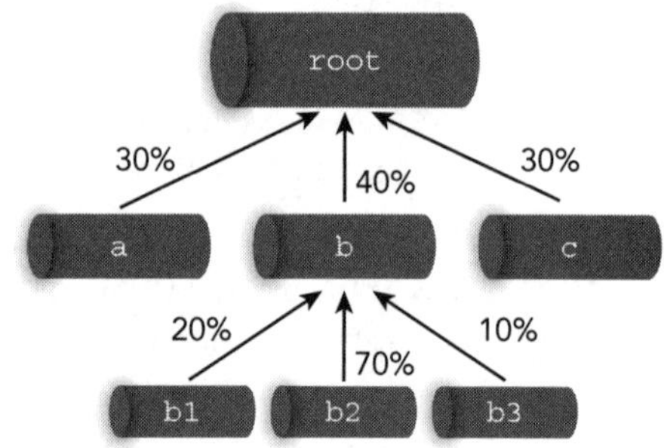

FIGURE 3-5

Later in this chapter we will cover the MapReduce architecture, which describes the shuffle and sort mechanism that is a core system of MapReduce. MapReduce guarantees that all inputs to reducer are sorted by key. This is done in a shuffle phase between map and reduce phases. A shuffle phase often affects the whole performance of the MapReduce application. Understanding the detail of the shuffle is useful for optimizing your MapReduce application.

The MapReduce application needs to read an input file from a filesystem such as HDFS. Hadoop MapReduce uses a class called `InputFormat` to define how each map task reads the input file.

Each map task processes a segment of the input file defined by `InputFormat`. The segment is called `InputSplit`, and `InputSplit` is processed by a map task. `InputSplit` has a length of a segment in a byte unit, and a list of hostnames where the `InputSplit` is located. `InputSplit` is transparently generated by `InputFormat`, and you don't have to pay attention to the implementation of `InputSplit` in many cases, given how `InputSplit` can be had by `InputFormat#getSplits`. This is called by a job client, which creates the split meta information on HDFS. An application master fetches the split meta information from the HDFS directory after launch. The application master passes the split meta information to each map task to read the corresponding field. The flow of the split info is described in Figure 3-6.

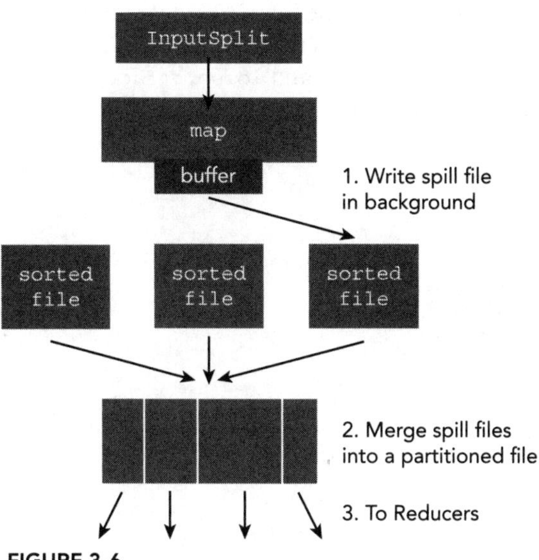

FIGURE 3-6

A map task reads a split of the input file. Split is a segment of the whole input file, as described earlier. The size of split is usually the same as the size of the block size of the filesystem, such as HDFS. You can write your own `InputFormat` class if you want to use the new text file format Hadoop MapReduce does not yet support. When a buffer is filled beyond a configured threshold (`mapreduce.map.sort.spill.percent`), the buffer content will be output on a disk. The file is called a spill file (see Figure 3.6). The writing on the disk can be done in the background, so it does not block map processing unless the memory buffer is not filled. Just before writing the spill file, the records are sorted for making partitions to distribute the next reducers. The spill files are merged into one file, if there are several spill files, before sending the output to reducers. The merged file is also sorted and separated into partitions, which will be sent to a corresponding reducer.

It is also efficient to compress map output, because it reduces the time to write map output on the disk and to transfer to reducers. You can enable map output compressed with `mapreduce.map.output.compress=true`. The default value is false, and the codec used by the map output compression can be set with `mapreduce.map.output.compress.codec`.

A reducer must fetch all of the output from mappers to complete the application, and the reduce task has threads for copying output data from mapper to the local disk. The number of threads can be controlled by `mapreduce.reduce.shuffle.parallel.copies`. The default value is 5, and the copy phase is conducted in parallel. When an output of the mapper is sufficiently small, which can be stored in the memory buffer, it will be stored in memory. Otherwise, it will be written to disk (see Figure 3-7). After finishing the copying of all data from `mapper`, the reduce task starts its merge phase. All map output that is in memory or on disks should be converted to a format that the reducer can read. Records have already been sorted by map tasks. In the merge phase, `reduce` tasks merge into one file. But the final file passed to reducer is not necessarily one file, nor even one disk. The input of reducer can be on both disk or memory if the overhead of merging to the last file is larger than the overhead of passing the data as it is to reducer. The input to reducer can be controlled by `mapreduce.task.io.sort.factor`. This value represents the number of open files when the merging starts at the same time. If the output of mappers are 50 and `io.sort.factor` is 10, the count of the merging cycle can be 5 (50 / 10 = 5). The reduce task tries to merge files with as few cycles as possible.

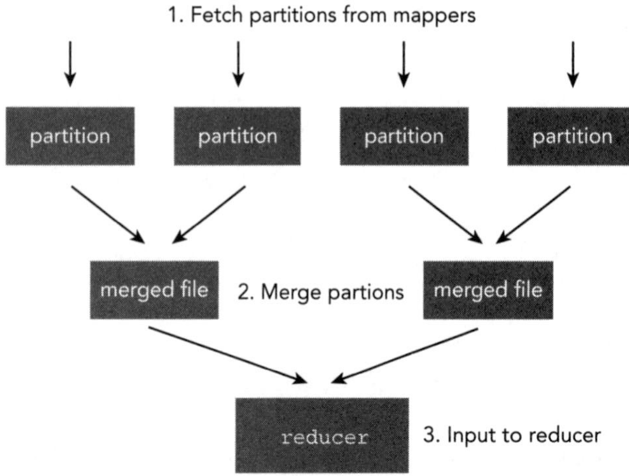

FIGURE 3-7

Shuffle is the most resource consuming process in the MapReduce application. Making shuffle phases more efficient often means directly making efficient MapReduce applications. Understanding the overview of the architecture of the MapReduce application will help you when tuning your MapReduce application.

HOW TO LAUNCH A MAPREDUCE JOB

We will now cover how to write a concrete MapReduce application based on the knowledge shown in previous sections. Hadoop MapReduce is a simple Java program. It is necessary to understand the basic knowledge of writing Java programs and compiling them, except for the MapReduce architecture described in previous sections, in order to develop a MapReduce application. The actual MapReduce applications are included in the Hadoop project under `hadoop-mapreduce-examples`.

If you installed Hadoop correctly, you can find the JAR file for examples under `$HADOOP_HOME/share/hadoop/mapreduce/hadoop-mapreduce-examples-*-.jar`. You can see the example application with the JAR command.

```
$ $HADOOP_HOME/bin/hadoop jar share/hadoop/mapreduce/hadoop-mapreduce-examples-↵
  3.0.0-SNAPSHOT.jar
```

An example program must be given as the first argument. Valid program names are:

- `aggregatewordcount`: An Aggregate based map/reduce program that counts the words in the input files.
- `aggregatewordhist`: An Aggregate based map/reduce program that computes the histogram of the words in the input files.
- `bbp`: A map/reduce program that uses Bailey-Borwein-Plouffe to compute exact digits of Pi.
- `dbcount`: An example job that counts the pageview count from a database.
- `distbbp`: A map/reduce program that uses a BBP-type formula to compute exact bits of Pi.
- `grep`: A map/reduce program that counts the matches of a regex in the input.
- `join`: A job that effects a join over sorted, equally partitioned datasets.

We will describe a transitional hello world program of MapReduce: the word count application. The word count application counts the number of appearances of each word found in documentation. In other words, we expect the output of this application to look like the following:

```
"wordA"    1
"wordB"    10
"wordC"    12
```

Let's continue by writing the map task.

Writing a Map Task

The input file is assumed to be a simple text file. One thing to do in map task is to conduct a morphological analysis. English text can be separated with the Java `StringTokenizer`.

```
import org.apache.hadoop.io.IntWritable;
     import org.apache.hadoop.io.Text;
     import org.apache.hadoop.mapreduce.Mapper;
     import java.io.IOException;
     import java.util.StringTokenizer;

public class TokenizerMapper
           extends Mapper<Object, Text, Text, IntWritable> {
    private final static IntWritable one
           = new IntWritable(1);
         private Text word = new Text();
    @Override
         protected void map(Object key, Text value, Context context) throws ↵
           IOException, InterruptedException {
        StringTokenizer iterator
               = new StringTokenizer(value.toString());
```

```
            while (iterator.hasMoreTokens()) {
                   word.set(iterator.nextToken());
                   context.write(word, one);
                }
            }
        }
```

Map task must inherit the `Mapper` class in Hadoop MapReduce. `Mapper` receives the key and value type of input and output as generics. Hadoop MapReduce uses `TextInputFormat` as the default `InputFormat`, and `TextInputFormat` makes splits in bytes. Each record is a key-value tuple whose keys are offset from the start of the file, with text values, except for terminal characters. For example, take a look at this example:

```
My name is Kai Sasaki. I'm a software
     engineer living in Tokyo. My favorite
     things are programming and scuba diving.
     Every summer I go to Okinawa to dive into the blue
     ocean. I'm looking forward to the beautiful summer.
```

This text is passed to Mapper through `TextInputFormat` with 5 tuples.

```
(0, "My name is Kai Sasaki. I'm a software")
     (38, "engineer living in Tokyo. My favorite")
     (75, "things are programming and scuba diving.")
     (115, "Every summer I go to Okinawa to dive into the blue")
     (161, "ocean. I'm looking forward to the beautiful summer.")
```

Each key is an offset from the start position of the file. This is not the line number of the file. `TokenizerMapper` defines the input key and value as `Object` and `Text`.

Map task in this case only records the appearance of a word. Map output is a tuple that has a word itself as a key and the count 1 as a value. The output of the `TokenizerMapper` task looks like this:

```
("My", 1)
     ("name", 1)
     ("is", 1)
     ("Kai", 1)
     ...
```

The outputs are sent to reduce task as described in the previous section. Tuples that have the same keys are collected by a reducer, and same word tuples are all collected by one reducer. It is necessary to aggregate all tuples that have the same word key in one machine to calculate the total count. Although some types of application don't need to reduce a task, the workload that is doing aggregation requires a reduce task after a map task.

Writing a Reduce Task

Just like the map task that is an inherited `Mapper` class, the reduce task class inherits the `Reducer` class. `Reducer` also receives the generics to specify the key and value type of input and output.

```
import org.apache.hadoop.io.IntWritable;
     import org.apache.hadoop.io.Text;
     import org.apache.hadoop.mapreduce.Reducer;
```

```
    import java.io.IOException;
public class CountSumReducer extends
        Reducer<Text, IntWritable, Text, IntWritable> {
    private IntWritable result = new IntWritable();
    @Override
        protected void reduce(Text key,
            Iterable<IntWritable> values, Context context)
            throws IOException, InterruptedException {
          int sum = 0;
          for (IntWritable value : values) {
            sum += value.get();
          }
          result.set(sum);
          context.write(key, result);
        }
    }
```

Reduce task receives a key and a list of values, so `reduce` is called for the same key. The input to the reduce task can be written like this:

```
("My", [1, 1, 1, 1, 1, 1])
```

All that reduce task has to do is calculate the sum of the list of values. The output is also a tuple whose key is a word (`Text`), and value is a total count of appearance (`IntWritable`). The output is written with `Context#write`. To store results `IntWritable` is reused in the reduce task because it is resource consuming to re-create the `IntWritable` object over the time the reduce method is called.

We have now finished writing a map task and a reduce task class. The last thing to write is the `Job` class to submit an application on the Hadoop cluster.

Writing a MapReduce Job

The `Job` class has a setting for referring a map task, a reduce class, and the configuration values and input/output path.

```
import org.apache.hadoop.conf.Configuration;
import org.apache.hadoop.fs.Path;
import org.apache.hadoop.io.IntWritable;
import org.apache.hadoop.io.Text;
import org.apache.hadoop.mapreduce.Job;
import org.apache.hadoop.mapreduce.lib.input.FileInputFormat;
import org.apache.hadoop.mapreduce.lib.output.FileOutputFormat;
public class WordCount {
public static void main(String[] args)
          throws Exception {
   Configuration conf = new Configuration();
   Job job = Job.getInstance(conf, "Word Count");
   job.setJarByClass(WordCount.class);
   // Setup Map task class
   job.setMapperClass(TokenizerMapper.class);
   job.setCombinerClass(CountSumReducer.class);
   // Setup Reduce task class
   job.setReducerClass(CountSumReducer.class);
```

```
            // This is for output of reduce task
            job.setOutputKeyClass(Text.class);
            job.setOutputValueClass(IntWritable.class);
            // Set input path of an application
            FileInputFormat
              .addInputPath(job, new Path("/input"));
            // Set output path of an application
            FileOutputFormat
              .setOutputPath(job, new Path("/output"));
            System.exit(job.waitForCompletion(true) ? 0 : 1);
        }
    }
```

The `Job` class can be instantiated by the `Job.getInstance` static method. The Hadoop MapReduce runtime has to find the classes for executing the MapReduce application on the distributed cluster. The classes needed to run the application are archived in a JAR format, and the `Job#setJarByClass` method specifies the JAR file including the `WordCount` class. The Hadoop MapReduce runtime finds the necessary class path automatically with this setting. Map task and reduce task classes are set with `setMapperClass` and `setReducerClass`. Combiner is a class used often in the merge phase between map task and reduce task. It is enough to set the reduce class as a combiner class, because it contributes mainly optimization for compressing output of the map task. The result must not be different, regardless of whether or not you set the combiner class. The input and output of a MapReduce application is specified as a filesystem directory, so the input directory can include multiple input files that are normal text files in a `WordCount` application. The output directory includes the result file and the status of an application.

```
-rw-r—r-- 1 root supergroup 0 2016-01-01 23:04 /output/_SUCCESS
-rw-r--r--   1 root supergroup 1306 2016-01-01 23:04 /output/part-r-00000
```

The result file is `part-r-XXXXX`.

It is better to use Apache Maven to compile the Hadoop MapReduce application. The dependency needed to import is `hadoop-client`. It is necessary to write below the dependency in your `pom.xml` file.

```
<dependencies>
   <dependency>
     <groupId>org.apache.hadoop</groupId>
     <artifactId>hadoop-client</artifactId>
     <version>2.6.0</version>
   </dependency>
 </dependencies>
```

Next, compile using the `maven` command.

```
$ mvn clean package -DskipTests
```

The necessary file to run your MapReduce application is the JAR archive, including all of the classes that you wrote. The JAR archive must be uploaded on a client or a master node of the Hadoop cluster. You can run the application with the `hadoop jar` command.

```
$ $HADOOP_HOME/bin/hadoop jar \
      /path/to/my-wordcount-1.0-SNAPSHOT.jar \
      my.package.WordCount
```

Configurations

The MapReduce application has a lot of configurations. Some of them are for optimizing performance, and some of them are the host name or port number of each component. It is usually beneficial to change the configuration in order to improve the performance of the application. Although it is often enough to use the default value for the ordinal workload, let's go over how to change the configurations for each application.

Hadoop prepares a utility interface for giving configuration values from the command line. The interface is `Tool`, and it has an interface to run an override method. The interface is necessary to run the MapReduce application using `ToolRunner`, which can handle parsing command line arguments and options. By combining with the `Configured` class, the `ToolRunner` set up configuration object is automatically based on the given configuration from the command line. The sample WordCount application implemented with `ToolRunner` is written here.

```
import org.apache.hadoop.conf.Configuration;
      import org.apache.hadoop.conf.Configured;
      import org.apache.hadoop.fs.Path;
      import org.apache.hadoop.io.IntWritable;
      import org.apache.hadoop.io.Text;
      import org.apache.hadoop.mapreduce.Job;
      import org.apache.hadoop.mapreduce.lib.input.FileInputFormat;
      import org.apache.hadoop.mapreduce.lib.output.FileOutputFormat;
      import org.apache.hadoop.util.Tool;
      import org.apache.hadoop.util.ToolRunner;
public class WordCountTool
          extends Configured implements Tool {
    public int run(String[] strings) throws Exception {
            Configuration conf = this.getConf();
        // Obtain input path and output path from
            // command line options
            String inputPath
              = conf.get("input_path", "/input");
            String outputPath
              = conf.get("output_path", "/output");
      Job job = Job
              .getInstance(conf, conf.get("app_name"));
      job.setJarByClass(WordCount.class);
            job.setMapperClass(TokenizerMapper.class);
            job.setCombinerClass(CountSumReducer.class);
            job.setReducerClass(CountSumReducer.class);
            job.setOutputKeyClass(Text.class);
            job.setOutputValueClass(IntWritable.class);
       FileInputFormat
              .addInputPath(job, new Path(inputPath));
       FileOutputFormat
              .setOutputPath(job, new Path(outputPath));
       return job.waitForCompletion(true) ? 0 : 1;
    }

    public static void main(String[] args)
              throws Exception {
```

```
        int exitCode
            = ToolRunner.run(new WordCountTool(), args);
          System.exit(exitCode);
        }
    }
```

The configurations can be given by using the `-D property=value` format on the command line. `WordCountTool` requires the application name, input path and output path. You can pass these configurations with the `hadoop jar` command.

```
$ $HADOOP_HOME/bin/hadoop jar \
        /path/to/hadoop-wordcount-1.0-SNAPSHOT.jar \
        your.package.WordCountTool \
        -D input_path=/input \
        -D output_path=/output \
        -D app_name=myapp
```

The configuration can be restored from every task by using the `Context#getConfiguration` method. The necessary information to run your application can be set on the `Configuration` object. Therefore, almost all configurations must be passed with the `Configuration` object. But there may be times when you want to pass a relatively large resource for your application, such as binary data, rather than a string. This data can be passed from the command line correctly, but so too can a large configuration that pressures a task in JVM memory. It is wasteful to pass custom resources to each task, and the solution to this problem will be introduced in the next section.

ADVANCED FEATURES OF MAPREDUCE

Let's now examine some of the advanced MapReduce features that you can tap into.

Distributed Cache

Distributed cache distributes read-only data to slave nodes for each task that can use the data. The distributed data is archived in slave nodes. The copy process runs only once to save network bandwidth inside the cluster, and `ToolRunner` can specify the files to be distributed in a cluster using the `-files` option.

```
$ $HADOOP_HOME/bin/hadoop jar \
        /path/to/hadoop-wordcount-1.0-SNAPSHOT.jar \
        your.package.WordCountTool \
        -files /path/to/distributed-file.txt
```

The distributed file can be put on any filesystem that is integrated in Hadoop, such as the local filesystem, HDFS, and S3. If you do not specify the schema, the distributed file is automatically found on the local filesystem. You can specify archive files such as JAR, ZIP, TAR, and GZIP files by using the `-archives` option. You can also add classes on the task JVM class path by using the `-libjars` option.

Distributed files can be private or public, and this designation determines how the distributed files are used on the slave nodes. A private version of distributed files is cached onto the local directory, and is only used by a user who submits an application with the distributed file. These files cannot be accessed by applications submitted by other users. So, the public version of a distributed file is put in the global directory that can be accessed by all users, and this accessibility is achieved by the HDFS permissions system.

Distributed files are then accessed by each task, and the restore can be done with a relative file path. In the above case, the filename is `distributed-file.txt`. You can obtain this resource file using the ordinal reading of a text file:

```
new File("distributed-file.txt")
```

`ToolRunner` (correctly `GenericOptionsParser`) automatically handles the distributed cache mechanism. You can use the distributed cache API specifically for your application, and there are two types of APIs for distributed cache. One is an API for adding distributed cache to your application. The other is an API for referring a distributed cache data from each task. The former can be set with the `Job` class, and the latter can be set with the `JobContext` class.

```
public void Job#addCacheFile(URI)
public void Job#addCacheArchive(URI)
public void Job#setCacheFiles(URI[])
public void Job#setCacheArchives(URI[])
public void Job#addFileToClassPath(Path)
public void Job#addArchiveToClassPath(Path)
```

In the list, the `addCacheFile` and `setCacheFiles` methods add the files to the distributed cache. These methods do the same to the `-files` option on the command line. `addCacheArchive` and `setCacheArchives` do the same to the `-archives` option from the command line, just as `addFileToClassPath` does the same to the `-libjars` option. One major difference between using options on the command line and the Java API shown above is that the Java API does not copy a distributed file on HDFS from the local filesystem. So, if you specify a file with the `-files` option, ToolRunner automatically copies the file on HDFS. But, you have to always specify the HDFS (or S3, etc.) path, because the Java API cannot find the distributed file on the local file system by itself.

These APIs are for referring distributed cache data:

```
public Path[] Context#getLocalCacheFiles()
public Path[] Context#getLocalCacheArchives()
public Path[] Context#getFileClassPath()
public Path[] Context#getArchiveClassPath()
```

These APIs return the distributed file paths of corresponding files, and they are used from the `Context` class, and passed to the map task and reduce task respectively. `Mapper` and `Reduce` have a `setup` method to initialize objects used in each task. The `setup` method is called once before the `map` function.

```
 String data = null;
@Override
  protected void setup(Context context)
```

```
            throws IOException, InterruptedException {
        Path[] localPaths = context.getLocalCacheFiles();
        if (localPaths.length > 0) {
            File localFile = new File(localPaths[0].toString());
            data = new String(Files.readAllBytes(localFile.toPath()));
        }
    }
```

With Hadoop 2.2.0, `getLocalCacheFiles` and `getLocalCacheArchives` are deprecated. It is recommended to use `getCacheFiles` and `getCacheArchives` instead.

Counter

It is necessary to obtain custom metrics as the need arises in order to tune your application. For example, it is necessary to know the number of read/write operations in order to reduce I/O overload, and the total number of splits and records are useful to optimize input data size. Counter provides a functionality to collect any type of metrics to measure the performance of your application, and you can set application-specific counters. It is useful to know how many invalid records are included in the data set for improving data set quality. In this section we will describe how to use pre-defined counters and user-defined counters.

Here are some types of pre-defined counters in Hadoop MapReduce.

- **File System counters:** The metrics around filesystem operations. This counter includes like number of bytes read, number of bytes written, number of read operations, and number of write operations.
- **Job counters:** The metrics about job execution. This counter includes the number of launched map tasks, launched reduce tasks, rack-local map tasks, and total time spent by all map tasks.
- **MapReduce framework counters:** The metrics are managed mainly by the MapReduce framework. This counter includes the number of combined input records, spent CPU time, and elapsed garbage collection time.
- **Shuffle errors counter:** The metrics count the number of errors that occurred in the shuffle phase such as BAD_ID, IO_ERROR, WRONG_MAP, and WRONG_REDUCE.
- **File input format counters:** The metrics about InputFormat used by an application. This counter includes the bytes read by each task.
- **File output format counters:** The metrics about OutputFormat used by an application. This counter includes the bytes written by each task.

These counters are counted by each task and the total of the job. These counter values are automatically calculated by the MapReduce framework.

In addition to these counters, you can also define custom counters by yourself. Counter has a group name and a counter name, and counters can be used through the `Context#getCounter` method.

```
context.getCounter("WordCounter", "total word count").increment(1)
```

The output can be confirmed by the console just after the job has finished, or the web UI of the Job history server that is described in the next section.

```
WordCounter
            total word count=179
```

You can also obtain counter values from the command line: `hadoop job -counter`.

Job History Server

The Job history server aggregates log files generated from each task in your application. It is necessary to see log files to debug the application and ensure it is running correctly. The log files of an application usually are removed when the application has finished, but it is necessary to collect log files before they are removed, and the Job history server does this. The server aggregates all logs for each application and stores them in HDFS. You can see the logs of past applications through the web UI (see Figure 3-8). The default post number of the Job history server is 19888. You can access `http://<Resource Manager hostname>:19888`.

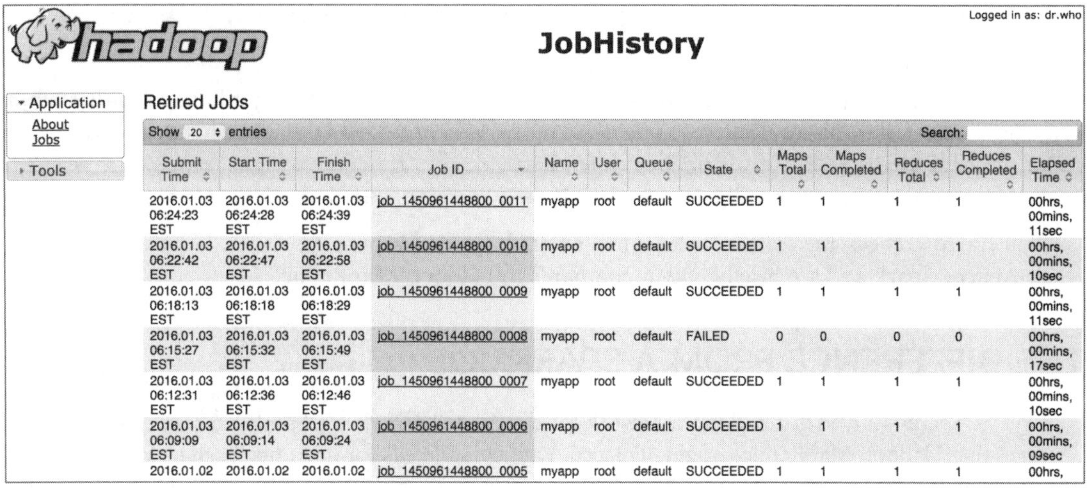

Submit Time	Start Time	Finish Time	Job ID	Name	User	Queue	State	Maps Total	Maps Completed	Reduces Total	Reduces Completed	Elapsed Time
2016.01.03 06:24:23 EST	2016.01.03 06:24:28 EST	2016.01.03 06:24:39 EST	job_1450961448800_0011	myapp	root	default	SUCCEEDED	1	1	1	1	00hrs, 00mins, 11sec
2016.01.03 06:22:42 EST	2016.01.03 06:22:47 EST	2016.01.03 06:22:58 EST	job_1450961448800_0010	myapp	root	default	SUCCEEDED	1	1	1	1	00hrs, 00mins, 10sec
2016.01.03 06:18:13 EST	2016.01.03 06:18:18 EST	2016.01.03 06:18:29 EST	job_1450961448800_0009	myapp	root	default	SUCCEEDED	1	1	1	1	00hrs, 00mins, 11sec
2016.01.03 06:15:27 EST	2016.01.03 06:15:32 EST	2016.01.03 06:15:49 EST	job_1450961448800_0008	myapp	root	default	FAILED	0	0	0	0	00hrs, 00mins, 17sec
2016.01.03 06:12:31 EST	2016.01.03 06:12:36 EST	2016.01.03 06:12:46 EST	job_1450961448800_0007	myapp	root	default	SUCCEEDED	1	1	1	1	00hrs, 00mins, 10sec
2016.01.03 06:09:09 EST	2016.01.03 06:09:14 EST	2016.01.03 06:09:24 EST	job_1450961448800_0006	myapp	root	default	SUCCEEDED	1	1	1	1	00hrs, 00mins, 09sec
2016.01.02	2016.01.02	2016.01.02	job_1450961448800_0005	myapp	root	default	SUCCEEDED	1	1	1	1	00hrs,

FIGURE 3-8

The log files are stored in the path configured by `mapreduce.jobhistory.intermediate-done-dir` and `mapreduce.jobhistory.done-dir`. Log files are categorized into two types: intermediate files and done files. Intermediate files are unfinished application logs. These log files are for the application running right now. Done files are for applications that are finished. After the application has finished, the Job history server moves intermediate files to the done directory.

The Job history server provides a REST API to enable users to get the overall information and statuses about applications. Table 3-1 contains the list of APIs for obtaining MapReduce related information.

TABLE 3-1: APIs for MapReduce information

AVAILABLE INFO	REST API URI
List Jobs	http://<Job history server hostname>/ws/v1/history/mapreduce/jobs
Job information	http://<Job history server hostname>/ws/v1/history/mapreduce/jobs/<Job ID>
Configuration of Job	http://<Job history server hostname>/ws/v1/history/mapreduce/jobs/<Job ID>/conf
List Tasks	http://<Job history server hostname>/ws/v1/history/mapreduce/jobs/<Job ID>/tasks
Task information	http://<Job history server hostname>/ws/v1/history/mapreduce/jobs/<Job ID>/tasks/<Task ID>
List Task Attempts	http://<Job history server hostname>/ws/v1/history/mapreduce/jobs/<Job ID>/tasks/<Task ID>/attempts
Task Attempts information	http://<Job history server hostname>/ws/v1/history/mapreduce/jobs/<Job ID>/tasks/<Task ID>/attempts/<Attempt ID>

The Attempts ID specifies the actual execution of each task. One task might have several attempts where some failures have occurred. There are more APIs provided by the Job history server, and all of the APIs are listed in the official document here: (`http://hadoop.apache.org/docs/current/hadoop-mapreduce-client/hadoop-mapreduce-client-hs/HistoryServerRest.html`).

You can also check the counter values incremented by your application tasks. Next we'll take a look at Apache Spark and see briefly how it compares to Hadoop MapReduce.

THE DIFFERENCE FROM A SPARK JOB

Apache Spark is a next generation framework for distributed processing. Spark improves some disadvantages that Hadoop MapReduce originally faced. Launching JVMs for operating each task, and writing intermediate files on distributed filesystem between each task, often causes a huge overhead. The overhead cannot fit with the machine learning workload that is doing the calculations. Spark was introduced as a new general on-memory distributed computational engine, but Spark is now a unique ecosystem and community. The main difference between Hadoop MapReduce and Spark job is shown here in Table 3-2.

TABLE 3-2: Differences between Hadoop MapReduce and Spark job

HADOOP MAPREDUCE	SPARK JOB
Write intermediate data on HDFS	On-memory processing
Java API and Hadoop streaming	Scala, Java, Python, and R
Running on YARN	Running on YARN, Mesos, and Standalone
Set only map task and reduce task	Flexible abstraction of tasks

The main advantage of Spark jobs is the sophisticated API and the workload speed that is has. The number of core lines you have to write in a Spark job are usually smaller than those for a MapReduce application. Although writing a Spark application in Scala or Python requires some knowledge about closure or lambda functions, it can enable you to write distributed applications more easily. This is the example of an application of counting words that we wrote in a previous section.

```
val wordCounts = textFile
                    .flatMap(line => line.split(" "))
                    .map(word => (word, 1))
                    .reduceByKey((a, b) => a + b)
wordCounts.collect
```

This is one of the biggest reasons why Spark gets so much attention from data scientists and data engineers. But one thing to note here is that Spark is a relatively new platform compared to Hadoop MapReduce. In terms of scalability and reliability, Hadoop MapReduce often defeats a Spark application, so it is best to decide which platform to use based on your workload.

SUMMARY

In this chapter, we explained the basics of Hadoop MapReduce. Understanding the basic architecture of Hadoop MapReduce helps you develop better applications. Hadoop MapReduce relies on other distributed frameworks such as HDFS or YARN. Although omitted here, MapReduce can also run on new frameworks. Apache Tez and Apache Spark can also work as an execution engine supporting a MapReduce application, so the number of users of the MapReduce framework continues to grow.

We also covered how to write a MapReduce application, showing how MapReduce is a simple framework, but it can provide sufficient flexibility to develop and to write any kind of distributed platform applications.

Finally, in order to compare and know the difference between MapReduce and a relatively new platform, we examined Apache Spark, which is currently under active development, and is worthwhile paying attention to.

User Experience

WHAT'S IN THIS CHAPTER?

- Using Hive for data warehouse
- Using Pig for data analysis
- Using Hue for web-based analysis
- Using Oozie for job management

The Hadoop MapReduce program is designed to process a large amount of data at a low cost. Hadoop has been in use for almost 10 years, and it was initially used to focus on massive parallel processing. As covered in Chapter 3, however, it's tiresome to use the MapReduce program every time you need to process and analyze data. A lot of code, builds, and deploy processes are required to perform just a simple word count program, and developers get tired of frequently occurring repetitive tasks. And non-developers, such as data analysts or general users, who don't have a strong development background, struggle to use this method in their environment.

General users don't need to know every detail about MapReduce operating principles or shuffle phases, such as having to know the operational principles of Oracle, in order to extract the desired value from a database. The framework of Hadoop MapReduce makes developers concentrate on logic by dividing the work into fault-tolerance and node management. Hadoop-related projects, on the other hand, can provide an interface that you can use on data flows, regardless of any complex events.

This chapter focuses on how the Hadoop ecosystem works to improve user experiences. The Hadoop ecosystem has been developed continuously, so it benefits from cluster provisioning, data collection, analysis, and visualization. It isn't necessary to build your architecture using the whole ecosystem that is shown in Figure 4-1. Most of the analysis can proceed smoothly with just a combination of a few ecosystems. And in the case of simple data analysis, DBMS or Excel can actually be more efficient. Therefore, you must choose the right ecosystem for the characteristics of your data. In this chapter we will cover Hive, Pig, Hue, and Oozie, since these are typically used with Hadoop. Let's start by first looking at Apache Hive.

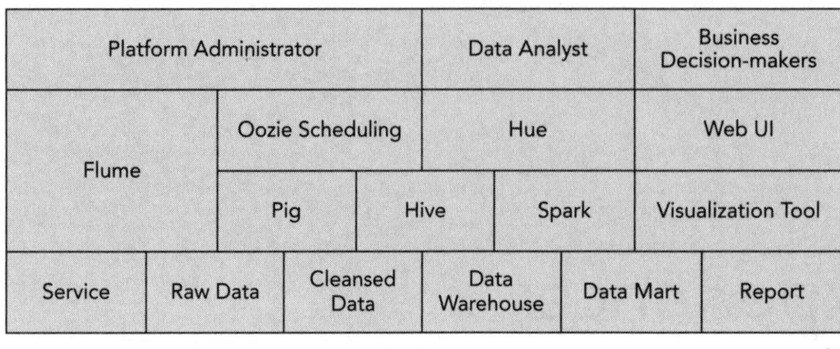

FIGURE 4-1

APACHE HIVE

Apache Hive is similar to the SQL language. Hive doesn't always follow ANSI SQL grammar, but it can convert SQL grammar to MapReduce jobs to use a parallel processing mechanism for the Hadoop ecosystem. This is beneficial not only for a database administrator who runs an existing legacy system, but also for casual users who use SQL. Since Hadoop is basically an application for handling data, and most data warehouse applications have implemented the SQL language, Hive is the most famous and widely used project among Hadoop ecosystems.

A simple Hive architecture diagram is shown in Figure 4-2.

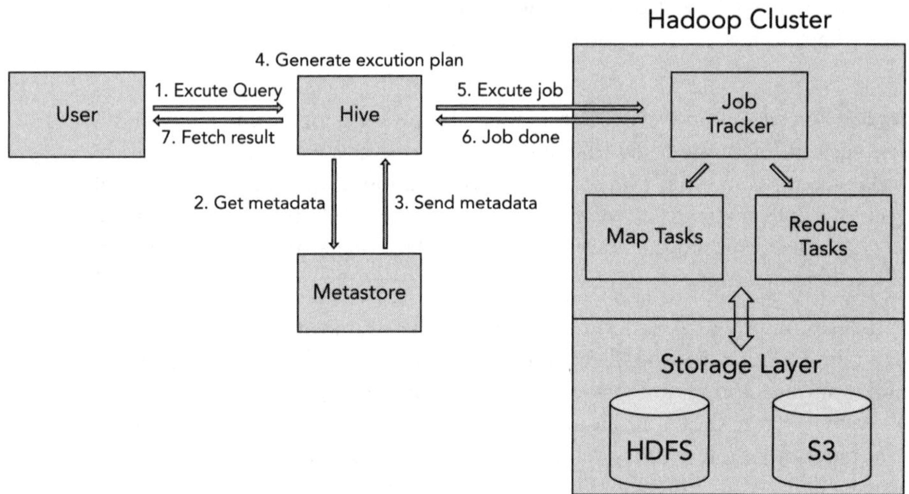

FIGURE 4-2

Before using Hive, consider the following:

- Hive is not a Relational Database Management System (RDBMS). Although it uses a SQL-like language, most jobs become converted into MapReduce jobs, following the nature of MapReduce. For example, unlike RDBMS where a simple `SELECT COUNT (*)` instantly converts the result, Hive needs the startup because it can take a long time for map and reduce to launch. Also, `COMMIT` and `ROLLBACK` are not yet supported, which are crucial for online transactional purposes.
- Hive works on files. Hive data exists in the form of HDFS or AWS S3 files, and a Hive table or partition exists in a physical form at the file location. Therefore, the dataset possessed by Hive can be converted by external factors, and it's also possible to load the external data.
- Using the built-in functions of Hive, it may be difficult to obtain the desired result. For this case, Hive supports User Defined Function (UDF) and Serializer/Deserializer (SerDe). This will be dealt with in more detail later in this chapter.

Hive Installation

This book provides a Hive 1.2.1 installation example. The latest version of Hive can be downloaded from the following URL: `http://hive.apache.org/downloads.html`.

1. Download Hive and uncompress:

```
$ wget http://www.us.apache.org/dist/hive/hive-1.2.1/apache-hive-1.2.1-bin.tar.gz
  apache-hive-1.2.1-bin.tar.gz
$ tar xvfz apache-hive-1.2.1-bin.tar.gz
```

2. Set the environment variable (or add it to your shell profile):

```
$ cd apache-hive-1.2.1-bin
$ export HIVE_HOME=$PWD
$ export PATH=$HIVE_HOME/bin:$PATH
$ export HADOOP_HOME=<your_hadoop_home> to conf/hive-env.sh
```

3. Set the configuration variable:

   Create `conf//hive-site.xml` according to `conf/hive-default.xml`, except for the `<property>` section.

   Add properties that you need to `hive-site.xml`. The list for all of the properties is found here:

`https://cwiki.apache.org/confluence/display/Hive/Configuration+Properties`

4. Set the metastore configuration.

   Hive uses the embedded Derby database with the default metastore, but in the production environment it is recommended that you use a different database. These configurations show how to use the Metastore with MySQL:

```
<property>
  <name>javax.jdo.option.ConnectionDriverName</name>
  <value>com.mysql.jdbc.Driver</value>
  <description>Driver class name for a JDBC metastore</description>
</property>
```

```
<property>
  <name>javax.jdo.option.ConnectionURL</name>
  <value>jdbc:mysql://dbAddress/metastore</value>
  <description>JDBC connect string for a JDBC metastore</description>
</property>
<property>
  <name>javax.jdo.option.ConnectionUserName</name>
  <value>hiveuser</value>
  <description>Username to use against metastore database</description>
</property>
<property>
  <name>javax.jdo.option.ConnectionPassword</name>
  <value>password</value>
  <description>password to use against metastore database</description>
</property>
```

HiveQL

As mentioned earlier, Hive defines a process with a SQL-like language. This is called the Hive Query Language (HiveQL). The Data Definition Language (DDL) and Data Manipulation Language (DML) exist similarly to SQL. We will cover DDL and DML later in this chapter. Click on this link if you are interested in seeing the complete description of HiveQL:

https://cwiki.apache.org/confluence/display/Hive/LanguageManual

Hive Command Line Options

HiveQL-executing methods are used most frequently through the use of the command line. In the Hive batch mode, one or more SQL queries from a file are distinguished by a semicolon, and can be executed directly by the user with the Query as a factor. The interactive shell mode is the conversation type that is usually used when running the ad hoc query. Table 4-1 lists the command line options most often used in batch mode.

TABLE 4-1: Batch mode command line options

OPTION	DESCRIPTION	EXAMPLES
`-e <quoted-query-string>`	SQL from command line	`hive -e 'SELECT a.col from tab1 a'`
`-f <filename>`	SQL from files	`hive -f /home/hive/hiveql.hql`
`--hiveconf <property=value>`	Using Hive configuration variables	`hive --hiveconf fs.default.name=localhost`
`--hivevar <key=value>`	Using Hive variables	`hive --hivevar tname="user"`

In the Hive interactive shell mode, the property can be defined by the set order as well as the execution of Hive QL or the JAR file used for UDF (see Table 4-2). It is also possible to execute an OS order by attaching "!" before the command, or to fulfill the HDFS-related command through DFS.

TABLE 4-2: Hive interactive shell mode properties

COMMAND	DESCRIPTION	EXAMPLES
`exit or quit`	Exiting the interactive shell	`exit;`
`set <key>=<value>`	Sets the value of a configuration variable	`set hive.exec.parallel=true;`
`add JAR <Jar file location>`	Adds jar file to distributed cache	`add jar s3://mybucket/abc.jar`
`list JAR`	Shows a list of JAR that already added to distributed cache	`list jar;`
`source <HQL file location>`	Executes a HQL script from file system	`source /home/hadoop/ex.hql`

Data Definition Language

Data Definition Language (DDL) statements are used to define and modify data structures such as create, alter, or drop database/table schemas. It is useful to divide files based on the duty and schedule under the classified folders by projects when managing documents in the computer. It is also convenient to designate the bundle of relevant datasets by table, and to bind the relevant tables to manage by database when it comes to Hive. This method has been widely used in the past.

You can think of it as the database being a set of related tables. Hive uses the default database, until you assign a database to use as the `USE <database_name>` statement. You can use the `SCHEMA` keyword instead of the `DATABASE` keyword when running any database related commands. Here are some simple database command examples:

- `CREATE DATABASE` **statement:** This uses the `IF NOT EXISTS` clause, even though the database with the same name exists, and does not return an error. You can add a descriptive comment using the `COMMENT` command. When creating a database, it creates a `db_name.db` directory under the directory defined in `hive.metastore.warehouse.dir` (default value: /user/hive/warehouse). You can change the position to be stored using the `LOCATION` command.

```
CREATE DATABASE [IF NOT EXISTS] db_name
 [COMMENT database_comment]
 [LOCATION database_path]
 [WITH DBPROPERTIES (key1=value1, ...)];
```

- `ALTER DATABASE` **statement:** This is a command to modify key-value pairs in `DBPROPERTIES`, but you can't change its location or database name.

```
ALTER DATABASE db_name
SET DBPROPERTIES (key1=value1, ...);
```

- `DROP DATABASE` **statement:** Remember that you can't drop the database unless there are no existing tables in the database. If you want to drop the database and its entire table, append the `CASCADE` keyword to the end of the command.

```
DROP DATABASE [IF EXISTS] db_name [CASCADE];
```

Hive does not use the data of a completely formatted form like RDBMS. It just reads and writes the file. Therefore, it is important to define the table schema in accordance with the form of inserted data. Hive Table DDL can designate the terminate key of the row format to process the input file format of various forms, and prevents the full scan of the entire data by designating the partition. In addition, using the ORC (Optimized Row Columnar) and Parquet file format, should allow column-oriented data processing. The following example demonstrates how to use the table command.

- `CREATE TABLE` **statement:** It defines the table schema. Hive supports various types of column data types such as String, Int, Timestamp, etc. In addition, nested types like Arrays and Maps are also supported. These complex data types can pack a lot of data into a single column, but it can cause performance degradation when running repetitive operations.

```
CREATE [EXTERNAL] TABLE [IF NOT EXISTS] [db_name.]table_name(
   column_name data_type, ...)
[COMMENT table_comment]
[PARTITIONED BY (col_name data_type, ...)]
[STORED AS file_format]
[LOCATION table_path]
```

- `ALTER TABLE` **statement:** It enables you to change the table schema and includes table name, add/delete/modify columns, partition information, SerDe properties, etc.

```
ALTER TABLE table_name
SET property_name property_value
```

- `DROP TABLE` **Statement:** It deletes table information from the metastore. Remember that in the case of Managed Table, it will delete the table location's data (file), but for the External Table it only deletes metadata.

```
DROP TABLE [IF EXISTS] table_name
```

Hive keeps the partition information in metastore, but the new partition can be directly added to the file system. Because Hive can't know about this new partition information, HiveQL targets this partition and returns a null. In this case, the user can add the partition manually by `ALTER TABLE table_name ADD PARTITION` commands or check the whole partition using `MSCK REPAIR TABLE table_name`.

Data Manipulation Language

Data Manipulation Language (DML) statements are used to work with the data in tables. `SELECT`, `INSERT`, `UPDATE`, and `DELETE` are some well-known examples. It is difficult to describe all of the instructions here, so we will cover features assuming that you already have a basic knowledge of SQL.

- **Dynamic partition inserts:** When using the `INSERT` data in a partitioned table, it can be used to manually specify the partition. But it is difficult to manage after the partition item has increased. In that case, you can use a dynamic partition insert statement by enabling the `hive.exec.dynamic.partition` configuration to true. With HiveQL you can use dynamic partitions instead of using the multiple statement, and manually specifying the country code.

  Here is a static partition insert statement example:

```
FROM daily_Table
INSERT OVERWRITE TABLE to_table PARTITION(dt='2016-05-26', ctCode='USA')
      SELECT col1, col2, col3 WHERE countryCode = 'USA'
INSERT OVERWRITE TABLE to_table PARTITION(dt='2016-05-26', ctCode='FRA')
      SELECT col1, col2, col3 WHERE countryCode = 'FRA'
INSERT OVERWRITE TABLE to_table PARTITION(dt='2016-05-26', ctCode='BEL')
      SELECT col1, col2, col3 WHERE countryCode = 'BEL';
```

  And here is a dynamic partition insert statement example:

```
FROM daily_Table
INSERT OVERWRITE TABLE to_table PARTITION(dt='2016-05-26', countryCode)
      SELECT col1, col2, col3, countryCode;
```

  Pay attention to the following points when using the dynamic partition insert:

  - A dynamic partition can't be the parent of a static partition.
  - Problems will occur when there are broken words in values of dynamic partition.
  - Performance degradation can occur when there are too many dynamic partitions.

- **Multi Table/File inserts:** Hive can send output into multiple tables or file systems with a single statement.

```
FROM daily_Table
INSERT OVERWRITE TABLE to_table1 SELECT * WHERE ctCode = 'USA'
INSERT OVERWRITE TABLE to_table2 SELECT * WHERE ctCode = 'FRA'
INSERT OVERWRITE LOCAL DIRECTORY '/out/bel.out' SELECT * WHERE ctCode = 'BEL';
```

- **Update and Delete operation:** Update and Delete commands have been available since Hive 0.14, but your table has to support ACID.

UDF/SerDe

UDF and SerDe help you use Hive's function by expanding. Both have the embodied built-in function so you can use them to reach your goals.

User Defined Functions

In Hive, the built in function (see Table 4-3) and the user defined function are called UDF. You can inquire the list of functions currently loaded by means of `SHOW FUNCTION`, and you can confirm the description document on the relevant `function_name` by using `DESCRIBE FUNCTION <function_name>`.

TABLE 4-3: Built in functions

BUILD-IN FUNCTION	DESCRIPTION	EXAMPLES

Mathematical Functions	Used for the mathematical operation such as the square root, round off, or exponential function	`round(DOUBLE a)`
		`sqrt(DOUBLE a)`
		`log2(DOUBLE a)`

Collection Functions	Functions that operate in the nested data structure like Map or Array	`size(MAP|ARRAY a)` `sort_array(Array a)`
Type Conversion Functions	Use this to try to change the data type to another type	`cast('1' as DOUBLE)`
Date Functions	A function to extract time information from string and Unix time-related functions	`unix_timestamp()` `date_add(string date, '1')`
Conditional Functions	Control Statement such as `IF` or `CASE-WHEN-THEN`	`nvl(value, default_value)` `case a when b then c end`
String Functions	String manipulation functions	`concat(string a, string b...)` `length(string a)`

In addition, there are Built-in Aggregate Functions (UDAF) and Built-in Table-Generating Functions (UDTF). For example, `sum0` of UDAF receives a column from several rows to fulfill the aggregation and the `explode()` of UDTF receives the array as input to return to individual rows.

When the user tries to write directly to UDF, the operation is processed in the following order:

1. Create a new class that extends the `org.apache.hadoop.hive.ql.exec.UDF` class.
2. Implement the `evaluate()` method.
3. Package the JAR file and add it to classpath (or upload to HDFS, S3).
4. Add the JAR file to the distributed cache using the `ADD JAR <jar_file_name>` command.
5. Register your function name using the `CREATE TEMPORARY FUNCTION AS <function_name> AS <class_name_including_package>` command.

Serializer/Deserializer

Hive accesses the data of the table through SerDe, which is an input/output interface that allows it to handle files on HDFS. It shows the data read from HDFS in forms of rows and columns by means of SerDe's deserializer. Serializer is used when writing the file on HDFS. Like UDF, Hive provides the built-in SerDes and can handle the frequently used forms by using AvroSerDe, RegexSerDe, OpenCSVSerde, and JsonSerDe.

You can write SerDe directly using the following methods:

- Create a new class that extends the `org.apache.hadoop.hive.serde2.SerDe` class.
- Implement `deserialize()` and `serialize()` methods.
- Package the JAR file and add it to classpath (or upload to HDFS, S3).
- Add the JAR file to the distributed cache using the `ADD JAR <jar_file_name>` command.
- Add the `ROW FORMAT SERDE 'serde_name_including_package'` clause at table creation time or by altering the table property.

Hive Tuning

You can use Hive without a special setting, but if you understand the property of Hive, you can improve the job's performance through simple settings.

- **Partitioning:** HiveQL sets the condition with the Where clause to extract the desired data. Since Hive accesses the file, if you approach the table to extract the data of a certain date, you should refer to all files in the folder of the relevant table. Partitioning is used in this situation, and it makes a physical folder under the table by subdividing into certain conditions (date, time, national code) that are frequently used. It is created by using the Partitioned By sentence in the Create Table statement and the folder is created in a form of `<partition>=<value>` and the multi-level partitioning is also possible. If the partition condition is included in the Where clause when fulfilling the Select query, Hive reads the entire folders belonging to Table while accessing only the folder applying to the given condition. Most data can be divided by time and code standard information, and users are likely to be interested only in the data belonging to a certain condition, so a well-designed partition policy is very helpful in reducing the job performance time.
- **Parallel execution:** Complex HiveQL is commonly converted into a number of MapReduce jobs. It runs sequentially by default, but sometimes it may lead to resource waste. The `hive.exec.parallel` property can execute independent jobs in parallel. Either add to `hive-site.xml`, or use the `set hive.exec.parallel=true` command to apply this option.
- **Use ORC files:** Although you select only one column when performing HiveQL, the file is saved based on the row, and it accesses the entire row to read unnecessary data so the performance decline happens. The columnar input format, such as ORC, was developed to improve this. If you use ORC, you can obtain the advantage, such as the increase in read/write performance, and the storage space efficiency through compression can easily be used. Specify `STORED AS ORC` with `CREATE TABLE` syntax, or add `SET FILEFORMAT ORC` in the `ALTER TABLE` statement. It also supports a compression such as `SNAPPY` or `ZLIB`.
- **Small Files Problem:** Hadoop is designed for high volume systems, but there are two problems when dealing with a number of split small files rather than large ones. These problems are the NameNode memory problem and performance problems that affect MapReduce. In the default input format, like TextInputFormat, each file should have at least one split. So, if there is a large number of mappers launching, it can cause a JVM startup overhead.

To solve this problem, set the `hive.hadoop.supports.splittable.combineinputformat` configuration to true. Enabling this property will increase performance, because mapper can handle more than one file.

APACHE PIG

Pig is a tool for analyzing the bulk dataset. It defines the job by the inherent language (Pig Latin). It is similar to Hive in that it converts into MapReduce internally, yet SQL used by Hive is declarative, while Pig Latin is the procedural language. Although Pig Latin is not familiar to users compared to SQL, it is advantageous when performing the different treatment to split the data stream, or by reading the anti-formal data.

A simple Pig architecture diagram is shown in Figure 4-3.

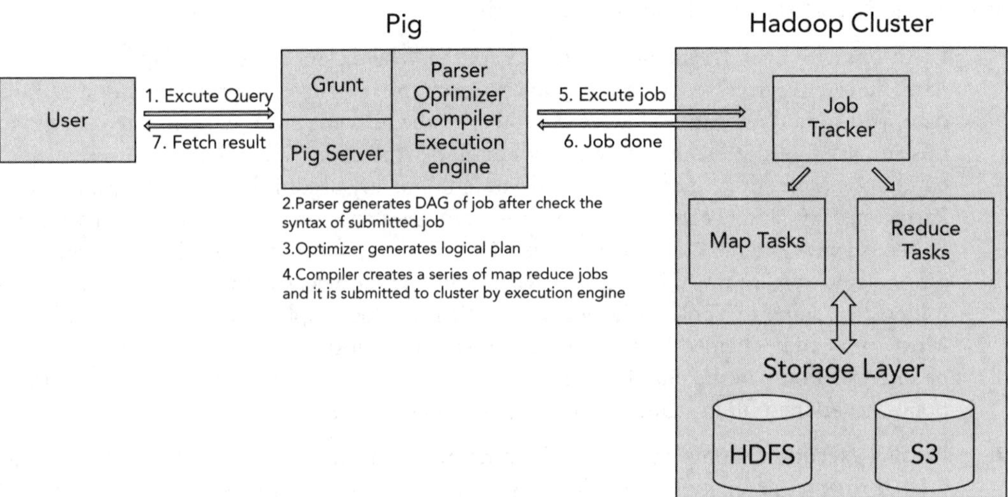

FIGURE 4-3

Pig Installation

Next we will cover a Pig 0.15.0 installation example. The latest version of Pig can be downloaded from the following URL: `http://pig.apache.org/releases.html`.

1. Download Pig and uncompress it:

```
$ wget http://apache.mirror.cdnetworks.com/pig/pig-0.15.0/pig-0.15.0.tar.gz
$ tar xvfz pig-0.15.0.tar.gz
```

2. Set the environment variable (or add it your shell profile):

```
$ cd pig-0.15.0
$ export PIG_HOME=$PWD
$ export PATH=$PIG_HOME/bin:$PATH
$ export HADOOP_HOME=<your_hadoop_home>
$ export PIG_CLASSPATH=<your_hadoop_conf_dir>
```

3. Make sure that the installation was successful:

```
$ pig -h
Apache Pig version 0.15.0 (r1682971)
compiled Jun 01 2015, 11:44:35
```

Pig Latin

Pig converts the script that describes the data stream into MapReduce. Pig Latin is the language used at this time. Pig Latin can process the data by a few codes, and can describe the job without caring about the MapReduce structure. Also, it can be expanded by using UDF, and can use Piggy Bank that gathers useful UDF or writes UDF directly. See the following link for a complete description of Pig Latin:

`http://pig.apache.org/docs/r0.15.0/start.html.`

Pig Command Line Options

A method of executing from the command line is most often used in Pig. By default, Pig runs in the MapReduce mode, and it can be specified via the `-x` option.

- **Local mode:** It runs through the `pig -x local` command, carrying a single JVM with the local filesystem. It's useful when prototyping and debugging your program.
- **MapReduce mode:** It runs through the `pix -x mapreduce` command or with no option. It uses cluster computing resources and HDFS.
- **Tez mode:** Runs Pig on the Tez framework using the `pix -x tez` command.

Pig also has the Interactive shell mode and batch mode. It is distinguished by the input type.

- **Batch mode:** It is the way to run a file that is pre-written by Pig Latin. Use as the `pig <pigLatin_file_name>` command. When you perform a multiquery written to the file, Pig tries to run all of the jobs in the file, even if it fails in the middle of the job. It can be classified as return code: 0 is Success, 2 is failed all of the job, and 3 is a partial failure. Table 4-4 shows command-line options most often used in batch mode.

TABLE 4-4: Batch mode on the command line

OPTION	DESCRIPTION	EXAMPLES
`-e(or -execute) <quoted-command-string>`	Command to execute	`pig -e 'sh ls'`
`[-f] <filename>`	Execute from files	`pig [-f] <pig_script_location>`
`-p(or -param) <property=value>`	Use Pig variables	`pig -p k: ey1=value1 pigLatin.pig`
`-P(or -propertyFile) <property_file>`	Specify a property file	`pig -P pig.properties`
`-F(or -stop_on_failure)`	Stop Pig job immediately when one of multiple query failed	`pig -F pig.properties`

- **Interactive shell mode:** Execute a shell that calls Grunt, and within this, type the Pig Latin phrase, "do the Job." Table 4-5 shows the commands that are frequently used in the interactive shell mode.

TABLE 4-5: Interactive shell mode commands

COMMAND	DESCRIPTION	EXAMPLES
`fs`	Use the Hadoop file system shell	`fs -ls`
`sh`	Use the `shell` command	`sh ls`
`exec`	Run a Pig script. All aliases in the script will not reference to Grunt.	`exec <pig_script_location>`
`run`	Run a Pig script. All aliases will be available to Grunt.	`run <pig_script_location>`
`kill`	Kill the MapReduce job with `jobid`	`kill <job_id>`

When writing Pig Latin, the processing logic is defined in the following order.

1. **Specifying Input Data:** Data can be read using the Load statement. `A = LOAD 'inputfile.txt' USING PigStorage('\t')` statement, and read `inputfile.txt` classified as a tab from the filesystem, storing it in the relation `A`.
2. **Define Data processing that you loaded:** Find out in Table 4-6 how to use the frequently used operator.
3. **Outputting the processed data:** Use the `STORE` command to save results to the filesystems or use a `DUMP` command to display to the screen.

TABLE 4-6: Frequently used operators

OPERATOR	DESCRIPTION	EXAMPLES
`FILTER`	Select tuples that meet the condition	`X = FILTER A BY a1 >= 2016;`
`FOREACH GENERATE`	Operation that works with specified columns	`X = FOREACH A GENERATE a1, a2;`
`GROUP`	Aggregate data to the specified field	`X = GROUP A BY a1;`
`DISTINCT`	Remove duplicate tuples	`X = DISTINCT A;`
`ORDER BY`	Sort the given data	`X = ORDER A BY a1;`

UDF

Pig has several functions to help you with a job. In most cases, this can be solved with built-in functions, or provided by the Piggybank, but sometimes you may be able to solve the problem when you must create your own function. UDF is used in this case, and it can be developed using various languages such as Java, Python, Ruby, etc.

When the user tries to write UDF directly to use, operations can be done in the following order:

1. Create a new class that extends the `org.apache.pig.EvalFunc(or FilterFunc)` class.
2. Implement the `exec()` method.
3. Package the JAR file and add it to the classpath (or upload to HDFS, S3).
4. Register the JAR file to the distributed cache using `REGISTER <jar_file_name>` command. If you use a language other than Java, paste the `USING` keyword behind the register statement.

HUE

Hue provides an interface that allows you to easily approach the Hadoop ecosystem using a web-based application. It changes the way you work with HDFS or user management on CLI to the GUI. You can execute the Hive, Impala, and Spark job directly on the web. Also, the result is automatically expressed as a graph, and you can make a chart using a simple operation. If you are wondering what functions Hue has, refer to this website:

`http://demo.gethue.com/#tourStep3`

A simple Hue architecture diagram is shown in Figure 4-4.

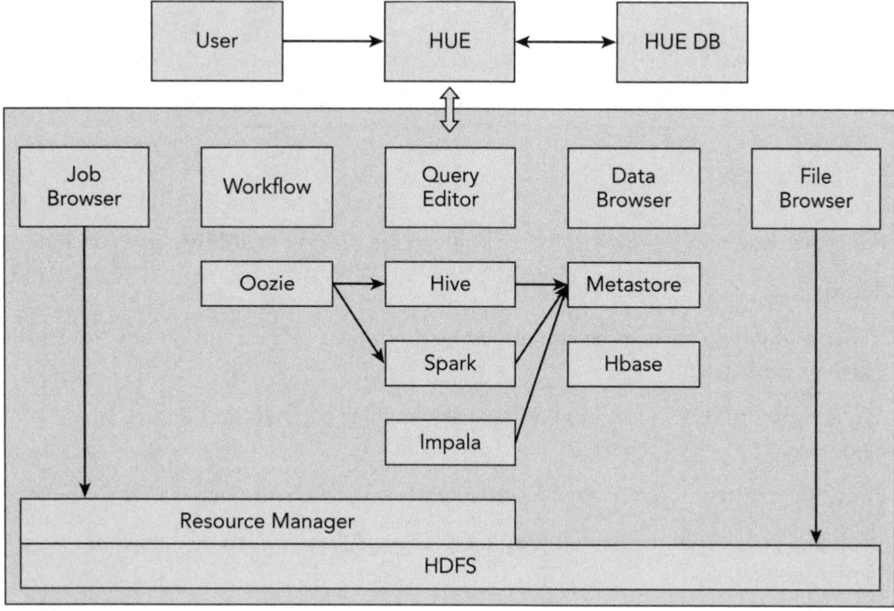

FIGURE 4-4

Features

Hue is intuitive to use, and most of the functions require no learning in order to use, because it runs a GUI environment. Given these characteristics, Hue is mainly responsible for providing the interface in contact with the end user. In Figure 4-5, you can see the chart using an executed Hive query in Hue.

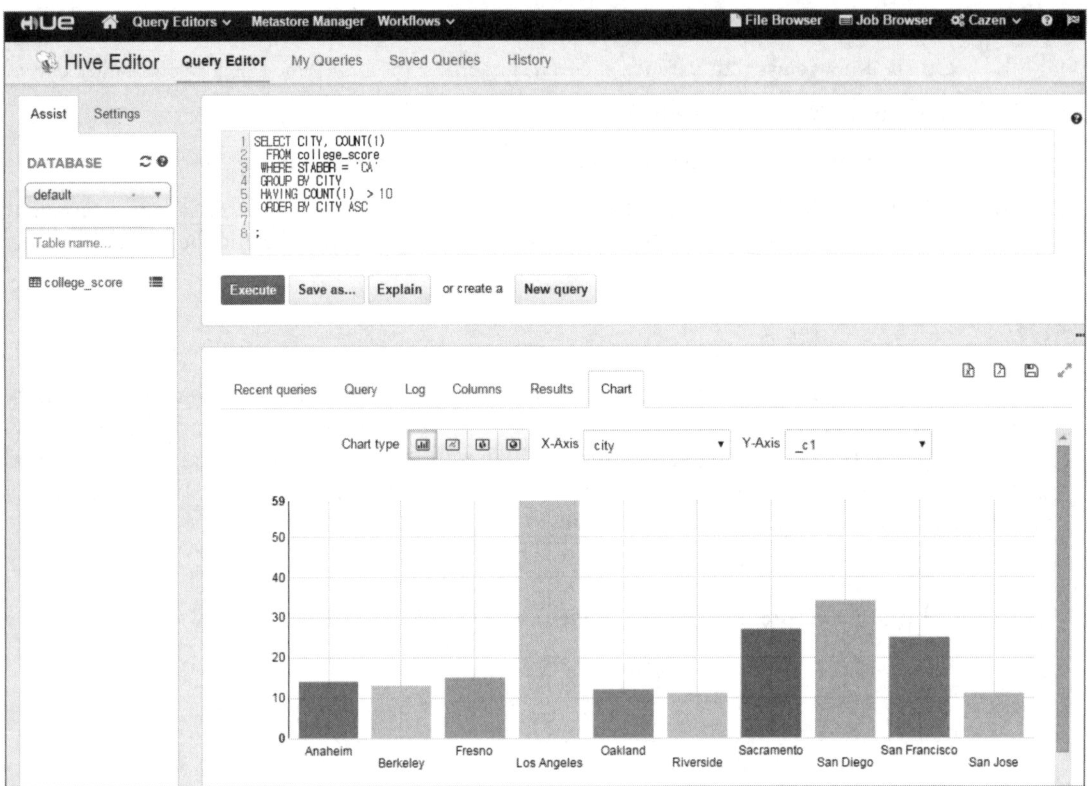

FIGURE 4-5

Let's examine the chart shown in Figure 4-5 where you can see an executed Hive query in Hue.

- **Query Editor**
  - Hive and Pig scripts can be run directly, and Impala (MPP solution of Cloudera) is also possible to query in.
  - In addition to this, traditional DB queries, such as MySQL and Oracle, are also possible.
  - Save the written query to the filesystem and you can recall queries in the job history.
  - Job Designer capabilities help simple Oozie workflow jobs to be defined in a graphic environment.

  - Parameterize supported. This feature is useful when performing repetitive tasks given a variable. For example, if you obtain a count of a particular device model from a log, it is convenient and can be reused with specified variables.
- **Data Browser**
  - The Hive metastore CRUD is possible in the data browser.
  - You can visually see the structure of the database and table you manage, and you can also check the sample data.
  - Browsing tables of Hbase is possible.
  - It supports the import/export job managing of the Sqoop.
- **Workflow**
  - This is the Oozie job related menu. In the Dashboard you can check a list of the workflow, coordinator, and bundled jobs.
  - Click on each job to see the detailed view, status, job logs and submitted XML file.
  - The Workflow Editor can manage the Oozie job. Even users who are not familiar with the Oozie can easily create and apply their own logic, because unlike traditional XML methods, it defines a job with an interactive UI.
- **File browser**
  - It provides a function of managing the file in HDFS via the web. Create, modify, delete, as well as a permission change, can be performed as well.
  - Upload files with drag and drop. Uncompressing the uploaded file is also supported.
- **Job browser**
  - Display the list of jobs based on information in the resource manager.
  - You can click the job id to query the status of the task and the logs.
  - Search by username, and containing text is also possible.

APACHE OOZIE

Oozie is a workflow scheduler for Hadoop. Although Hadoop jobs can be executed by connecting map and reduce, the use of scheduler is required because of the inconvenience of writing and management in realizing the complex business logic. Since Oozie supports most jobs of the Hadoop ecosystem (such as MapReduce, Spark, Pig, Hive, Shell, and Distcp), it is widely used.

Oozie workflow jobs are Direct Acyclic Graphs (DAGs) of actions and Oozie coordinator jobs can fulfill repeatedly by using the parameter of the start time, end time, and frequency that received the workflow jobs as a variable. It is possible to use the condition sentence, comparative sentence, and the Expression Language (EL). Thanks to this property, it is possible to easily embody generally used business logic, such as the input file check, hourly job, and various kinds of job chaining.

If you want to use Oozie, the considerations are as follows:

- ➤ Each workflow action creates control dependency DAG. It means that the second job is not executed until the end of the first job, and there is no circulation in the same workflow.
- ➤ The Oozie web console is a useful tool to get coordinator/workflow status information. The Oozie web console is disabled by default because the ExtJS library has different license agreements with Oozie. You can enable it in the following way:

```
$ mkdir libext
$ cd libext
$ wget http://extjs.com/deploy/ext-2.2.zip
$ cd ../bin
$ ./oozie-setup.sh prepare-war
```

The screenshot of the Oozie web console is shown in Figure 4-6.

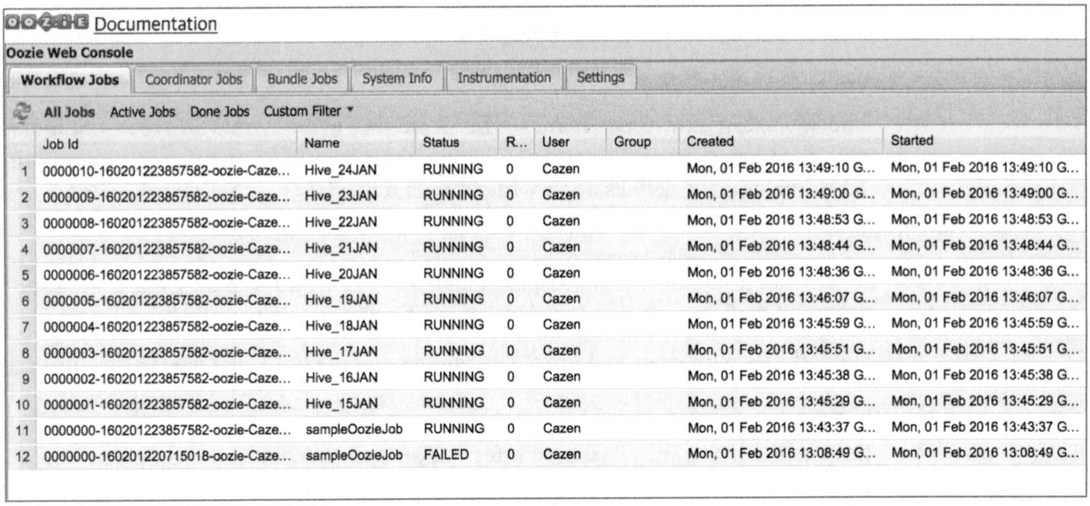

Documentation

Oozie Web Console

Workflow Jobs | Coordinator Jobs | Bundle Jobs | System Info | Instrumentation | Settings

All Jobs Active Jobs Done Jobs Custom Filter ▾

	Job Id	Name	Status	R...	User	Group	Created	Started
1	0000010-160201223857582-oozie-Caze...	Hive_24JAN	RUNNING	0	Cazen		Mon, 01 Feb 2016 13:49:10 G...	Mon, 01 Feb 2016 13:49:10 G...
2	0000009-160201223857582-oozie-Caze...	Hive_23JAN	RUNNING	0	Cazen		Mon, 01 Feb 2016 13:49:00 G...	Mon, 01 Feb 2016 13:49:00 G...
3	0000008-160201223857582-oozie-Caze...	Hive_22JAN	RUNNING	0	Cazen		Mon, 01 Feb 2016 13:48:53 G...	Mon, 01 Feb 2016 13:48:53 G...
4	0000007-160201223857582-oozie-Caze...	Hive_21JAN	RUNNING	0	Cazen		Mon, 01 Feb 2016 13:48:44 G...	Mon, 01 Feb 2016 13:48:44 G...
5	0000006-160201223857582-oozie-Caze...	Hive_20JAN	RUNNING	0	Cazen		Mon, 01 Feb 2016 13:48:36 G...	Mon, 01 Feb 2016 13:48:36 G...
6	0000005-160201223857582-oozie-Caze...	Hive_19JAN	RUNNING	0	Cazen		Mon, 01 Feb 2016 13:46:07 G...	Mon, 01 Feb 2016 13:46:07 G...
7	0000004-160201223857582-oozie-Caze...	Hive_18JAN	RUNNING	0	Cazen		Mon, 01 Feb 2016 13:45:59 G...	Mon, 01 Feb 2016 13:45:59 G...
8	0000003-160201223857582-oozie-Caze...	Hive_17JAN	RUNNING	0	Cazen		Mon, 01 Feb 2016 13:45:51 G...	Mon, 01 Feb 2016 13:45:51 G...
9	0000002-160201223857582-oozie-Caze...	Hive_16JAN	RUNNING	0	Cazen		Mon, 01 Feb 2016 13:45:38 G...	Mon, 01 Feb 2016 13:45:38 G...
10	0000001-160201223857582-oozie-Caze...	Hive_15JAN	RUNNING	0	Cazen		Mon, 01 Feb 2016 13:45:29 G...	Mon, 01 Feb 2016 13:45:29 G...
11	0000000-160201223857582-oozie-Caze...	sampleOozieJob	RUNNING	0	Cazen		Mon, 01 Feb 2016 13:43:37 G...	Mon, 01 Feb 2016 13:43:37 G...
12	0000000-160201220715018-oozie-Caze...	sampleOozieJob	FAILED	0	Cazen		Mon, 01 Feb 2016 13:08:49 G...	Mon, 01 Feb 2016 13:08:49 G...

FIGURE 4-6

Oozie Installation

Here is an installation example of Oozie 4.2.0. The latest version of Oozie can be downloaded from the following URL: `http://http://oozie.apache.org/`.

1. Download Oozie and uncompress it:

```
wget http://apache.mirror.cdnetworks.com/oozie/4.2.0/oozie-4.2.0.tar.gz
tar xvfz oozie-4.2.0.tar.gz
```

2. Build and set up Oozie from source. Remove the following codehaus repository from `pom.xml` before building:

```
<repository>
      <id>Codehaus repository</id>
      <url>http://repository.codehaus.org/</url>
```

```
        <snapshots> <enabled>false</enabled> </snapshots>
    </repository>

bin/mkdistro.sh -P hadoop-2,uber -DskipTests
--cp distro/target/oozie-4.2.0-distro.tar.gz ../
cp -R distro/target/oozie-4.2.0-distro/oozie-4.2.0/ ../oozie
cd ../oozie
```

3. Set the environment variable (or add it your shell profile):

```
export OOZIE_HOME=$PWD
export PATH=$OOZIE_HOME/bin:$PATH
```

4. Set the configuration variable. Add properties that you need to `conf/oozie-site.xml`.

5. Set the metastore and shared lib configuration.

   In general, Oozie uses an external metastore. The below configurations are examples of using the Metastore with MySQL. To use the external metastore, the proper driver has to exist in the libext folder.

```
<property>
    <name>oozie.service.JPAService.jdbc.driver</name>
    <value>com.mysql.jdbc.Driver</value>
</property>
<property>
    <name>oozie.service.JPAService.jdbc.url</name>
    <value>jdbc:mysql://dbAddress:port/database</value>
</property>
    <property>
    <name>oozie.service.JPAService.jdbc.username</name>
    <value>oozieuser</value>
</property>
<property>
    <name>oozie.service.JPAService.jdbc.password</name>
    <value>password</value>
</property>
```

6. Set the library path and the proxy user:

```
<property>
    <name>oozie.service.WorkflowAppService.system.libpath</name>
    <value>hdfs://<namenode>:<port>/user/hadoop/share/lib</value>
    </property>
<property>
    <name>oozie.service.ProxyUserService.proxyuser.<oozieuser>.hosts</name>
    <value>*</value>
    </property>
<property>
    <name>oozie.service.ProxyUserService.proxyuser.<oozieuser>.groups</name>
    <value>*</value>
</property>
```

7. Add the following property to `conf/hadoopconf/core-site.xml`:

```
<property>
    <name>fs.default.name</name>
    <value>hdfs://namenode:port</value>
</property>
```

8. After that, create the db schema and sharelib:

```
bin/oozie-setup.sh db create -run
bin/oozie-setup.sh sharelib create -fs namenodeurl:port
```

9. Start Oozie and check the status.

```
bin/oozied.sh start
bin/oozie admin -oozie http://localhost:11000/oozie -sharelibupdate
```

After performing the command, it is successful if the shared library list is displayed as follows:

```
$ bin/oozie admin -oozie http://localhost:11000/oozie -shareliblist
[Available ShareLib]
oozie
hive
distcp
hcatalog
sqoop
mapreduce-streaming
spark
hive2
pig
```

How Oozie Works

Apache Oozie is a web application that supports the Rest API and runs on Tomcat (see Figure 4-7). It consists of the Oozie Server and Client and uses the metastore storage (RDBMS). You can perform a simple workflow job with Oozie as follows:

1. The Oozie Client uses the `Job.properties` to submit jobs to the Job Oozie Server.
2. The Oozie Server executes the job, calling a ResourceManager.
3. ResourceManager executes the Oozie Launcher (Map-Only Job) using the received information.
4. The Oozie Launcher runs the job defined in the workflow.
5. A task invokes the callback URL to the Oozie server when it has either completed or failed.
6. Be sure to finish the job.

Oozie has been prepared in accordance with a design principle that separates the scheduler and the job. Since a Job is run by the Oozie Launcher in the cluster, such as configuration files, `workflow.xml`, and `coordinator.xml`, it should be placed on HDFS. Also, if you want to use a JAR file, create a lib folder under the `workflow.xml` folder of HDFS, or specify `oozie.libpath job.properties`.

Performing a Job can be cumbersome, given how you need to add each workflow library, but Oozie manages a library of commonly used job types by using sharelib. The folder structure created on HDFS is produced similarly to the following (The latest version has been added for the version management `lib_timestamp` directory under lib).

```
/user/oozie/share/lib/lib_20160126002346/hive
/user/oozie/share/lib/lib_20160126002346/hive/ST4-4.0.4.jar
/user/oozie/share/lib/lib_20160126002346/hive/activation-1.1.jar
/user/oozie/share/lib/lib_20160126002346/hive/ant-1.9.1.jar
/user/oozie/share/lib/lib_20160126002346/hive/ant-launcher-1.9.1.jar
```

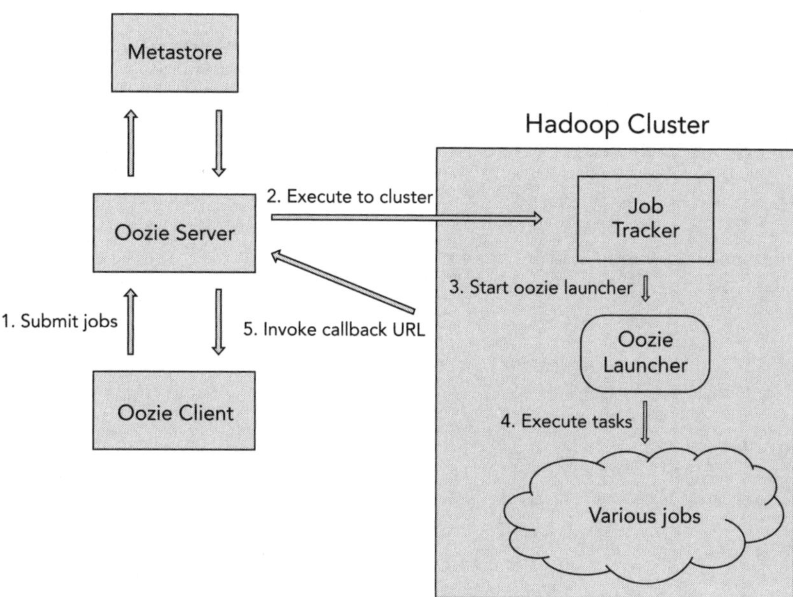

FIGURE 4-7

Workflow/Coordinator

In order to accomplish your business goals, you have to fulfill one or more jobs. For example, a Pig script can bring the raw log saved in HDFS by grouping and designating it as an external table. You can also use the script to add the partition, and conduct a Hive job, making the report and informing the user of success and failure by email. Both of these items can be bound as one workflow. That is, the workflow is a gathering of the job, control, and the flow. Also, the above workflow is executed regularly during a certain time, or is dependent on other workflow or data. The coordinator is used to control this situation. In addition, the bundle and a set coordinator also exist, although we won't be discussing this here.

Workflow

The Oozie workflow is written in XML, based on xPDL (XML Process Definition Language), and it consisted of two types of nodes:

- **Action node:** Execute the actual job such as MR, Pig, Hive, SSH, etc.
- **Control flow node:** State control such as start, fork, join, kill, and end.

By combining these nodes, you can define the workflow. The following example is a simple Hive job with success at the end, which leaves a failed log.

workflow.xml

```
<workflow-app xmlns="uri:oozie:workflow:0.3" name="sampleOozieJob">
    <start to="hive_sample_job" />
    <action name="hive_sample_job">
```

```
        <hive xmlns="uri:oozie:hive-action:0.2">
            <job-tracker>${jobTracker}:${jobTrackerPort}</job-tracker>
            <name-node>hdfs://${nameNode}:${nameNodePort}</name-node>
            <configuration>
      <property>
          <name>oozie.use.system.libpath</name>
          <value>true</value>
      </property>
      <property>
          <name>mapred.job.queue.name</name>
          <value>q2</value>
      </property>
      <property>
          <name>oozie.launcher.mapred.job.queue.name</name>
          <value>q1</value>
      </property>
            </configuration>
            <script>sample.hql</script>
            <param>targetDate=20160129</param>
        </hive>
        <ok to="end" />
        <error to="fail" />
    </action>
    <kill name="fail">
        <message>Job failed, [${wf:errorMessage(wf:lastErrorNode())}]</message>
    </kill>
    <end name="end" />
</workflow-app>
```

job.properties

```
jobTracker=<jobtracker_address>
nameNode=<namenode_address>
jobTrackerPort=<jobtracker_port>
nameNodePort=<namenode_port>
oozie.wf.application.path=hdfs://${nameNode}:${nameNodePort}/{location_of_workflow}
oozie.use.system.libpath=true
```

You can run and check the Oozie workflow job using the following command:

```
$ oozie job -oozie http://localhost:11000/oozie -config job.properties -run
job: 160106012758058-oozie-bpse-W
$ oozie job -oozie http://localhost:11000/oozie -info 160106012758058-oozie-bpse-W
Job ID : 160106012758058-oozie-bpse-W
------------------------------------------------------------------------
Workflow Name : sampleOozieJob
App Path      : hdfs://10.3.50.73:8020/user/cazen/
Status        : RUNNING
Run           : 0
User          : hadoop
Group         : -
Created       : 2016-01-27 07:11 GMT
Started       : 2016-01-27 07:11 GMT
Last Modified : 2016-01-27 07:11 GMT
Ended         : -
CoordAction ID: -
```

```
Actions
------------------------------------------------------------------------
ID                             Status    Ext ID       Ext Status Err Code
------------------------------------------------------------------------
160106012758058-oozie-bpse-W@:start:                     OK
------------------------------------------------------------------------
160106012758058-oozie-bpse-W@hive_sample_job             RUNNING
------------------------------------------------------------------------
```

Coordinator

If you carefully examine the workflow sample above, you can see a `targetDate` variable that has passed to the job. The coordinator can perform workflow jobs at specified times via `startTime`, `endTime`, and also the frequency. A simple coordinator example that calls the Job at a certain time while passing a variable is shown next:

coordinator.xml

```
<coordinator-app name="sample_oozie_coord" frequency="${coord:days(1)}"
start="2016-01-01T00:20Z" end="2016-12-31T00:25Z"
 timezone="UTC" xmlns="uri:oozie:coordinator:0.4">
   <action>
      <workflow>
         <app-path>hdfs://${nameNode}:${nameNodePort}/user/cazen/</app-path>
         <configuration>
            <property>
    <name>targetDate</name>
<value>${coord:formatTime(coord:dateOffset(coord:nominalTime(), -1, 'DAY'),
 'yyyyMMdd')}
</value>
            </property>
         </configuration>
      </workflow>
   </action>
</coordinator-app>
```

coord.properties

```
jobTracker=<jobtracker_address>
nameNode=<namenode_address>
jobTrackerPort=<jobtracker_port>
nameNodePort=<namenode_port>
oozie.coord.application.path=hdfs://${nameNode}:${Port}/{location_of_workflow}
oozie.use.system.libpath=true
```

You can run and check the Oozie coordinator job by using the following command:

```
$ oozie job -oozie http://localhost:11000/oozie -config coord.properties -run
job: 160106012758058-oozie-bpse-C
$ oozie job -oozie http://localhost:11000/oozie -info 160106012758058-oozie-bpse-C
Job ID : 160106012758058-oozie-bpse-C
------------------------------------------------------------------------
Job Name     : sample_oozie_coord
App Path     : hdfs://10.3.50.73:8020/user/cazen
Status       : RUNNING
```

```
Start Time   : 2016-01-01 00:20 GMT
End Time     : 2016-12-31 00:25 GMT
Pause Time   : -
Concurrency : 1
----------------------------------------------------------------------
ID            Status    Ext ID            Err Code  Created    Nominal Time
160106012758058-oozie-bpse-C@1         RUNNING
----------------------------------------------------------------------
160106012758058-oozie-bpse-C@2         READY
----------------------------------------------------------------------
160106012758058-oozie-bpse-C@3         READY
----------------------------------------------------------------------
160106012758058-oozie-bpse-C@4         READY
----------------------------------------------------------------------
```

Oozie CLI

Oozie can be operated via the CLI, and the frequently used commands are listed next. Using an alias and export `OOZIE_URL` makes it more convenient.

```
Run a job             : oozie job -config job.properties -run
Check status          : oozie job -info <job_id>
Kill a job            : oozie job -kill <job_id>
Rerun a job           : oozie job -rerun <coord_id> -action=<job_num>
Check err log         : oozie job -errorlog <job_id>
List all coordinator : oozie jobs -jobtype coord
List all workflow     : oozie jobs -jobtype wf
Validate xml          : oozie validate workflow.xml
Update share library : oozie admin -sharelibupdate
Check share library  : oozie admin -shareliblist
```

SUMMARY

In this chapter on user experience, a project that increased the user convenience was based on the Hadoop environment was discussed. Hive and Pig enabled you to analyze by script, without an effort of writing the program code directly, thanks to the high level language called HiveQL and Pig Latin. Hue enabled you to execute the analysis and HDFS file management that was completed in the CLI environment by means of the web interface. Oozie helped to manage repetitive jobs in production. These projects can be used for free under the Apache license 2.0, and can be easily installed.

5

Integration with Other Systems

WHAT'S IN THIS CHAPTER?

- Fitting Hadoop into existing IT environments
- Connecting Hadoop with structured data stores
- Streaming data into the Hadoop Data Lake
- Moving data faster and processing data in real time

Hadoop is introduced into an organization's IT environment when the organization needs to more effectively manage big data. Of course databases, enterprise data warehouses, and other IT systems already exist in your organization's IT environment. And, it is likely that new systems, especially emerging technologies, will be added into the data center in the near future.

Before Hadoop, your organization ran analytical workloads in the data warehouse provided by vendors such as Teradata, Netezza or Vertica. After adding Hadoop into the data center, it is common practice to migrate the heavy Extract, Transform and Load (ETL) process to Hadoop. First, you extract data from the source systems, such as the Relational Database Management System (RDBMS) into HDFS (introduced in Chapter 2). You can leverage Hadoop's parallel processing to transform the data into target data models. Then the transformed data is loaded from Hadoop into the data warehouse. Apache Sqoop, from the Hadoop ecosystem, is the tool that can be used for this kind of integration. In this chapter we will first introduce Sqoop, to learn how it can efficiently transfer bulk data between Hadoop and structured data stores such as relational databases.

In addition to database systems, application servers have data your organization wants to capture. One example is web server logs that can be collected for website user click stream analysis, network security, and system operation monitoring. Hadoop is designed to be useful for this kind of processing, so this chapter will also introduce Apache Flume, which is a tool originally designed to stream server logs into Hadoop.

Hadoop MapReduce (introduced in Chapter 3) is designed as a batch-oriented data paradigm, taking in massive bounded data sets and processing them in a batch. It does not support streaming processing, because even the data is streamed into its storage. The batch processing naturally introduces high latency from the time when business events occur, to the time businesses can use the analysis results to make decisions. Business moves faster in the Internet era, so near-real time or real time data analysis is required. New technologies are coming out from the Hadoop ecosystem to advance the processing capability of Hadoop. For instance, Apache Spark makes it possible to process data faster in Hadoop. Apache Ignite boosts the performance of both the computation and storage layer. In this chapter, we will also introduce the other two cousins from the Apache family: Kafka and Storm, which together enable moving data faster to process data in real time. In this chapter we will take a detailed look at all of these technologies that are part of the Hadoop ecosystem.

APACHE SQOOP

Apache Sqoop is a command line tool built for efficiently transferring bulk data between Hadoop and structured data stores such as RDBMS, enterprise data warehouses, NoSQL and mainframe systems. It became a top-level Apache project in March of 2012.

Sqoop was initially developed as a tool to transfer data from RDBMS to Hadoop (its name Sqoop actually means "SQL-to-Hadoop"). It later became a standalone open source project on Github submitted by Cloudera. It can import existing tables or databases from RDBMS into HDFS, and can even populate tables in Hive and HBase (see Figure 5-1). This is really helpful for organizations that have recently set up a new cluster. Conversely, Sqoop can also be used to export data from Hadoop into external structured data stores.

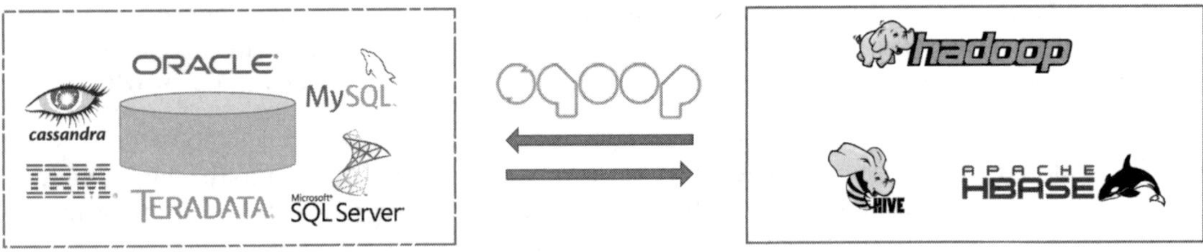

FIGURE 5-1

At the time of writing, the latest stable version of Sqoop is 1.4.6. You may also be aware that the next generation of Sqoop (a.k.a. Sqoop2) is also under active development. In this book we focus on version 1 and do not cover any new features from Sqoop2.

How It Works

With Sqoop, you can import data from a database or a mainframe system into HDFS. For this input, you can use either database table(s) or mainframe dataset(s). For databases, Sqoop will read the table row-by-row into HDFS. For mainframe data sets, Sqoop will read records from each mainframe dataset into HDFS. The output of this process yields a set of files containing a copy of the imported table or data set. The import process is performed in parallel, and for this reason, the output will be in multiple files. The files' format may be text delimited (CSV or TSV for example), a SequenceFile, or Avro, etc.

After processing data in Hadoop (for example, with Hive or Pig) you may have a result data set that you can then export to the relational database for consumption by external applications or users. Sqoop's export process will read a set of delimited text files from HDFS in parallel, parse them into records, and insert them as new rows in a target database table, or update existing rows if you specify the column name as an update-key.

The import process from a database to Hadoop is done in two steps as depicted in Figure 5-2. First, Sqoop introspects the database to gather the necessary table metadata for the data being imported. Second, there is a map-only MapReduce job that Sqoop submits to Hadoop. This job uses DBInputFormat, which is backed with JDBC to interact with the database. With the proper JDBC driver installed, Sqoop can interact with any database system implemented by JDBC. DBInputFormat is a subclass of InputFormat, which can split up the input (here in a database table) into logical InputSplits; each of the splits will be assigned to an individual Mapper. When the Sqoop import command is invoked, it retrieves the table's metadata, and generates a class definition that can be used to de-serialize the data emitted from DBInputFromat, and then submit the job to start importing data. The job spawn mapper transfers data into HDFS in parallel. Sqoop also outputs to Mapper according to the specified arguments in the command line.

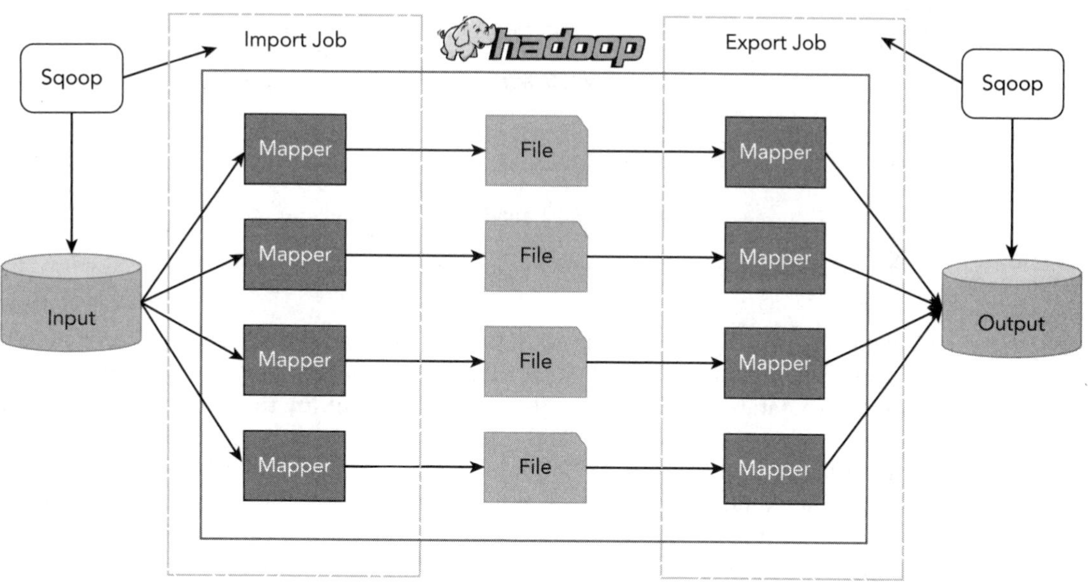

FIGURE 5-2

The export process from Hadoop to a database is done in two steps, but in a reversed way as depicted in Figure 5-2. The first step is to introspect the database for metadata of the target table, followed by the second step of transferring the data with a map-only job. Sqoop divides the input dataset into splits with the help of the concrete FileInputFormat, and then uses individual map tasks to write the splits into the target table with the configured ExportOutputFormat. Note that DBOutputFormat is not involved in actual write operations, but it's only used for configuration by Sqoop's default export job.

Let's use MySQL as an example to see how to import data into HDFS:

```
$ $SQOOP_HOME/bin/sqoop import --connect jdbc:mysql://mysqlhost/db --table ↵
  employees --target-dir /sqoop/mysqlimport/employees
16/01/29 22:32:00 INFO sqoop.Sqoop: Running Sqoop version: 1.4.6
16/01/29 22:32:00 INFO manager.MySQLManager: Preparing to use a MySQL streaming ↵
  resultset.
16/01/29 22:32:00 INFO tool.CodeGenTool: Beginning code generation
16/01/29 22:32:00 ERROR sqoop.Sqoop: Got exception running Sqoop: java.lang.
Runtime↵
  Exception:
  Could not load db driver class: com.mysql.jdbc.Driver
java.lang.RuntimeException: Could not load db driver class: com.mysql.jdbc.Driver
```

From the error message in the terminal, you can see Sqoop requires a JDBC driver to work with the source database. Install the driver JAR under the $SQOOP_HOME/lib folder and rerun the import command:

```
$ ls  -l $SQOOP_HOME/lib/mysql*
-rw-r--r--  1 sqoop  hadoop   855946 Jan 29 22:34 mysql-connector-java-5.1.13.jar

$ $SQOOP_HOME/bin/sqoop import --connect jdbc:mysql://mysqlhost/db --table ↵
  employees --target-dir /sqoop/mysqlimport/employees
16/02/09 23:12:06 INFO sqoop.Sqoop: Running Sqoop version: 1.4.6
16/02/09 23:12:06 INFO manager.MySQLManager: Preparing to use a MySQL streaming ↵
  resultset.
16/02/09 23:12:06 INFO tool.CodeGenTool: Beginning code generation
16/02/09 23:12:07 WARN manager.MySQLManager: It looks like you are importing from ↵
  mysql.
16/02/09 23:12:07 WARN manager.MySQLManager: This transfer can be faster! Use the ↵
  --direct
16/02/09 23:12:07 WARN manager.MySQLManager: option to exercise a MySQL-specific ↵
  fast path.
```

Sqoop recognizes that the import source is MySQL, and suggests that the transfer can be faster if you use an additional option: `--direct`. Transferring large volumes of data through JDBC is often inefficient, since database vendors usually provide native utility tools that imports/exports data in a more high-performance manner. With the option `--direct`, mysqldump can be used by Sqoop to import data from MySQL to Hadoop, and mysqlimport can be used for the export process. Sqoop provides a pluggable mechanism for optimal connectivity to external systems. It provides a convenient framework for building new connectors, which can be dropped into Sqoop installations to provide connectivity to various systems. Sqoop itself comes bundled with various connectors that can be used for popular database and data warehousing systems. Apart from the built-in connectors, many companies have developed their own connectors that can be plugged into Sqoop. These range from specialized connectors for enterprise data warehouse systems to NoSQL datastores. To leverage those native utility tools and optimal connectors in Sqoop jobs, you need to make sure they are installed properly along with Sqoop on Hadoop worker nodes (where the mapper tasks run).

APACHE FLUME

Apache Flume is a distributed, reliable, and available service for efficiently collecting, aggregating, and moving large amounts of log data. It has a simple and flexible architecture based on streaming data flows. It is robust and fault tolerant with tunable reliability mechanisms and many failover and recovery mechanisms. It uses a simple extensible data model that allows for online analytic application. It became a top-level Apache project in June of 2012.

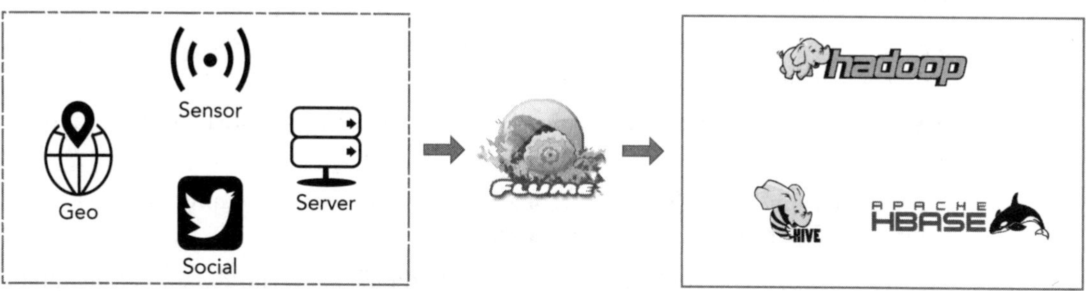

FIGURE 5-3

Sqoop lets users ingest structure data into Hadoop, while Flume enables users to ingest high-volume streaming data into HDFS, Hive and HBase (See Figure 5-3). Flume was initially created by Cloudera to enable reliable and simplified collection of log information from many distributed sources, for example, web servers of large internet companies. It's also designed to be extensible for other typical streaming sources like sensor and machine data, geo-location data, and social media posts. Hadoop is an ideal system to store and process a large volume and variety of those types of data, but it's not able to handle a large number of low-bandwidth connections and small files being continuously generated. Flume is designed to address all of these challenges.

The current stable version of Flume is 1.6.0. You may find that some old books, documents or web blogs mention "Flume NG." It is actually the current version of Apache Flume (1.x). Back in 2011 it was the next generation of Flume, compared to the original implementation (pre 1.0) open sourced by Cloudera in 2009. In this book, we only talk about the current version.

How It works

Flume is designed to be a flexible distributed system to provide reliable and scalable ways of efficiently collecting, aggregating and transporting large amounts of data from many different sources to a centralized datastore. Below is the list of its key concepts. By understanding these concepts, you can better understand the architecture of Flume and how it works:

- **Event:** The unit of data transported by Flume from its origination to its destination. Event has a byte array payload accompanied by an optional header, which is a collection of string key-value pairs.
- **Client:** The entity that generates events and sends them to one or multiple agents. An example of a client is Flume log4j Appender. A client is not needed if your application embedded a Flume agent.

- **Agent:** The unit of Flume deployment that is a container (single JVM process) of hosting sources, channels, sinks, and other components that enable the transportation of events from one place to another.
- **Source:** The active component that receives events from a specialized place and is put into one or multiple channels.
- **Channel:** The passive component that buffers incoming events from a source until they are drained by sinks.
- **Sink:** The active component that pulls events out of a channel and transmits them to a final destination or the next agent in the flow.
- **Interceptor:** An optional component that can transform events before they are put into a channel.
- **Flow:** The pipeline starts from the origination where the event is coming from to its final destination. The simplest flow has one agent.

Table 5-1 is a summary of commonly used components in the Flume agent. For a more comprehensive list of components that Flume supports, you can refer to Flume's user guide. Like Sqoop, Flume is also designed to be extensible. The plugin-based architecture enables users to build custom components. The flexible architecture and those reusable components allow you to design a large range of possible deployment scenarios.

TABLE 5-1: Common Flume Agent Components

TYPE ALIAS	DESCRIPTION	IMPLEMENTATION CLASS
Source		
-avro	Receives Avro events from upstream	org.apache.flume.source.AvroSource
Source		
-http	Starts http server and turns POST request into events	org.apache.flume.source.http.HTTPSource
Source		
-jms	Converts JMS message into events	org.apache.flume.source.jms.JMSSource
Source		
-spooldir	Monitors a directory and create events from the data file under the directory	org.apache.flume.source.SpoolDirectorySource
Channel		
-memory	Holds events in memory	org.apache.flume.channel.MemoryChannel

continues

TABLE 5-1: *(continued)*

TYPE ALIAS	DESCRIPTION	IMPLEMENTATION CLASS
Channel		
-file	Persists events to local disk to avoid data loss in memory	org.apache.flume.channel.file.FileChannel
Channel		
-kafka	Buffering events with Kafka	org.apache.flume.channel.kafka.KafkaChannel
Sink		
-avro	Sends Avro events downstream	org.apache.flume.sink.AvroSink
Sink		
-hbase	Writes events into HBase	org.apache.flume.sink.hbase.HBaseSink
Sink		
-hdfs	Writes events into HDFS	org.apache.flume.sink.hdfs.HDFSEventSink

In Figure 5-4, you can see a common scenario with Flume being used in a log collection. A large number of web servers (log producing clients) are sending data to a few tier 1 Agents, while connecting to a tier 2 Agent, which consolidates the data that is then written to HDFS.

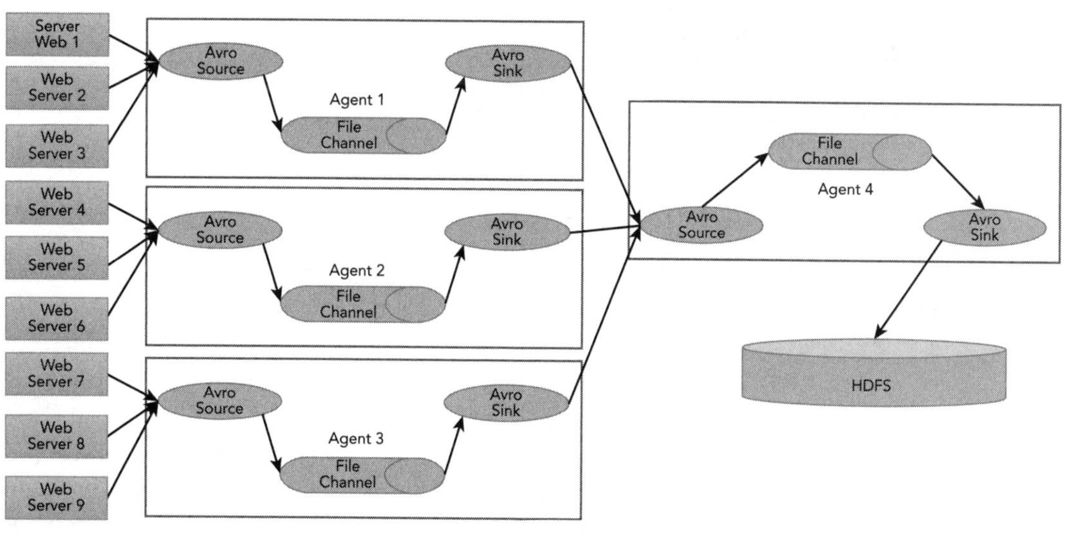

FIGURE 5-4

Each agent should be started using a Flume shell script called flume-ng. You need to specify the agent name, the config directory, and the config file on the command line:

```
$ $FLUME_HOME/bin/flume-ng agent -c <config-dir> -f <config-file> -n <agent-name>
```

The configuration file follows the Java properties file format, and describes the data flow within the agent. Here is a template for the configuration file.

```
# list the sources, sinks and channels for the agent
<agent-name>.sources = <Source>
<agent-name>.sinks = <Sink>
<agent-name>.channels = <Channel1> <Channel2>

# set channel for source
<agent-name>.sources.<Source>.channels = <Channel1> <Channel2> ...

# set channel for sink
<agent-name>.sinks.<Sink>.channel = <Channel1>

# properties for sources
<agent-name>.sources.<Source>.<someProperty> = <someValue>

# properties for channels
<agent-name>.channels.<Channel>.<someProperty> = <someValue>

# properties for sinks
<agent-name>.sources.<Sink>.<someProperty> = <someValue>
```

Based on the template, the Agent 4 in Figure 5-4 can be defined as:

```
agent4.sources = source-4-avro
agent4.sinks = sink-4-hdfs
agent4.channels = channel-4-file

agent4.sources.source-4-avro.channels = channel-4-file
agent4.sinks.sink-4-hdfs.channel = channel-4-file

agent4.sources.source-4-avro.type = avro
agent4.sources.source-4-avro.bind = localhost
agent4.sources.source-4-avro.port = 10000

agent4.channels.channel-4-file.type = memory
agent4.channels.channel-4-file.capacity = 1000000
agent4.channels.channel-4-file.transactionCapacity = 10000
agent4.channels.channel-4-file.checkpointDir = /mnt/flume/checkpoint
agent4.channels.channel-4-file.dataDirs = /mnt/flume/data

agent4.sinks.sink-4-hdfs.type = hdfs
agent4.sinks.sink-4-hdfs.hdfs.path = hdfs://namenode/flume/weblogs
```

Flume provides channel-based transactions to guarantee reliable event delivery. When an event moves from one agent to another, two transactions are started, one on the agent that delivers the event and the other on the agent that receives the event. The first transaction is initiated by sending agent's sink, while the second one is initiated by receiver's source. The commit of first transaction depends on the second transaction. The receiving agent returns a success indication if its transaction committed properly (the event successfully put into the channel), then the sending agent commits

its transaction. This ensures guaranteed delivery semantics with the host that the flow makes. This mechanism also forms the basis for failure handling in Flume. Failure can be propagated from downstream to upstream through the flow. When the upstream agent is not able to pass the event downstream (due to network connection error, for example), it starts buffering the events in its channel. Once the connection has recovered, the buffered event will be drained out toward the final destination. The memory channel simply holds the events in memory, which is fast, but it's not recoverable if any crash happens. As a result, use the file channel, which is backed by the local filesystem and is recommended if you need durability and recoverability. Using a Kafka channel is even better, because Kafka is a high-throughput distributed messaging system that keeps strong durability and fault-tolerance guarantees. We will continue to discuss Kafka in the next section.

APACHE KAFKA

Apache Kafka is a high performance system for moving data in real time. From a high level, Kafka looks like a messaging system—clients publish messages to Kafka and messages are delivered in milliseconds. But Kafka works more like a distributed database: When you write a message to Kafka, it is replicated to multiple servers and committed to disk. Kafka is designed as a modern distributed system. The cluster is elastically scalable and fault tolerant, and applications can transparently scale out to produce or consume massive distributed streams. Kafka has become a key enabler for real time data processing.

Kafka was originally developed by LinkedIn, and subsequently became an open source project in 2011. In October 2012, it graduated from the Apache Incubator and started flourishing in the open source community. Initially, Kafka was designed as an efficient and scalable event queueing solution for user activity tracking on LinkedIn's website. Later it was extended to feed all activity events to the data warehouse and Hadoop for offline batch analysis. Because of its high throughput, reliable event delivery, and horizontal scalability, Kafka is being widely used as a general-purpose messaging system to support various use cases, which include:

- Website activity tracking
- Metrics collection and monitoring
- Log aggregation
- Stream processing and real time analytics
- Internet of Things

The original engineers of Kafka departed LinkedIn and started a company named Confluent to focus on building out the Kafka ecosystem to broaden its community. The major product of the company is the Confluent Platform (see Figure 5-5), which includes Kafka as the core and several components around Kafka to make it enterprise ready. The Confluent Platform is open source, free to use, and was released with an Apache license. The company provides commercial support for the platform, so it runs the same business model as Hortonworks for Hadoop.

The latest version of Kafka is 0.9.0, whereas the latest stable version is 0.8.2.2. We are going to use the version 0.9.0 for discussion in this section, because in this release, several new features have been introduced, which make Kafka enterprise ready. Those features include security, user defined quota, and Kafka Connect.

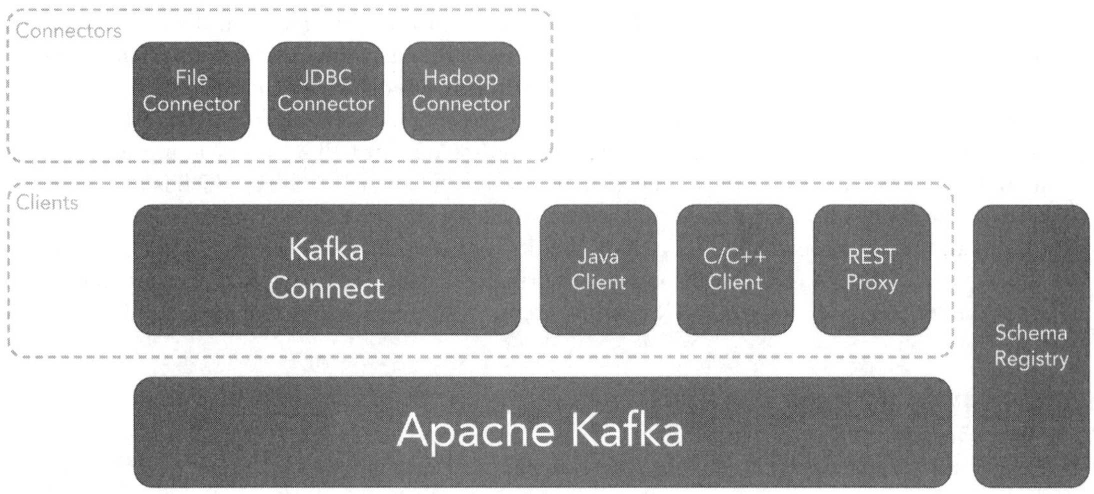

FIGURE 5-5

How It Works

Kafka basically provides a distributed, partitioned, and replicated commit log service to its users. It has a simple high level design that can be depicted, as shown in Figure 5-6.

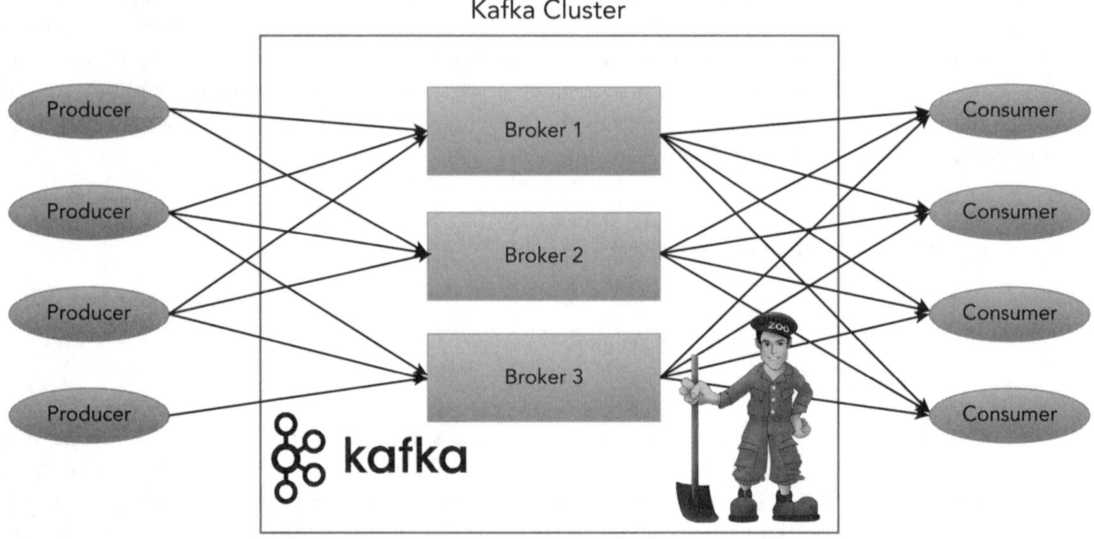

FIGURE 5-6

From the architecture perspective, Kafka provides the functionality for message producing and consuming. **Topic** is the category or feed name to which messages are published. **Producer** is the client process that publishes messages to a Kafka topic. Messages are simply byte arrays and can hold any object in any format, such as: String, JSON, and Avro. **Consumer** is the client process that subscribes to topics. Kafka itself runs as a cluster with one or more servers, each process of which is called a **Broker**. Kafka maintains feeds of messages in categories called topics. As for coordination and facilitation of distributed systems, **ZooKeeper** is used, for the same reason the Kafka cluster is using it. ZooKeeper is used for managing and coordinating Kafka brokers. Starting from 0.9, ZooKeeper's dependency from the clients (both Producer and Consumer) can be completely removed, but it is required internally by Kafka cluster.

The topic can be partitioned, and each partition is an ordered, immutable sequence of messages that is continually appended to—a commit log. The messages in the partitions are each assigned a sequential id number called the **offset** that uniquely identifies each message within the partition. The partition allows the log to scale beyond a size that will fit on a single server. Each partition must fit on the servers that host it, but a topic may have many partitions so it can handle an arbitrary amount of data. The partitions of the log are distributed over the brokers in the cluster, with each server handling data and requests for a share of the partitions. More partitions allow greater parallelism. A partition can be replicated across a configurable number of servers for fault tolerance. Each partition has one broker that acts as the leader, and zero or more brokers that act as followers. The leader handles all read and write requests for the partition, while the followers passively replicate the leader. If the leader fails, one of the followers will automatically become the new leader (coordinated by Zookeeper). Each broker acts as a leader for some of its partitions, and a follower for others, so the load is well balanced within the cluster. To illustrate, let's create a topic with a Kafka command line tool; "mytopic" is created with two partitions and two replicas across two brokers:

```
$ $KAFKA_HOME/bin/kafka-topics.sh --create --zookeeper localhost:2181
  --replication-factor 2 --partitions 2 --topic mytopic

$ $KAFKA_HOME/bin/kafka-topics.sh --describe  --zookeeper localhost:2181 --topic ↵
  mytopic
Topic:mytopic  PartitionCount:2    ReplicationFactor:2 Configs:
       Topic: mytopic     Partition: 0  Leader: 0     Replicas: 0,1     Isr: 0,1
       Topic: mytopic     Partition: 1  Leader: 1     Replicas: 1,0     Isr: 1,0
```

Here is an explanation of output. The first line gives a summary of all of the partitions, and each additional line gives information about one partition.

- `Leader` is the broker node responsible for all reads and writes for the given partition. Each node will be the leader for a randomly selected portion of the partitions.
- `Replicas` is the list of nodes that replicate the log for this partition, regardless of whether they are the leader or even if they are currently alive.
- `Isr` is the set of in-sync replicas. This is the subset of the replicas list that is currently alive and has caught-up to the leader.

The producer is responsible for choosing which message to assign to which partition within the topic. This can be done in a round-robin fashion, simply to balance the load, or it can be done according to some semantic partition function (based on some key in the message). The cluster retains all messages—whether or not they have been consumed—for a configurable period of time or size of data. Once the configured retention time or size is reached, old messages will be discarded to free up space.

The only metadata retained on a per-consumer basis is the offset. The consumer tracks the maximum offset it has consumed in each partition, and periodically commits its offset vector, so that it can resume from those offsets in the event of a restart. Consumer can also reset the offset for consumption if it needs to consume old messages. Since version 0.9.0, the Consumer offset can be managed through a special compacted Kafka topic, without Zookeeper, which was seen as the potential bottleneck in previous versions of Kafka.

As a distributed messaging system, Kafka is able to provide different levels of message delivery guarantees. Kafka guarantees at-least-once delivery (messages are never lost but may be redelivered) by default, and allows you to implement at-most-once delivery (messages may be lost, but are never redelivered) by disabling retries on the producer, and committing its offset prior to processing a batch of messages. Exactly-once delivery (strongest guarantee, since each message is delivered once and only once) requires cooperation with the destination system, but Kafka provides the offset that makes implementing this straight forward.

Kafka Connect

Kafka's flexible and scalable design allows Consumers to periodically consume batch data loads that periodically bulk-load data into an offline system such as Hadoop.

Before Kafka 0.9, there were two ways to load Kafka messages into Hadoop: Use a customized MapReduce job or use Kafka as source in Flume. Camus is the most famous solution of the first approach, which is also initiated in LinkedIn. From the previous section in this chapter, you have learned how Flume works. Now, you can see how there is significant overlap in the functions of Flume and Kafka. Flume has many built-in sources and sinks, and Kafka source and sink is among them. Flume can also use Kafka as a reliable channel. If you have already set up Flume to work with your Hadoop cluster, then Kafka can be easily integrated with the cluster through Flume (see Figure 5-7).

FIGURE 5-7

Kafka Connect is a new feature added in version 0.9. It is the standard framework for Kafka connectors, which standardizes integration of other data systems with Kafka, thus simplifying connector development, deployment, and management. You may realize that the primary goal of Kafka Connect, copying data between systems, has been tackled by a variety of frameworks and tools. So why do we need another framework? The detailed motivation and rationale can be found in the original proposal (KIP-26) for this feature. In short, most of the existing solutions do not integrate optimally with Kafka. Kafka Connect abstracts the common problems the third party connectors need to solve: fault tolerance, partitioning, offset management, and message delivery semantics.

Since Kafka is becoming the de facto standard stream data store, Kafka Connect will be the solution to make Kafka the central hub for data exchange between different systems.

The Kakfa HDFS Connector is one of the connectors created for Kafka Connect, which moves data from Kafka into HDFS, integrating it with Hive. The connector periodically polls data from Kafka and writes it to HDFS. The data from each Kafka topic is partitioned by the provided partitioner and divided into chunks. Each chunk of data is represented as an HDFS file with the topic, the Kafka partition, and the start and end offsets of this data chunk in the filename. If no partitioner is specified in the configuration, the default partitioner preserves the Kafka partitioning that will be used. The size of each data chunk is determined by the number of records written to HDFS, and the time written to HDFS and schema compatibility. This connector can optionally integrate with Hive. When enabled, the connector automatically creates an external Hive partitioned table for each Kafka topic and updates the table according to the available data in HDFS.

The Kafka JDBC Connector is another connector shipped with Confluent Platform. It allows loading data from any JDBC-compatible database into Kafka. Data is loaded by periodically executing a SQL query, and creating an output record for each row in the result set. By default, all tables in a database are copied, each to its own output topic, making it easy to ingest entire databases into Kafka. The database is monitored for new or deleted tables, and adapts automatically. When copying data from a table, the connector can load only new or modified rows by specifying which columns should be used to detect changes. Using HDFS and JDBC Connector together, you can build a scalable data pipeline to export data from RDBMS and load it into Hadoop. Does it sound like a similar functionality as Sqoop? Yes, but it is implemented in a totally different way. But unlike Sqoop, the only destination of the database records is Hadoop. With Kafka Connect, however, the destination could be stream processing systems, illustrating its unique feature set.

Stream Processing

Stream processing in our context is the processing of data streams being produced as data arrives in the system. It enables continuous computation, real time data processing, and transformation. Kafka provides guaranteed message delivery with low end-to-end latency. A single Kafka broker can handle hundreds of megabytes of reads and writes per second from thousands of clients. It makes stream processing a common use case of Kafka, because it is the ideal system of both source and sink for stream processing.

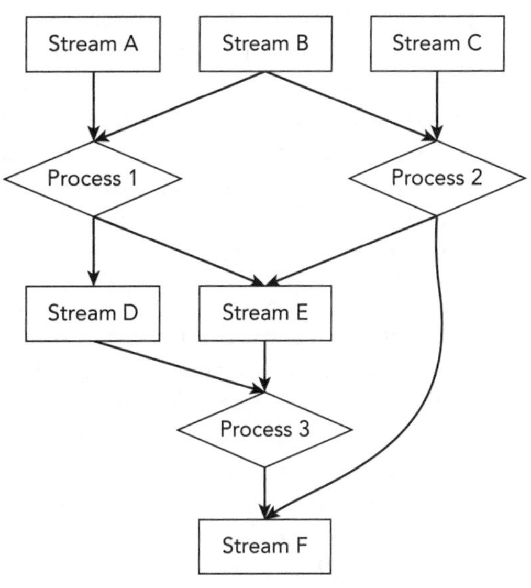

FIGURE 5-8

Stream processing can be modeled as a transformation between streams, seen as a Directed Acyclic Graph (DAG, shown in Figure 5-8). A stream processing job continually reads from one or more data streams, and outputs one or more data streams of output. For example, data is consumed from topics of raw data and then aggregated, enriched, filtered, and transformed into new Kafka topics for further consumption. Publishing data back into Kafka like this provides a number of benefits. First, it decouples parts of the processing graph. One set of processing jobs may be written by one team and another by another. And they may be built using different technologies. Most importantly, we don't want a slow downstream processor to be able to cause back-pressure to seize up anything that feeds data to it. Kafka acts as this buffer between the processors that can let an organization happily share data.

The most basic approach is writing an application, directly using the Kafka APIs, to create a custom Consumer to read input data stream, process that input, and produce output stream as a custom Producer. This can be done in a simple program in any programming language. However, this type of application can be made easier and more scalable with the help of a stream processing framework—such as Storm, Samza, Flink, or Spark's Streaming module—that provides richer stream processing primitives. All of them provide good integration with Kafka.

APACHE STORM

Apache Storm is a distributed real time computation system for processing large volumes of high-velocity data. Storm makes it easy to reliably process unbounded streams of data, doing for stream processing what MapReduce did for batch processing. Storm provides a simple API and enables developers to write Storm topologies using any programming language. It adds reliable real time processing capabilities to the Hadoop ecosystem. Using Storm, a Hadoop cluster can efficiently process a full range of workloads, from real time to interactive to batch.

In September 2013, Storm entered the Apache Software Foundation (ASF) as an incubator project. It became a top level Apache project in September of 2014. There are several major branches in Storm's codebase: 0.9.X, 0.9.6 (the latest stable release version), and 0.10.X. 0.10.0 is another release version that includes security, multi-tenant deployment support, and a couple of performance improvements: 1.x is targeting the next major release (V1) and also 2.x, and the community is actively working on merging JStorm's codebase into Storm. JStorm was originally a fork of Storm, where Clojure implemented the core module reimplemented in Java by Alibaba. After 4 years of active development and production deployment at Alibaba's scale, JStorm has been proven to be more stable, feature rich, and better than Storm. In October 2015, JStorm was officially donated to the Apache Foundation, and the community decided to merge it into Storm. In this book we are using version 0.9.6 of Storm.

The past decade has seen a revolution in data processing. MapReduce, Hadoop, and Spark related technologies have made it possible to store and process data at previously unthinkable scales. Unfortunately, these data processing technologies are not real time systems, nor are they meant to be. There's no hack that will turn Hadoop into a real time system. Spark Streaming is still a batch system at heart. Real time data processing has a fundamentally different set of requirements than batch processing. However, real time data processing at a massive scale is becoming more and more of a requirement for businesses. The lack of a "Hadoop of real time" has become the biggest hole in the data processing ecosystem. Storm fills that hole. Storm is extremely fast, with the ability to process over a million records per second per node. It is scalable, fault-tolerant, guarantees the data will be processed, and is easy to set up and operate.

Storm has many use cases: real time analytics, online machine learning, continuous computation, distributed RPC, ETL, and more. Theoretically, Storm can integrate with any message queues and database systems.

How It Works

As a distributed computing system, Storm follows the classic master and slave style architecture. There is one master node that runs a daemon called **Nimbus**, which is responsible for distributing a job around the cluster, assigning tasks to machines, and monitoring for failures. There are multiple slave nodes, each of them running a daemon called the **Supervisor.** The supervisor listens for work assigned to its machine and starts and stops worker processes as necessary, based on what Nimbus has assigned to it. All coordination between Nimbus and the Supervisors is done through a **Zookeeper** cluster (see Figure 5-9). Additionally, the Nimbus and Supervisor daemons fail-fast and are stateless, given that all state is kept in Zookeeper or on a local disk. If the Nimbus dies, supervisors will continue to run.

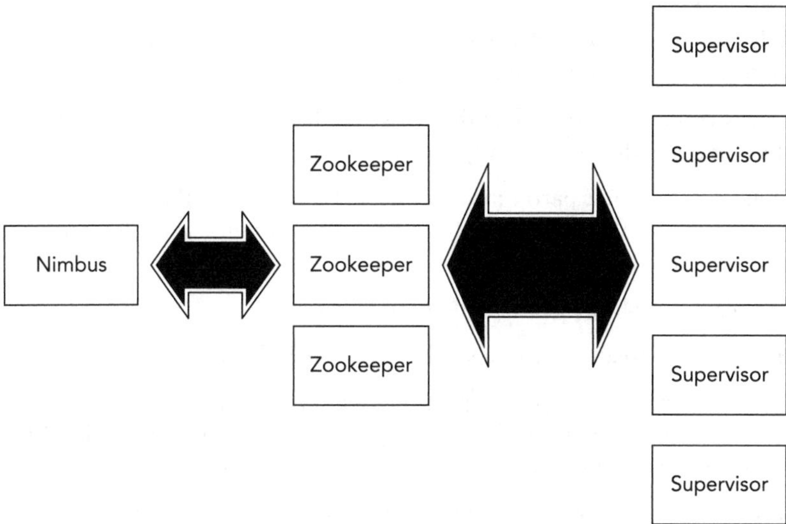

FIGURE 5-9

Storm uses two basic programming primitives to simplify distributed and parallel stream processing: **Spout** and **Bolt**. A Spout is a source of streams. For example, Kafka can be a type of Spout. A Bolt consumes any number of input streams, does some processing, by possibly emitting new streams or writing data into a data store. Complex stream transformations may require multiple steps and thus multiple Bolts (Figure 5-10). Networks of Spouts and Bolts are packaged into a **Topology,** which is the top-level abstraction that you submit to Storm clusters for execution. A topology can be represented as a graph of computation. Each node is a Spout or Bolt, and edges between nodes indicate how data should be passed around between them.

Storm uses **Tuple** as its key data structure to model the data being processed in a topology. A tuple is a named list of values, and a field in a tuple can be an object of any type. Out of the box, Storm supports all the primitive types, strings, and byte arrays as tuple field values. It also allows you to define

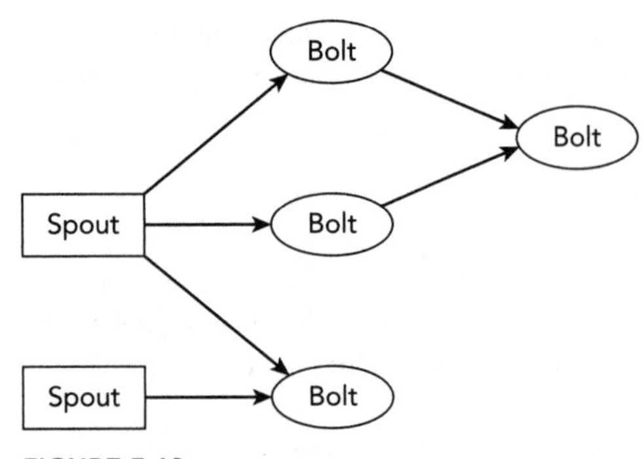

FIGURE 5-10

your own type of tuple. A Spout can emit a stream of tuples from a data source. A Bolt can do anything from run functions, filter tuples, do streaming aggregations, do streaming joins, talk to databases, and so on.

Storm can spawn multiple worker processes across different Supervisors for a single topology. Each worker process is a physical JVM process that can spawn one or more executor threads. Each executor can run one or more actual data processing tasks for the same topology component (Spout or Bolt). Storm API allows you to configure the parallelism of a topology: number of worker processes, number of executors, and number of tasks.

Strom provides different kinds of stream grouping strategies to allow you to define how the stream should be partitioned across tasks and how tuples should be shuffled from Spout to Bolt, or from Bolt to Bolt. Here is a list of the grouping strategies:

- **Shuffle grouping:** Tuples are randomly distributed across the Bolt's tasks in a way such that each Bolt is guaranteed to get an equal number of tuples.
- **Fields grouping:** The stream is partitioned by the fields specified in the grouping. Tuples with the same value of the specified fields will always go to the same task.
- **Partial Key grouping:** The stream is partitioned by the fields specified in the grouping, like the Fields grouping, but are load balanced between two downstream Bolts, which provide better utilization of resources when the incoming data is skewed.
- **All grouping:** The stream is replicated across all of the Bolt's tasks.
- **Global grouping:** The entire stream goes to a single one of the Bolt's tasks.
- **Direct grouping:** This is a special kind of grouping. A stream grouped this way means that the producer of the tuple decides which task of the Consumer will receive this tuple. Direct groupings can only be declared on streams that have been declared as direct streams.
- **Local or shuffle grouping:** If the target Bolt has one or more tasks in the same worker process, tuples will be shuffled to only those in-process tasks. Otherwise, this acts like a normal shuffle grouping.

A topology runs forever, or until you kill it. Storm will automatically reassign any failed tasks. Additionally, Storm guarantees that there will be no data loss, even if machines go down and messages are dropped. Storm guarantees that every tuple emitted by Spout will be fully processed by the topology. It does this by tracking the tree of tuples triggered by every Spout tuple, thus determining when that tree of tuples has been successfully completed. Every topology has a "message timeout" associated with it. If Storm fails to detect that a Spout tuple has been completed within that timeout, then it fails the tuple and replays it later.

The Storm code base includes a sub-project storm-starter, and it's a good place for you to get started with Storm programming. The official documentation also provides a good summary of the common Topology patterns, With the concepts introduced previously, you can build some exciting streaming processing applications.

Trident

In addition to a normal API for building topologies, Storm also provides Trident API, which is a high-level abstraction for doing real time computing on top of Storm. The concepts of Trident will be very familiar to you, if you are familiar with high level batch processing frameworks like Pig or Cascading. Trident lets you elegantly express real time computation while still getting maximal performance. It allows you to build fault-tolerant real time computation in a natural way without touching low level APIs to control the stream groupings, and to acknowledge tuples. In addition to this, Trident adds primitives for doing stateful, incremental processing, on top of any database or persistence store. Most importantly, Trident has consistent and exactly-once semantics, which normal APIs don't have. If you need to build some applications that require the strongest consistency, you should use the Trident API.

The following code snippet illustrates the word counting program implemented with Trident.

```
TridentTopology topology = new TridentTopology();
TridentState wordCounts =
     topology.newStream("spout1", spout)
       .each(new Fields("sentence"), new Split(), new Fields("word"))
       .groupBy(new Fields("word"))
       .persistentAggregate(new MemoryMapState.Factory(), new Count(), new Fields
         ("count"))
       .parallelismHint(6);
```

Assume that the topology reads an infinite stream of sentences from Spout. With Trident's fluent API, split sentence and aggregation can be done in a single line of code. The aggregated counting result is then continuously persistent into a state. In this example, `MemoryMapState.Factory`, means store in memory, but it can be easily replaced by Memcached, Cassandra, or some other store. This is just a little taste of the Trident API, since you can refer to project storm-starter for more examples.

Kafka Integration

The Storm community provides a bunch of components to integrate with other systems. Some of them are shipped with Storm as built-in components. They are released as external modules in tandem with Storm in order to maintain version compatibility. Storm version 0.9.6 includes 3 external modules: storm-hbase, storm-hdfs, and storm-kafka. Version 0.10.0 includes even more: storm-hive, storm-jdbc, and storm-redis etc. And more will be added in future releases.

In terms of integrating with Kafka, from Figure 5-8, it's very clear that Kafka can act as a Spout or a Blot. The storm-kafka module provides both implementations. Let's take a look at the examples. It is necessary to add the below dependencies into your application's `pom.xml` file:

```
<dependency>
       <groupId>org.apache.storm</groupId>
       <artifactId>storm-core</artifactId>
       <version>${storm.version}</version>
       <scope>provided</scope>
</dependency>
<dependency>
       <groupId>org.apache.storm</groupId>
```

```
        <artifactId>storm-kafka</artifactId>
        <version>${storm.version}</version>
</dependency>
<dependency>
        <groupId>org.apache.kafka</groupId>
        <artifactId>kafka_2.10</artifactId>
        <version>0.8.2.2</version>
        <scope>provided</scope>
        <exclusions>
            <exclusion>
                <groupId>org.apache.zookeeper</groupId>
                <artifactId>zookeeper</artifactId>
            </exclusion>
            <exclusion>
                <groupId>log4j</groupId>
                <artifactId>log4j</artifactId>
            </exclusion>
        </exclusions>
</dependency>
```

Both normal and Trident Spouts are supported:

```
BrokerHosts hosts = new ZkHosts(zkConnString);//kafka zookeeper
//the Zkroot will be used as root path in zookeeper to store consumer offset
    for this spout.
//The clientId should uniquely identify your spout.
SpoutConfig spoutConfig = new SpoutConfig(hosts, topicName, zkRoot, clientId);
//deserialize the message as string
spoutConf.scheme = new SchemeAsMultiScheme(new StringScheme());
//normal spout only accepts an instance of SpoutConfig
KafkaSpout kafkaSpout = new KafkaSpout(spoutConfig);


TridentKafkaConfig tridentSpoutConf = new TridentKafkaConfig(hosts, topicName);
tridentSpoutConf.scheme = new SchemeAsMultiScheme(new StringScheme());
//Trident spout takes TridentKafkaConfig
OpaqueTridentKafkaSpout spout = new OpaqueTridentKafkaSpout(tridentSpoutConf);
```

To write tuples into Kafka you can use the bolt `storm.kafka.bolt.KafkaBolt`. If you use Trident you can use:

`storm.kafka.trident.TridentState`, `storm.kafka.trident.TridentStateFactory`

or:

`storm.kafka.trident.TridentKafkaUpdater`

```
KafkaBolt bolt = new KafkaBolt()
    .withTopicSelector(new DefaultTopicSelector("testTopic"))
    .withTupleToKafkaMapper(new FieldNameBasedTupleToKafkaMapper());//from the
      package storm.kafka.bolt.mapper

TridentKafkaStateFactory stateFactory = new TridentKafkaStateFactory()
    .withKafkaTopicSelector(new DefaultTopicSelector("testTopic"))
    .withTridentTupleToKafkaMapper(new FieldNameBasedTupleToKafkaMapper("word",
      "count"));//from the package  storm.kafka.trident.mapper
```

SUMMARY

This chapter provides a broad overview of how to integrate Hadoop with other systems. We introduced four open source projects from the Apache family: Sqoop, Flume, Kafka, and Storm. Sqoop's main use case is to transfer bulk data between Hadoop and structured data stores, such as relational databases. Flume's main use case is to ingest data into Hadoop. Even Kafka and Storm can be used as the bridge to connect Hadoop with other systems. All of them are designed to be extensible to support a different data source, but they also have their own unique design and primary features. Kafka is the key enabler for stream processing, and can be used as a central message hub. Storm is designed to be a stream processing engine. Kafka, together with Storm, can move data faster and process data in real time. Now, you should have a better understanding of how to fit Hadoop into existing IT environments and extend its capability by integrating with these technologies.

Hadoop Security

WHAT'S IN THIS CHAPTER?

- Securing Hadoop Cluster
- Securing Data stored in Cluster
- Securing Applications running in Cluster

Given that Hadoop is used for storing and processing an organization's data, it is important to secure the Hadoop cluster. The security requirements vary depending on the sensitivity of data stored on the cluster. Some clusters are used to address a single use case with very few users (dedicated clusters). Some other clusters are general-purpose clusters used by many users belonging to different teams. The security requirements of a dedicated cluster are different from that of a shared cluster. In addition to storing lots of data for a long time, Hadoop accepts arbitrary programs from users, which are launched as independent Java processes on many machines in the cluster. If not properly constrained, these programs can create unwanted effects on the cluster, data, and programs run by other users.

When Hadoop was originally developed, the security features were limited, but over the years, many security features have been added. New features are being developed and existing features are being enhanced all of the time. In this chapter we will discuss various security features supported by Hadoop. We start with perimeter security to protect the network of the Hadoop cluster. We will go over the authentication mechanism supported by Hadoop to identify the user. Once a user is properly identified, the authorization rules specify the user's privileges to consume resources and the actions that can be performed by the user. It's possible to apply different levels of protection to the channel used to communicate with the cluster. Since Hadoop supports RPC and HTTP protocols to service different requests, we will learn how to apply a desired quality of protection for each protocol. In addition, we'll identify how to transmit data securely to and from the cluster.

Since data is the primary resource in a Hadoop cluster, features to protect that data require special attention. You can restrict access to this data using file permissions and ACLs. You must encrypt some of this data, and so HDFS encryption helps you address this requirement. Users can submit applications containing arbitrary data processing logic. To ensure authorization and accountability, applications needs to be executed using the identity of the submitter. The applications themselves can have ACLs control the users who can modify the application and view the application status including job counters. The access to computing resources can also be restricted using Queues and ACLs.

SECURING THE HADOOP CLUSTER

A Hadoop cluster can consist of hundreds or thousands of computers "glued" together to provide big data storage and computing. Securing the Hadoop cluster involves taking care of a number of things, including perimeter security, authentication of servers and users, and authorization of users to perform actions on cluster.

Perimeter Security

Perimeter security is comprised of mechanisms to control access to the computers that form the cluster. A Hadoop cluster consists of hundreds or even thousands of computers, so let's examine the various types of cluster classifications (see Figure 6-1):

- **Master nodes:** The master nodes run Hadoop servers like NameNode and ResourceManager.
- **Slave nodes:** The slave nodes are the workhorse machines. Hadoop servers like DataNodes and NodeManagers run on these machines. These machines also run user applications like mapreduce tasks.
- **Edge nodes:** On edge nodes, users run Hadoop commands.
- **Management nodes:** Management nodes are machines from which administrators perform installations, upgrades, fixes, etc.
- **Gateway nodes:** Servers like Hue servers or Oozie servers are installed on gateway nodes. These servers provide higher-level services on top of Hadoop.

Access to the machines inside the cluster can be restricted using firewalls and authorization rules on the local systems. Firewall rules limit the machines and ports accessible from outside the firewall, and authorization rules limit the users trying to connect to specific protocols (see Table 6-1).

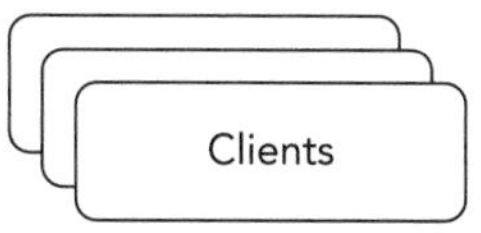

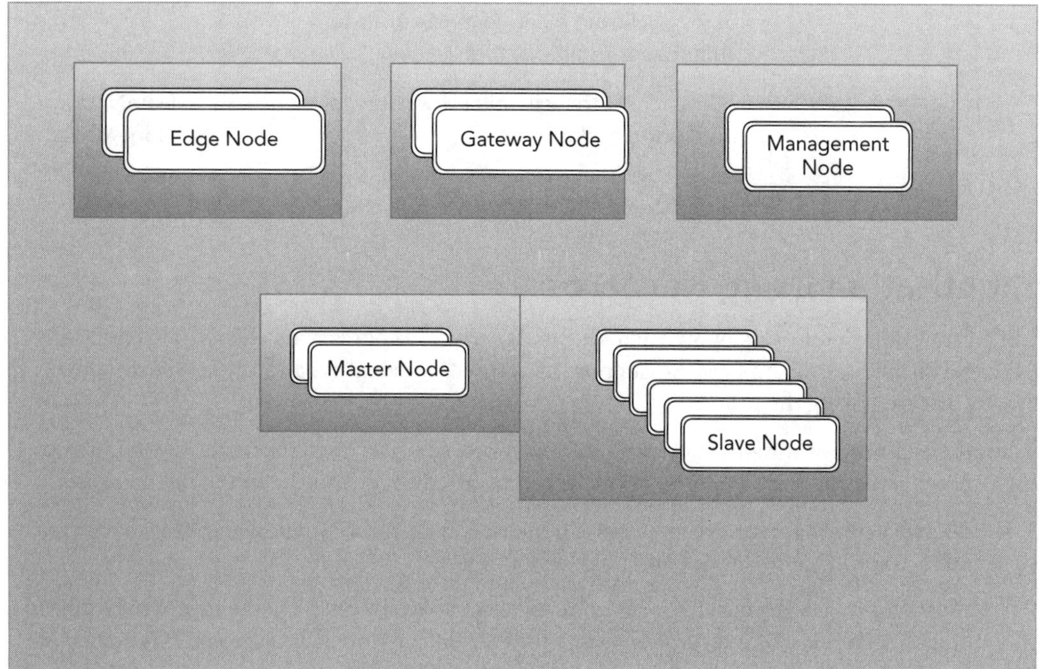

FIGURE 6-1

TABLE 6-1: Node types

NODE TYPES	ACCESS POLICY	EXAMPLES
Edge Nodes	Allow SSH from client machines for authorized Hadoop users.	Hadoop Client machines (CLIs)
Management Nodes	Allow SSH from clients for authorized Administrators.	Ansible/Puppet Hosts
Gateway Nodes	Allow access to well defined service ports from client machines. Allow SSH from clients for authorized Administrators.	Hive Servers, Hue Servers, Oozie servers

continues

TABLE 6-1: *(continued)*

NODE TYPES	ACCESS POLICY	EXAMPLES
Master Nodes	Allow access to well defined service ports from edge nodes. Allow SSH from management nodes for authorized Administrators.	NameNode, ResourceManager, Hbase Master
Slave Nodes	Allow access to well defined service ports from edge nodes. Allow SSH from management nodes for authorized Administrators.	DataNodes, NodeManagers, Region Servers

Authentication Using Kerberos

Authentication is the process by which a system or service recognizes its clients. This normally involves a client providing a proof to support its claim of an identity, and the server recognizes the identity after verifying the proof.

Hadoop uses Kerberos for authentication. Many systems use Secure Sockets Layer (SSL) for client-server authentication. Hadoop chose Kerberos over SSL due to the following reasons:

- **Better performance:** Kerberos uses symmetric key operations, and hence it is much faster than SSL, which use asymmetric key operations.
- **Simpler user management:** It's easy to revoke user access by disabling the user in the Authentication server. SSL uses revocation lists, which are difficult to synchronize and hence unreliable.

Kerberos Protocol

Kerberos is a strong authentication mechanism that involves three parties: client, service, and authentication server. The authentication server has two components: Authentication Service (AS) and Ticket Granting Service (TGS). Authentication server holds passwords belonging to all parties, and there can be multiple clients and multiple servers. A simplified interaction diagram between client, authentication server, and server (service) is shown in Figure 6-2.

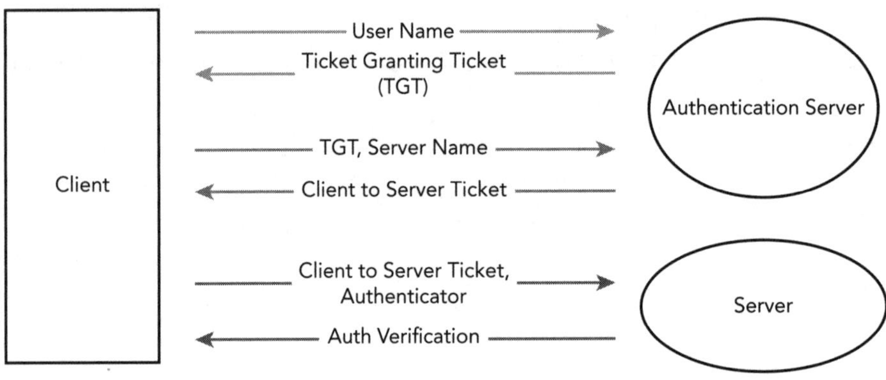

FIGURE 6-2

Let's go over the six steps involved when a client authenticates to service.

1. A user on the client machine starts the authentication process by typing **kinit**. Kinit prompts for a password for the user, and the Kerberos library on the client machine will transform the password into a secret key. It sends the user name to the authentication server. The authentication server looks up the user from its database, reads the password, and transforms the password to a secret key. The authentication server generates a Ticket Granting ticket (TGT). The TGT includes the client Id, the client network address, the ticket validity period, and the Client/TGS session key. The TGT will be encrypted using the secret key of the TGS. The server also sends a Client/TGS Session Key encrypted using the secret key of the client.
2. The client uses the secret key generated from its password to obtain the Client/TGS Session Key. The session key is used to obtain the TGT from the message received from the authentication server and caches TGT for later use. The session key is also cached and will be used for communication with the TGS.
3. When the client needs to authenticate to a server (service), the client sends its cached TGT and server (service) name to the authentication server. It also sends an authenticator, which is protected by encryption with the Client/TGS Session Key.
4. TGS decrypts TGT using TGS's secret key. The TGS obtains the Client/TGS Session Key from the TGT. Then it validates the authenticator using a Client/TGS Session Key. After validating the TGT, the server checks to see whether the Server (service) exists on the authentication server's database. If present, the TGS generates a client-to-server ticket. The client-to-server ticket includes the client ID, client network address, validity period, and Client/Server Session Key. The Client-to-server ticket will be encrypted using the server's secret key. The server also sends a Client/Server Session Key encrypted with the Client/TGS Session Key.
5. The client will send the client-to-server ticket to the server (service). The client also sends an authenticator, which includes the client ID, the time stamp and is encrypted using the Client/Server Session Key. The server (service) decrypts the client-to-server ticket using its secret key and obtains the Client/Server Session Key. Then it verifies the authenticator using the Client/Server Session Key. It also reads the Client ID from the client-to-server ticket. The server (service) increments the time stamp found in the authenticator and sends a confirmation message to the client. This will be encrypted using the Client/Server Session Key.
6. The client decrypts the confirmation message using the Client/Server Session Key. The client checks whether the time stamp is correct. If so, the client can trust the server (service) and can start issuing service requests to the server (service).

Advantages of Kerberos

1. A secure communication channel is **not** needed for authentication, because the password is never transmitted from one party to another.
2. Kerberos is stable and widely supported on all platforms.

Disadvantages of Kerberos

1. The authentication server is a single point of failure. This can be mitigated by the presence of multiple authentication servers.
2. Kerberos has strict time requirements, and the clocks of the involved hosts must be synchronized within configured limits.

Kerberos Principals

An identity on a Kerberos system is termed a Kerberos principal. The principal can have multiple components separated by `/`. The last component is the name of the realm, separated from the rest of the principal by `@`. The realm name is used to identify the Kerberos database, which houses a hierarchical set of principals. The examples of Kerberos principals are:

- `userA@example.com`: A two part principal that identifies userA who belongs to realm example.com.
- `hdfs/NameNode.networkA.example.com@example.com`: A three part principal that identifies a service running on the machine namenode.networkA.example.name. A three-part principal is normally associated with Hadoop servers like NameNode, DataNodes, and ResourceManager.

Kerberos assigns tickets to the Kerberos principal. In a Hadoop cluster, all of the servers and users should have a principal, and ideally, there should be a unique principal for each server.

Kerberos Keytabs

As described earlier, the client provides a password to generate the secret key while obtaining Kerberos tickets. But in a long running service like NameNode or DataNode, which needs to renew tickets periodically, it is not practical for a person to provide a password whenever a new ticket is required.

Keytabs solve this problem. The keytab is a file containing pairs of Kerberos principals and an encrypted copy of that principal's secret key. The secret key is derived from the password of the principal. So keytab is a very sensitive file and should be protected in the same way as the password. When the password of a principal changes, the keytab file should also be updated with the new secret key.

All of the Hadoop servers should have a principal and keytab file that contains the principal and its secret key. Hadoop servers use the keytab to stay authenticated with each other. The users who run periodic jobs without human intervention can also use keytabs.

Simple Authentication and Security Layer (SASL)

Simple Authentication and Security Layer (SASL) is a framework for authentication and data security that can be reused by application protocols. Different authentication mechanisms can be plugged in to the SASL framework. An application that incorporates SASL can potentially use any authentication mechanism supported by SASL. The mechanisms can also provide a data security layer offering data integrity and data confidentiality.

Hadoop uses SASL to incorporate the security layer for its communication protocol (RPC) and data transfer protocol. Using SASL, Hadoop supports Kerberos and Digest-MD5 authentication mechanisms.

The authentication sequence in Hadoop is based on SASL and it goes somewhat like this:

1. Client connects to Server and says, "hi, I want to authenticate."
2. Server says: "All right! I support Digest-MD5 and Kerberos in that order of preference."
3. Client says: "Cool, I don't have a Digest-MD5 token. So let's use Kerberos. Let me send you the Kerberos service ticket and authenticator."
4. Server says: "Great. That service ticket seems valid and I see that you are UserA. Let me send you the incremented time stamp value from the authenticator."
5. Client Says: "Got it. Now I am sure that you have authenticated me and you are indeed ServerA. Let's start the application protocol now. Here is my application specific request."
6. Server Says: "Cool. Let me process that request."

The SASL protocol in general follows this sequence:

- Client: INITIATE
- Server: CHALLENGE 1
- Client: RESPONSE 1
- Server: CHALLENGE 2
- Client: RESPONSE 2

There can be an arbitrary number of `{CHALLENGE, RESPONSE}` pairs until authentication is complete.

Hadoop Kerberos Configuration

Let's see how to configure Kerberos authentication in Hadoop.

The following change in core-site.xml is required on all Hadoop servers and clients to trigger the above mentioned SASL interaction.

```
<property>
        <name>hadoop.security.authentication</name>
        <value>kerberos</value>
</property>
```

Any client who makes a request against Hadoop needs to be sure that they have a valid Kerberos ticket. The Hadoop servers need to specify their unique principal in the configuration and the location of the associated keytab. The following configuration in hdfs-site.xml will be used by NameNode to specify its principal and keytab.

```
<property>
        <name>dfs.namenode.kerberos.principal</name>
        <value>hdfs/_HOST@YOUR-REALM.COM</value>
</property>
```

```
<property>
        <name>dfs.namenode.keytab.file</name>
        <value>/etc/hadoop/conf/hdfs.keytab</value>
</property>
```

Note that the principal is specified as `hdfs/_HOST@YOUR-REALM.COM`. `_HOST` will be substituted by the fully qualified domain name (fqdn) of the Hadoop server when the Hadoop server starts up.

Accessing a Secure Cluster Programmatically

Some use cases require accessing Hadoop via programs. When working with a secure cluster, the clients have to authenticate to the Hadoop servers. The client has to present a valid Kerberos ticket, and assuming that the user running the program has access to a keytab, there are two ways to make sure that there is a valid Kerberos ticket to authenticate to the server:

1. A utility process like k5start uses the keytab and caches a valid Kerberos ticket periodically before the current ticket expires. The program will look up the Kerberos ticket in the cache and use it.
2. The program itself will use the keytab and obtain the ticket. For this, it has to use method `UserGroupInformation.loginUserFromKeytab(principal, keytabFilePath)`. This method will obtain Kerberos ticket when invoked.

Service Level Authorization in Hadoop

Once a client is authenticated, the client's identity is known. Now, authorization rules/policies can be applied to allow or restrict access to resources. Hadoop has two levels of authorization: service level authorization and resource level authorization. While processing a request, the service level authorization policy is applied first, right after authentication. Service level authorization determines whether the user can access a specific service like HDFS. This is enforced by Access Control Lists (ACLs) associated with the service. The resource level is more fine grained and is enforced with ACLs associated with a resource like a file in HDFS.

Enabling Service Level Authorization

Service level authorization can be enabled via the following configuration in core-site.xml:

```
<property>
        <name>hadoop.security.authorization</name>
        <value>true</value>
</property>
```

This configuration needs to be present on all Hadoop servers where authorization has to be enforced. The ACLs are specified in a file named `hadoop-policy.xml`. After changing `hadoop-policy.xml`, the administrator can invoke the command `refreshServiceAcl` to make the changes effective without restarting any of the Hadoop services.

Benefits of Enabling Service Level Authorization

Service level Authorization is applied right after authentication. Hence an unauthorized access is denied much earlier on the server. For example, an unauthorized user trying to access a file on

HDFS will be denied access right after authentication by using `security.client.protocol.acl`. If service level authorization is disabled, then the HDFS namespace will be consulted to locate the ACL associated with the file, and this requires more CPU cycles.

Access Control Lists

The service level authorization policy is specified in terms of Access Control Lists (ACLs). An ACL normally specifies a list of user names and a list of group names. A user is allowed access if the user is in the list of user names. If not, then user's groups are fetched and checked to see if any of the user's groups are in the list of group names of the ACL.

The list of users and groups are a comma-separated list of names, with the two lists separated by a space. As an example, the following entry in `hadoop-policy.xml` restricts access to HDFS for a limited set of users and groups.

```
<property>
        <name>security.client.protocol.acl</name>
        <value>userA,userB  groupA,groupB</value>
  </property>
```

To specify only a list of group names, a list of group names should be preceded by a space. A special value of `*` implies that all users are allowed to access the service. Prior to Hadoop 2.6, `*` was the default value for an ACL, which means access to that service/protocol was allowed for all users. Starting with Hadoop2.6 and onward, it is possible to specify a default ACL value without using `*` by using the property `-security.service.authorization.default.acl`.

Users, Groups, and Group Memberships

ACLs depend on groups to a large extent, given how there is a large number of users who need access to a serve/protocol, so it isn't practical to be specified in the long list of users as a comma separated list. Instead of managing a long list of user names in an ACL, it is much easier to specify a group and add the users to the group.

How does Hadoop fetch the groups of a user? Hadoop depends on an interface named `GroupMappingServiceProvider`. The implementations of this interface can be plugged in via this configuration:

```
<property>
            <name>hadoop.security.group.mapping</name>
            <value>org.apache.hadoop.security.JniBasedUnixGroupsMapping</value>
      </property>
```

The default implementation is `ShellBasedUnixGroupsMapping`, which executes the `groups` shell command to fetch the group memberships of a given user.

Blocked ACLs

Using Hadoop 2.6, it is possible to specify ACLs to list the users to be blocked from accessing the service. The format of the blocked access control list is the same as that of the access control list. The policy key is formed by suffixing with ". blocked". For example, the property name of blocked access control list for `security.client.protocol.acl` is `security.client.protocol.acl.blocked`.

For a service, it is possible to specify both an ACL and a blocked ACL. A user is authorized if the user is in the ACL, and not in the blocked ACL. You can also specify a default value for blocked ACLs, and if that's not specified, then an empty list will be considered as a default blocked ACL.

Specifying the following configuration will enable everyone to access the HDFS client protocol except for a user named `userC`, and members of the group named `groupC`:

```
<property>
        <name>security.client.protocol.acl</name>
        <value>*</value>
      </property>
<property>
        <name>security.client.protocol.acl.blocked</name>
        <value>userC  groupC</value>
  </property>
```

The entry for `security.client.protocol.acl` can be omitted if it matches the default ACL.

Restricting Access Using Host Addresses

Access to a service can be controlled based on the IP address of the client accessing the service for Hadoop distributions starting with Hadoop 2.7. It is possible to restrict access to a service from a set of machines by specifying a list of IP addresses, host names, or IP-ranges. The IP-ranges can be specified in the CIDR format. The property name is the same as that of the corresponding ACL, except that the word "acl" is replaced with the word "hosts." For example, for the protocol `security.client.protocol`, the property name for the hosts list will be `security.client.protocol.hosts`.

As an example, adding the following snippet to `hadoop-policy.xml` restricts access of the HDFS client protocol to the hosts, which fall in the 162.34.31.0-162.34.31.255 IP range.

```
<property>
        <name>security.client.protocol.hosts</name>
        <value>162.34.31.0/24</value>
  </property>
```

Just like ACLs, it is possible to define a default hosts list, by specifying `security.service.authorization.default.hosts`. If the default value is not specified, then the value `*` is assumed, which gives access to all IP addresses.

You can also specify a blocked list of hosts. Only those machines that are in the hosts list, but not in the blocked-hosts list, will be granted access to the service. The property name is derived by suffixing with `.blocked`. For example, the property name of the blocked hosts list for the protocol `security.client.protocol` will be `security.client.protocol.hosts.blocked`. You can also specify a default value for the blocked list of hosts.

The following `hadoop-policy.xml` entries make sure that access to the HFS client protocol is allowed only for hosts, which fall in the 162.34.31.0-162.34.31.255 IP-range. It also makes sure that requests from 162.34.31.111 and 162.34.31.112 are denied, even though they fall in the IP-range specified in the hosts entry.

```
<property>
        <name>security.client.protocol.hosts</name>
        <value>162.34.31.0/24</value>
  </property>
```

```
<property>
        <name>security.client.protocol.hosts.blocked</name>
        <value>162.34.31.111, 162.34.31.112</value>
  </property>
```

List of Service Authorization Policies

Important service authorization policies are shown in Table 6-2. The important service authorization policies available for YARN are shown as well.

TABLE 6-2: Service Authorization policies

POLICY NAME	POLICY DESCRIPTION
security.client.protocol.acl	ACL for HDFS Client Protocol. Applied when invoking normal HDFS operations like listing a directory, reading and writing files.
security.datanode.protocol.acl	ACL for DataNode Protocol. Applied when a DataNode communicates with the NameNode.
security.inter.datanode.protocol.acl	ACL for Inter DataNode Protocol. Applied when a DataNode communicates with another DataNode for block replication.
security.admin.operations.protocol.acl	ACL applied when someone is invoking HDFS administrative operations.
security.refresh.user.mappings.protocol.acl	ACL applied when someone tries to the refresh the user to group mappings.
security.refresh.policy.protocol.acl	ACL applied when someone tries to the refresh the policies.
security.applicationclient.protocol.acl	ACL for Application Client Protocol. Applied when a client communicates with the YARN ResourceManager to submit and manage applications.
security.applicationmaster.protocol.acl	ACL for the Application Master Protocol. Applied when YARN application masters communicate with the ResourceManager

Impersonation

Hadoop Servers allow one user to impersonate another user. This is similar to the sudo functionality available in Unix-based systems. This feature is useful in different cases including the following:

- With a high level service like Hive server or Hue server, you can submit jobs or make HDFS calls on behalf of using user's privileges.

- An administrator who needs to diagnose an issue faced by a user can impersonate that user to accurately reproduce the issue.
- A team of users can impersonate a team account used to run periodic jobs belonging to the team.

To impersonate a user, you must first authenticate the user. In addition, the user needs permission to impersonate another user. Impersonation can be configured using the properties `hadoop.proxyuser.$superuser.hosts` along with either or both `hadoop.proxyuser.$superuser.groups` and `hadoop.proxyuser.$superuser.users` in `core-site.xml` on Hadoop servers.

For example, the following configuration entries allow the `super` user to impersonate users who are members of either group1 or group2. The `super` can impersonate from only two hosts: `host1` and `host2`.

```
<property>
        <name>hadoop.proxyuser.super.hosts</name>
         <value>host1,host2</value>
    </property>
    <property>
            <name>hadoop.proxyuser.super.groups</name>
            <value>group1,group2</value>
    </property>
```

Just like ACLs, the special value * allows a user to impersonate any user. If * is specified as the value of hosts, then the super user can impersonate from any host. The hosts can accept *, a comma separated list of host names, IP addresses, and IP-ranges specified in the CIDR format.

After changing `core-site.xml` to change impersonation entries, the administrator can invoke `refreshSuperUserGroupsConfiguration` to make the changes effective, without restarting any of the Hadoop services.

Impersonation via Command Line

To impersonate another user, the super user should first authenticate using kinit if the cluster is Kerberos enabled. Next, `HADOOP_PROXY_USER` needs to be set to the user to be impersonated. After that, Hadoop commands can be issued on behalf of the proxy user. A sample sequence is shown next in which the user named `super` impersonates the user named `joe`, and issues the Hadoop command as `joe`.

```
super@chlor:~$ kinit -kt ~/super.keytab super

super@chlor:~$ klist

Ticket cache: FILE:/tmp/krb5cc_1004
Default principal: super@DATAAPPS.IO

Valid starting       Expires              Service principal
12/14/2015 00:14:29  12/14/2015 10:14:29  krbtgt/DATAAPPS.IO@DATAAPPS.IO
      renew until 12/15/2015 00:14:29

super@chlor:~$ export HADOOP_PROXY_USER=joe
super@chlor:~$ ./bin/hadoop queue -showacls
```

```
Queue acls for user :  joe

Queue  Operations
=====================
root  ADMINISTER_QUEUE,SUBMIT_APPLICATIONS
admin  ADMINISTER_QUEUE,SUBMIT_APPLICATIONS
regular  ADMINISTER_QUEUE,SUBMIT_APPLICATIONS
```

Impersonation via Program

To impersonate as another user, the super user should first log in if the cluster is Kerberos enabled. Next, `proxyuserUGI` must be created to represent the impersonated user. After that, Hadoop commands can be issued using the proxy user. Sample code is shown next where the `super` user impersonates a user named `joe` and issues a Hadoop command as `joe`.

```
//'super' should first login
UserGroupInformation.loginUserFromKeytab("super@DATAAPPS.IO",
              "/home/super/.keytabs/super.keytab");

//Create ugi for joe. The login user is 'super'.
UserGroupInformation ugi =
        UserGroupInformation.createProxyUser("joe", UserGroupInformation.↵
          getLoginUser());
ugi.doAs(new PrivilegedExceptionAction<Void>() {
  public Void run() throws Exception {
    //Submit a job
    JobClient jc = new JobClient(conf);
    jc.submitJob(conf);
    //OR access hdfs
    FileSystem fs = FileSystem.get(conf);
    fs.mkdir(someFilePath);
  }
}
```

Customizing Impersonation Authorization

As mentioned, impersonation can be controlled by adding properties such as {`groups, users, hosts`} per user in the configuration file. This approach, though, has limitations. For example, when there are a large number of super users, it is difficult to specify each super user in the configuration file and make sure that the configuration is distributed across all of the Hadoop servers. Hadoop 2.5 and onward allows customizing the authorization of impersonation. This can be done by implementing the `ImpersonationProvider` interface and providing the implementation class name via the configuration property `hadoop.security.impersonation.provider.class`.

Securing the HTTP Channel

Hadoop supports access via the HTTP protocol, which provides authentication and protection for integrity and confidentiality. By default, there is no authentication enabled for HTTP to access. To enable authentication, the `org.apache.hadoop.security.AuthenticationFilterInitializer` initializer class should be added to the `hadoop.http.filter.initializers` property in `core-site.xml`. The RPC protocol limits authentication to Kerberos, so it is possible to configure custom authentication for access via HTTP. To configure this authentication, the following properties should be in the `core-site.xml` in all of the nodes in the cluster. Note that the properties in Table 6-3 are prefixed with `hadoop.http.authentication`, but they are omitted for conciseness.

TABLE 6-3: core-site.xml properties

PROPERTY NAME	DEFAULT VALUE	DESCRIPTION
`type`	Simple	Defines authentication used for the HTTP web-consoles. The supported values are: `simple | kerberos | #AUTHENTICATION_HANDLER_CLASSNAME#`.
`token.validity`	36000	Indicates how long (in seconds) an authentication token is valid before it has to be renewed.
`signature.secret.file`		The signature secret file for signing the authentication tokens. The same secret should be used for all nodes in the cluster: JobTracker, NameNode, DataNode, and TastTracker. This file should be readable only by the Unix user running the daemons.
`cookie.domain`		The domain to use for the HTTP cookie that stores the authentication token. For authentication to work correctly across all nodes in the cluster, the domain must be correctly set. If the value is not set, the HTTP cookie will work only with the hostname issuing the HTTP cookie.
`simple.anonymous.allowed`	True	Indicates whether anonymous requests are allowed when using simple authentication.
`kerberos.principal`		Indicates the Kerberos principal to be used for the HTTP endpoint when using Kerberos authentication. The principal short name must be HTTP, per the Kerberos `HTTP SPNEGO` specification.
`kerberos.keytab`		Location of the keytab file with the credentials for the Kerberos principal used for the HTTP endpoint.

To enable authentication other than `simple` or Kerberos, you must implement using the `org.hadoop.security.authentication.server.AuthenticationHandler` interface, and then specify the implementation class name as the value of `hadoop.http.authentication.type`.

Enabling HTTPS

HTTPS can be enabled for web UIs for NameNode, Resource Manager, DataNodes, and NodeManagers. To enable HTTPS, you have to specify a policy for HDFS and YARN. To enable HTTPS for HDFS web consoles, set `dfs.http.policy` to `HTTPS` or `HTTP_AND_HTTPS`.

SSL for the Hadoop server can be configured by setting properties in `core-site.xml`. The properties are shown in Table 6-4.

TABLE 6-4: core-site.xml for SSL properties

PROPERTY NAME	DEFAULT VALUE	PROPERTY DESCRIPTION
`hadoop.ssl.require.client.cert`	`False`	Whether client certificates are required.
`hadoop.ssl.hostname.verifier`	`DEFAULT`	The hostname verifier to provide for `HttpsURLConnections`. Valid values are: `DEFAULT`, `STRICT`, `STRICT_I6`, `DEFAULT_AND_LOCALHOST` and `ALLOW_ALL`.
`hadoop.ssl.keystores.factory.class`	`org.apache.hadoop.security.ssl.FileBasedKeyStoresFactory`	The `KeyStoresFactory` implementation to use.
`hadoop.ssl.server.conf`	`ssl-server.xml`	Resource file from which `ssl server keystore` information will be extracted. This file is looked up in the `classpath`, so typically it should be in the Hadoop conf/ directory.
`hadoop.ssl.client.conf`	`ssl-client.xml`	Resource file from which `ssl server keystore` information will be extracted. This file is looked up in the `classpath`, so typically it should be in the Hadoop conf/ directory.
`hadoop.ssl.enabled.protocols`	`TLSv1`	The supported SSL protocols (JDK6 can use TLSv1, JDK7+ can use TLSv1,TLSv1.1,TLSv1.2).

Keystores and Truststores

Additional SSL properties need to be configured in `ssl-server.xml` on the server side. Given how Hadoop servers can potentially act as clients of other Hadoop servers, `ssl-client.xml` needs to be set up as well. The properties include the location and passwords of the keystore and the truststore.

If the certificates and private keys are rotated (changed), the servers have to be restarted. This is costly and can be avoided by specifying that the truststore and keystore have to periodically be reloaded. Table 6-5 specifies the keystore and truststore properties to be specified in `ssl-server.xml`.

TABLE 6-5: ssl-server.xml keystore and truststore properties

PROPERTY NAME	DEFAULT VALUE	PROPERTY DESCRIPTION
`ssl.server.keystore.type`	`Jks`	Keystore file type.
`ssl.server.keystore.location`	`NONE`	Keystore file location. The user running the Hadoop server should own this file and have exclusive read access to it.
`ssl.server.keystore.password`	`NONE`	Keystore file password.
`ssl.server.truststore.type`	`Jks`	Truststore file type.
`ssl.server.truststore.location`	`NONE`	Truststore file location. The user running the Hadoop server should own this file and have exclusive read access to it.
`ssl.server.truststore.password`	`NONE`	Truststore file password.
`ssl.server.truststore.reload.interval`	`10000 (10 seconds)`	Truststore reload interval, in milliseconds.

Similar properties need to be specified in `ssl-client.xml` to specify truststore and keystore properties when the Hadoop server is interacting as a client.

SECURING DATA

For an organization, data is a vital asset. Hadoop now allows the storing of petabytes of data in a single system. In addition to making sure that the data is available and reliable, the data should be made secure. Securing the data in a Hadoop cluster needs to take care of the following:

- Data should be transferred over a secure channel between the client and the Hadoop cluster. The channel should offer confidentiality and data integrity depending on the data classification.
- When data is stored on the cluster, its access should be restricted based on the data classification.
- If the data classification demands encryption, then the data should be encrypted when stored in the Hadoop cluster. Only users who have access to the secret key should be able to decrypt the data.
- Based on the data classification, access to the data should be regularly audited.

As you can see, all security measures on the data are taken based on the classification of data.

Data Classification

Data can be classified into different categories based on the sensitivity of the elements in the data, and also based on data compliance requirements. Classification of a specific dataset helps to determine how to transport the data in and out of the Hadoop cluster, how to restrict access to data when stored on the cluster, and how to protect the data during processing. This data can be classified into the following categories:

- **Public:** This is information that is publicly available, so there is no need to restrict access to this data. Information about different cities of the world available on the Internet, but stored on the Hadoop cluster for faster data processing, fall into this category.
- **Limited or private:** This is information that should not be public. Such data may not have any sensitive elements, but it should remain private since the data gives the company a competitive advantage. An example of private data could be datasets purchased by the company from outside the company. Access to limited or private data should be restricted.
- **Confidential:** This is a data set, which contains elements that should be kept confidential. An example would be datasets that contain personally identifiable information (PII) such as an email address, a phone number, etc. Access to this dataset may be restricted and the sensitive data elements may need to be encrypted or masked.
- **Restricted:** This dataset contains data that should not be read by anyone other than an approved set of users. A dataset containing financial information from customers or health records fall into this category. Access to these datasets should be strictly restricted and elements may need to be encrypted so that only approved users who have access to a secret key should be able to read the data.

Sensitive Data Discovery

In some cases, users store data in the HDFS without properly classifying it or restricting the access. Administrators will have to review the schema associated with the data to decide the appropriate classification. In some cases, the schema may not contain sufficient information to accurately classify the data. In such cases, the only option is to scan data to see if it contains sensitive elements.

There are tools available to make this scan for sensitive elements. These tools use the YARN framework to run applications, which scan the data and report if there are sensitive elements. One such tool is DataApps.io's Chlorine available at `www.dataapps.io`. Chlorine scans datasets and reports the presence of sensitive elements. Chlorine supports all of the standard file formats, including Avro, parquet, RC, ORC, and sequence files. Chlorine allows deep and quick scans, as well as scheduled incremental scans. Chlorine also enables a user to scan for new patterns and add custom scan logic.

Bringing Data to the Cluster

Depending on how it's classified, data should be protected in transit to and from the cluster. Sending sensitive data over an insecure channel makes it susceptible to eavesdropping, requiring that datasets be sent over channels that guarantee confidentiality and integrity.

Different methods of data transfer are involved, depending on the size of the data, the nature of data transfer, the latency, and the performance requirements. The data transfer should be secured independent of the data channel involved based on the data's classification. The scope of the discussion in this section is limited to transferring data securely to HDFS from another system. The source can be another database, an application server, a Kafka queue, a Knox proxy, or another Hadoop cluster.

Data Protocols

Hadoop supports two protocols to transfer data to HDFS.

- **RPC + streaming:** A client first talks to the NameNode via RPC to obtain the block locations. Then the client talks to the DataNode identified by the block locations to stream the data. Both RPC and streaming protocols are based on TCP, because this method is used when data is transferred via the `hdfs -put/get` command. Use the DistCp tool, with the hdfs:/ schema prefix using both RPC and streaming protocols.
- **HTTP:** If the Hadoop cluster supports WebHDFS, the client can use webHDFS to transfer data. This protocol blocks locations that are obtained over HTTP and data that is transferred from the client to the ResourceManagers over HTTP. DistCp with webhdfs:/ or hftp:/ or the hsftp:/ schema prefix uses the HTTP protocol to transfer data. Similarly, HTTP based clients can use the webhdfs REST API to obtain block locations from NameNode and stream data to/from DataNodes.

Let's see how to protect data transfer conducted over both of these protocols.

Securing the RPC Channel

We have described how clients authenticate to Hadoop servers using Kerberos. As described, Hadoop uses the SASL framework in its RPC protocol to support Kerberos. But some data needs to be protected further during transit.

SASL allows different levels of protection. These are referred to as the quality of protection (QOPs). It is negotiated between the client and server during the authentication phase of the SASL exchange. The QOP taps into Hadoop's configuration property: `hadoop.rpc.protection`. This property can have values specified in Table 6-6.

TABLE 6-6: Hadoop.rpc.protection properties

	QUALITY OF PROTECTION (QOP)	DESCRIPTION
1	Authentication	Authentication only.
2	Integrity	Authentication with integrity protection. Integrity protection prevents the tampering of requests and responses.
3	Privacy	Authentication with integrity and privacy protection. Privacy prevents the unintended monitoring of requests and responses.

This property can be specified in the `core-site.xml` of the client and server. The SASL authentication fails if the client and server can't negotiate a common quality of protection.

To encrypt the requests and responses sent over RPC, the following entry needs to be in the `core-site.xml` on all Hadoop servers and clients.

```
<property>
       <name>hadoop.rpc.protection</name>
        <value>privacy</value>
   </property>
```

If `hadoop.rpc.protection` is not specified, then it defaults to `authentication`.

Selective Encryption to Improve Performance

Prior to Hadoop 2.4, `hadoop.rpc.protection` supported specifying only a single value: one of authentication, integrity, or privacy. To encrypt communication, `hadoop.rpc.protection` should be set to privacy. In most Hadoop clusters, different types of data will be stored in the cluster. Only a limited number of RPC communications need to be encrypted, so be sure not to set this value to privacy results in encryption across all of the RPC communication. By doing that you risk a performance degradation due to the cost of encrypting all RPC communication.

Starting with Hadoop 2.4, `hadoop.rpc.protection` can accept multiple values as a comma separated list. To avoid performance degradation, the Hadoop server can support multiple values. While transmitting confidential data, clients can set the value of `hadoop.rpc.protection` on the client side to privacy. Clients, when transmitting non-confidential data, can set the `hadoop.rpc.protection` to authentication to avoid incurring the cost of encryption.

Here is `hadoop.rpc.protection` on NameNode supports multiple QOPs:

```
<property>
       <name>hadoop.rpc.protection</name>
        <value>authentication,privacy</value>
   </property>
```

And `hadoop.rpc.protection` on the client, sending data over an encrypted channel:

```
<property>
       <name>hadoop.rpc.protection</name>
        <value>privacy</value>
   </property>
```

And here is `hadoop.rpc.protection` on the client involved in non-confidential data transfer:

```
<property>
       <name>hadoop.rpc.protection</name>
        <value>authentication</value>
   </property>
```

Note that in the above cases, the client determines the QOP. It is not always desirable for the client to decide. In some cases, you need to encrypt all data coming from a specific set of hosts. This decision logic can be plugged in by extending the class-`SaslPropertiesResolver`. It can be plugged on the server or the client side via `hadoop.security.saslproperties.resolver.class` in `core-site.xml`. `SaslPropertiesResolver` can provide the SASL properties as key value pairs for each connection.

Securing the Block Transfer

Data is transferred from client machines to DataNodes via the streaming protocol. Since DataNodes store blocks, it is important to make sure that only authorized clients should read a particular block. To enforce authorization for block access, you need to add the following property in `hdfs-site.xml` on all NameNode and DataNodes.

```
<property>
        <name>dfs.block.token.enable</name>
         <value>true</value>
    </property>
```

The client requests NameNode to access a file, and NameNode checks whether the client is authorized to access the file based on HDFS file permissions and ACLs and if authorized, the NameNode responds with the block locations. If `dfs.block.token.enable` is set to true, then it returns a block token along with block location information.

When the client contacts the DataNode to read the block, the client has to submit a valid block token. The block token contains the block ID and user identifier protected with a secret shared between the NameNode and the DataNode. The DataNode verifies the block token before allowing the client to stream the block. This handshake between client, NameNode, and DataNode makes sure that only authorized users can download the blocks.

But this does not enforce the integrity and privacy of the block transfer. To fully secure the block transfer, the following property needs to be set on the NameNode.

```
<property>
        <name>dfs.encrypt.data.transfer</name>
         <value>true</value>
    </property>
```

When the above property is set, the client fetches the encryption key from the NameNode before block transfer. The DataNodes already know this key and so the client and DataNode can use the key to set up a secure channel. SASL is internally used to enable encryption of the block transfer.

The algorithm used for encryption can be configured with `dfs.encrypt.data.transfer.algorithm`. It can be set to either 3DES or RC4. If nothing is set, then the default on the system is used (usually 3DES.) While 3DES is more cryptographically secure, RC4 is substantially faster.

Just as with RPC, setting `dfs.encrypt.data.transfer` to true will enable encryption for all data transfers, even if most of them don't need to be encrypted. This will slow down all block transfers. In most cases, encryption needs to be done only for a subset of block transfers. Under these conditions, encrypting all block transfers causes an unnecessary slowdown of the data transfers and data processing.

In Hadoop 2.6, a major rework was done around this feature so that privacy can be enabled for selected block transfers in a way very similar to that of RPC protocol. The QOP values {`authentication, integrity, privacy`} can be configured using the `dfs.data.transfer.protection` property. Like RPC, it is possible to select a QOP for each block transfer by specifying the QOP resolution logic via the configuration: `dfs.data.transfer.saslproperties.resolver.class`. The value should be a class, which extends the class `SaslPropertiesResolver`.

Securing WebHDFS-Based Data Transfer

It is possible to transfer data to and from the HDFS using HTTP via WebHDFS. WebHDFS can be secured by authenticating the access and encrypting the data transfer for confidentiality.

Authentication can be configured with Kerberos. The properties in Table 6-7 need to be specified via `dfs-site.xml` to enable WebHDFS authentication.

TABLE 6-7: dfs-site.xml properties

PROPERTY NAME	DESCRIPTION
`dfs.web.authentication.kerberos.principal`	Indicates the Kerberos principal to be used for the HTTP endpoint when using Kerberos authentication. The principal short name must be `HTTP` per the Kerberos `HTTP SPNEGO` specification.
`dfs.web.authentication.kerberos.keytab`	Location of the keytab file with the credentials for the Kerberos principal used for the HTTP endpoint.

To use an authentication scheme other than Kerberos, you must override the `dfs.web.authentcation.filter` property in `dfs-site.xml`. Setting `dfs.http.policy` to `HTTPS` or `HTTP_AND_HTTPS` can encrypt the data transmitted using the WebHDFS protocol. There are enhancements in WebHDFS security that enables the usage of `OAUTH` to gain access.

Protecting Data in the Cluster

We have discussed how to protect data, and how it comes into the Hadoop cluster by specifying the desired quality of protection. Once the data is on the Hadoop cluster, access to the data has to be restricted based on the data classification. The following controls are available in HDFS to protect and restrict access to data stored in HDFS.

- File Permissions—Unix like file permissions
- Access Control Lists (ACLS)—fine-grained permissions
- Encryption

Using File Permissions

HDFS has a permissions model for files and directories, which is very similar to the POSIX model. Each file/directory has an owner and a group. Similar to POSIX, `rwx` permissions can be specified for the owner, group, and all other users. To read a file, `r` permission is required. To write or append to a file, `w` permission is required. The `x` permission has no relevance for a file. Similarly, `r` permission is required to list the contents of the directory, and `w` permission is required to create or delete files under the directory, and `x` permission is required to access the children of the directory.

The file permissions are sufficient to satisfy most of the data protection requirements. As an example, consider a dataset, which is generated by a user named `marketer` in the marketing division. A bunch of users from different organizations need to use this data. Ideally, the dataset needs to be modified only by `marketer` and read by different users. This can be accomplished using file permissions and groups as follows:

1. Create a directory, say /marketing_data, to hold the files belonging to the marketing dataset.
2. Generate a group, say `marketing_data_readers` and add users who need to read marketing data to `marketing_data_readers`.
3. Set the owner of `marketing_data`, and all of the files and directories under it, to marketer and group to `marketing_data_readers`.
4. Recursively change permissions of `marketing_data` to `rwrr_x___`. This setting allows full control (read, write, and browse) to marketer, read capability (read and browse), to members of `marketing_data_readers`, and no access to others.

To make ownership, group, and permissions changes use the following commands: `chown` (Change Owner), `chgrp` (Change Group), and `chmod` (Change mode/permissions) commands can be used respectively.

Limitations of File Permissions

While file permissions are sufficient to satisfy most common access requirements, it has significant limitations. These limitations are due to the fact that it is possible to associate only one user and one group for a file or a directory. Let's go through a few cases of these limitations.

- **Case 1:** In the above example regarding marketing data, consider the case when more than one user needs to read/write the data and a limited group of users need to have read only access. It is not possible to express it in a straightforward way using file permissions, since there can be only one user associated with a file or directory.
- **Case 2:** Consider the case where a set of users who already belong to `sales_data_readers` needs to access `marketing_data`. These users can read `marketing_data` only if they are made members of `marketing_data_readers` as well. While this is possible, it is easier to specify `sales_data_readers` as a reader group of marketing data.

Using ACLS

To overcome the limitations of file permissions, HDFS supports ACLs. This is similar to POSIX ACLs. The best practice is to use file permissions for most of the cases, and have a few ACLs in cases, which demand more fine-grained access. HDFS ACLs are available starting with Hadoop 2.4.

Setting `dfs.namenode.acls.enabled` to `true` on the NameNode, and then restarting the NameNode can enable ACLs. The ACLs on files and directories are managed using two new commands added to HDFS: `setfacl` and `getfacl`.

Once ACLs are enabled, the owner can define ACLs per user and per group for a file. The specifications use the form `user:username:permission` and `group:groupname:permission`. These are the named user and named group ACLs.

Let's see how ACLs can satisfy the cases described in the previous section.

- **Case 1:** In case1, you'd like to add a set of users to have read/write access to the dataset and a different set to have read only access. To accomplish this, create a new group called `marketing_data_writers` and add an ACL from the following form `group:marketing_data_writers:rwx`. The ACL can be set on the marketing data as follows:

```
hdfs dfs -setfacl -R -m group:marketing_data_writers:rwx /marketing_data
```

- **Case 2:** In case 2, you want to add one more groups named `sales_data_reader` to have read access to the dataset. To accomplish this, you add a group ACL. The `setfacl` command is as follows:

```
hdfs dfs -setfacl -R -m group:sales_data_reader:r_x /marketing_data
```

Encrypting the Data

Encryption is the process of encoding messages using a key so that the message can then be decoded using a key. Encryption involves an algorithm to encode a message as well as a key. The strength of encryption depends on properly securing the keys, and the keys are stored and managed by a Key Store. The Key Store can be a software or hardware based key management system.

Encrypting data ensures that only a client possessing a key can decrypt the message. The authorization measures like permissions and ACLs prevent data from being accessed by unauthorized users. But administrators who can change the authorization rules can read the data. Users who have access to the DataNodes where data is stored can also read data. Encrypting the data makes sure that only those who have access to the key can decrypt it. By having different sets of administrators for the key management system and Hadoop, even administrators will not be able to read the data by side-stepping authorization controls.

Privacy and security regulations also require an organization to encrypt sensitive data at rest. Some examples of regulations requiring encryption are:

- Health care and HIPAA regulations
- Card payment and PCI/DSS regulations
- US government and FISMA regulations

HDFS supports the transparent encryption of the data based on the concept of an encryption zone, which is created by the Hadoop administrator and associated with an HDFS directory. All files stored in the encryption zone are stored under the directory associated with the encryption zone. All of these files will be encrypted.

Hadoop KMS

HDFS encryption depends on a new Hadoop server, namely Hadoop KMS. Hadoop KMS does key management for HDFS (see Figure 6-3). Hadoop KMS internally depends on a keystore to store and manage its keys. Hadoop KMS communicates with the keystore using the KeyProvider API. If the organization already has a keystore to store secret keys, then a KeyProvider interface can be implemented to interact with keystore. The KeyProvider implementation needs to be configured in Hadoop KMS to integrate the keystore with Hadoop KMS.

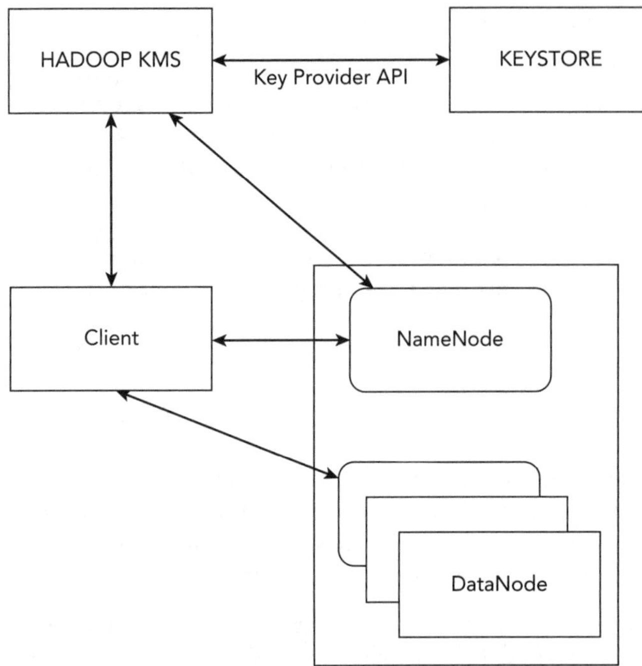

FIGURE 6-3

Encryption Zones

An encryption zone can be created using command line tools using the newly added `crypto` subcommand. Every encryption zone has an Encryption Zone Key (EZkey), associated with it. The EZkey serves as the master key for all files in the encryption zone. All keys, including EZkeys, are stored in a keystore and Hadoop KMS accesses the keys from the keystore using KeyProvider implementations. It is assumed that a key administrator oversees the keystore and KMS.

The key administrator must create a key in the keystore before the HDFS administrator can create an encryption zone. The EZkey may be rotated or changed as needed. Key metadata like key and version names, initialization vectors, and cipher information are stored in extended attributes of the encryption zone directory.

Once Hadoop KMS is set up so that HDFS clients and NameNode can access it for key management, encryption zones can be set up and data can be stored in the encrypted form in the encryption zones. Let us go through the full sequence of setting up an encryption zone, storing files in the encryption zone, and reading files from the encryption zone.

To set up an encryption zone:

1. The key administrator creates a key (Ezkey) and gives it a name, say `master_key`.
2. The HDFS administrator creates a directory, which is going to contain files that will be encrypted. The command will be of the form:

   ```
   "hadoop fs -mkdir /path/to/dataset"
   ```

3. The HDFS administrator then sets up an encryption zone associating the directory with the master key using the following command:

```
hdfs crypto -createZone -keyName master_key -path /path/to/dataset
```

4. The name of the key (`master_key`) and current version of `master_key` (obtained from Hadoop KMS) are stored as an extended attribute on the directory (/path/to/dataset).

Storing Files in Encryption Zones

When storing a file inside an encrypted zone, a key is generated and the data is encrypted using the key. For each file, a new key is generated and the encrypted key is stored as part of the file's metadata on the NameNode. The key to encrypt the file is referred to as a Data Encryption Key (DEK). The sequence is as follows:

1. The client issues a command to store a new file under /path/to/dataset.
2. The NameNode checks if the user has access to create a file under the specified path based on file permissions and ACLs. The NameNode requests Hadoop KMS to create a new key (DEK) and also provide the name of the encryption zone key namely `master_key`.
3. The Hadoop KMS generates a new key, DEK.
4. The Hadoop KMS retrieves the encryption zone key (`master_key`) from the key store and encrypts the DEK using `master_key` to generate the Encrypted Data Encryption Key (EDEK).
5. The Hadoop KMS provides the EDEK to the NameNode and NameNode persists the EDEK as an extended attribute for the file metadata.
6. The NameNode provides the EDEK to the HDFS client.
7. The HDFS client sends the EDEK to the Hadoop KMS, requesting the DEK.
8. The Hadoop KMS checks if the user running the HDFS client has access to the encryption zone key. Note that this authorization check is different from file permissions or ACLs. If the user has permissions, then the Hadoop KMS decrypts the EDEK using the encryption key and provides the DEK to the HDFS client.
9. The HDFS client encrypts data using the DEK and writes the encrypted data blocks to HDFS.

Reading Files from Encryption Zones

When reading a file stored in an encryption zone, the client needs to decrypt the encrypted key stored in the metadata file, and then use the key to decrypt the content of the blocks. The sequence of events for reading an encrypted file is as follows:

- The client invokes a command to read the file.
- The NameNode checks if the user has authorization to access the file. If so, the NameNode provides the EDEK associated with the requested file to the client. It also sends the encryption zone key name (`master_key`) and the version of the encryption zone key.
- The HDFS client passes the EDEK and encryption zone key name and version to the Hadoop KMS.

- The Hadoop KMS checks if the user running the HDFS client has access to the encryption zone key. If the user has access, Hadoop KMS requests the EZK from the key server and decrypts the EDEK using the EZK to obtain the DEK.
- The Hadoop KMS provides the DEK to the HDFS client.
- The HDFS client reads the encrypted data blocks from DataNodes, and decrypts them with the DEK.

SECURING APPLICATIONS

Once the data is stored on the Hadoop cluster, users interact with the data using a variety of mechanisms. You can use MapReduce programs, Hive queries, Pig scripts, and other frameworks to process the data. In Hadoop 2, YARN facilitates execution of the data processing logic.

Several security measures are available in Hadoop to ensure that the data processing logic doesn't cause unwanted effects on the cluster. Since YARN can manage computing resources, access to computing resources can be controlled. Similarly, mechanisms are available for users to control access to their applications.

In this section we'll review how Hadoop enables applications to run using the application submitter's identity, so that proper access controls can be enforced based on the correct identity. We'll go over the process of dividing the computing resources to different parties to enable authorized users to administer and use the computing resources. We will also identity how users can apply access controls to their data processing logic that is run as applications on the Hadoop cluster.

YARN Architecture

Users store their data on HDFS, and the Hadoop ecosystem offers multiple frameworks or technologies to process this data. It is up to you to choose which specific framework to use based on your requirements and expertise.

In Hadoop 1, there was only one framework to execute data processing logic, namely MapReduce. Daemons like Job Tracker and Task Trackers enabled the management and scheduling of computing resources to execute the data processing logic on many DataNodes. In Hadoop 2, a generalized application execution framework, namely YARN was added, which takes care of resource management and scheduling (see Figure 6-4). The separation of resource management from the execution of data processing logic enables you to use different ways of executing data processing logic, including MapReduce, Spark, and others (see Figure 6-4).

Application Submission in YARN

You submit data processing logic as applications to the ResourceManager. During the application submission the job resource, including JAR files, job configuration, etc. is stored on HDFS in a staging directory. The staging directory is accessible only to the user who is submitting the application.

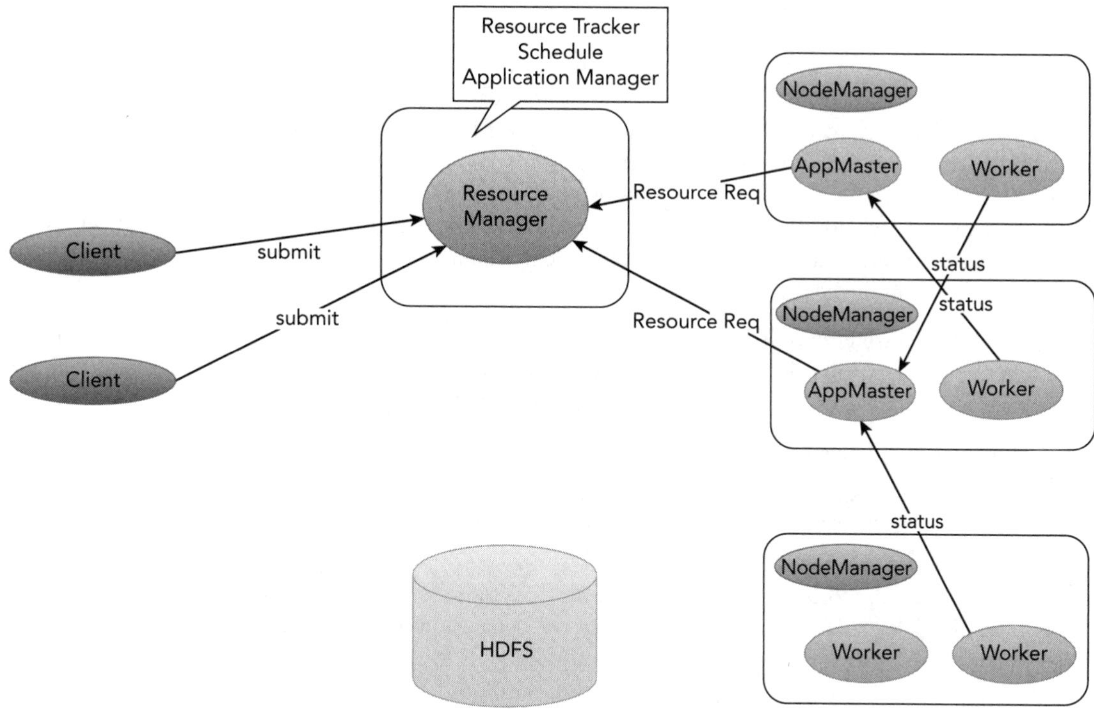

FIGURE 6-4

If the cluster is a secure cluster with Kerberos authentication, then the client needs to have a valid Kerberos ticket to authenticate to the ResourceManager. If service authorization is enabled, then ResourceManager will verify if the user is authorized to submit applications to the Resource Manager by applying the `security.applicationclient.protocol.acl`.

Controlling Access to Computing Resources Using Queues

YARN manages the computing resources of the Hadoop cluster with ResourceManager, which uses its scheduler component to determine which application gets which resource. The scheduler logic is pluggable, and the Capacity Scheduler and Fair Scheduler are commonly used schedulers, which are part of the Hadoop distribution.

Capacity Scheduler supports the notion of queues to manage resources. The queues can be hierarchical and can be modeled after the organizational hierarchy of the institution. Queue definitions include ACLs to determine who can submit applications to the queue and who can administer the queue. These ACL labels are `yarn.scheduler.capacity.root.<queue-path>.acl_submit_applications` and `yarn.scheduler.capacity.root.<queue-path>.acl_administer_queue`. The ACLs follow the general pattern of comma-separated lists of users and groups. These ACLs are evaluated for an application as part of the application submission.

Role of Delegation Tokens

During data processing, the application is divided into smaller work units and will be executed from slave machines on YARN containers. These containers need to access HDFS to read and write data. In a secure cluster, accessing HDFS will require users to authenticate. While Kerberos is the primary authentication mechanism, the container will not be able to obtain the Kerberos tickets since they don't have the user's credentials to obtain Kerberos tickets. To solve this problem, Hadoop supports the usage of delegation tokens. The NameNode issues the delegation token. The delegation token identifies the user, so it can be used to authenticate the user. The delegation token can be obtained only if the client authenticates using Kerberos.

The delegation token has an expiry time, and can be renewed for a configurable period of time. By default, delegation tokens are valid for 24 hours and can be renewed for 7 days. It is possible to specify a separate user as renewer for a delegation token.

The format of a delegation token is as follows:

```
TokenID = {ownerID, renewerID, realUserID, issueDate, maxDate, sequenceNumber, keyID}
TokenAuthenticator = HMAC-SHA1(masterKey, TokenID)
Delegation Token = {TokenID, TokenAuthenticator}
```

The `realUserId` will be set as a different user than `OwnerId` if a super user on behalf of the owner obtains the delegation token. The security of the delegation token can be configured using a set of properties, and these properties are specified in Table 6-8.

TABLE 6-8: Security delegation token properties

PROPERTY NAME	DEFAULT VALUE	PROPERTY DESCRIPTION
`dfs.namenode.delegation.key.update-interval`	1 day	The secret key used to generate the delegation token is updated periodically. This property specifies the update interval in milliseconds.
`dfs.namenode.delegation.token.renew-interval`	1 day	The token validity time in milliseconds before the token needs to be renewed.
`dfs.namenode.delegation.token.max-lifetime`	7 days	The delegation token has a maximum lifetime beyond which it cannot be renewed anymore. This value is also specified in milliseconds.

Note that if you have an application that has to run beyond 7 days, then `dfs.namenode.delegation.token.max-lifetime` needs to be set to a higher value. Once generated, delegation tokens are independent of Kerberos tickets. It is honored and can be renewed even if the user's Kerberos credentials are revoked on the Kerberos KDC. To properly revoke a user from accessing Hadoop, the user also needs to be removed from Hadoop related groups. Revoking a user's group membership can cause authorization checks to fail, so users will not be able to access the resources.

During the application submission, the client obtains a delegation token from NameNode, and the ResourceManager is set as the renewer for delegation tokens. The delegation token will be stored in HDFS as part of the application resources. The individual containers of the application retrieve the delegation token as part of the application resources and use the delegation token to authenticate as the application submitter to HDFS to read and write files. Once the application is done, the delegation token is canceled.

Block Access Tokens

The data is stored as blocks on DataNodes and indexed by block identifiers (block ids). To access some data, the client needs to specify the block identifier. In an insecure cluster, the client just needs to specify the block identifier. The protocol by default does not enforce authentication and authorization, so this is a loophole since it enables unauthorized clients to access any data if they happen to know the block identifier corresponding to the data.

This security issue is resolved using block access tokens. To enable this feature, `dfs.block.access.token.enable` should be set to true. When a client tries to access a file, the client first contacts the NameNode. The NameNode will authenticate the client and make sure that the client has permissions to access the file. Instead of handing over the list of block identifiers for blocks belonging to the file, the NameNode will generate block access tokens for each block belonging to the file. The Block Access Token has the following format:

- Block Access Token = `{TokenID, TokenAuthenticator}`
- TokenID = `{expirationDate, keyID, ownerID, blockPooID, blockID, accessModes}`
- TokenAuthenticator = HMAC-SHA1 `(key, TokenID)`

The NameNode and DataNodes share a secret key, which is used to generate the TokenAuthenticator. The block access token is valid across all DataNodes irrespective of where the actual block resides. The key is updated periodically and can be configured via the `dfs.block.access.key.update.interval` property. The default value is 10 minutes, and each block access token has a lifetime beyond which it expires. The lifetime can be configured using the `dfs.block.access.key.update.interval` property.

Since users may have limited permissions to a file, the access modes in the block access token indicate the operations permitted for a user. The access modes could be combination of `{READ, WRITE, COPY, REPLACE}`.

Using Secure Containers

The data processing logic of the application is executed on different containers on different machines. The NodeManager starts the containers, and this process is usually started as the YARN user. By default, the process owner of any processes started by the NodeManager will be YARN. Since the user application runs on the containers, running as YARN will enable these user applications to perform operations that only the YARN user can perform. This includes stopping the NodeManager or other containers. The user application running as YARN can also access log files belonging to other users.

In a secure cluster, YARN uses the operating system facilities to enable execution isolation for containers. Secure containers execute under credentials of the application submitter, which should be different from that of the user running the NodeManager.

In a Linux environment, NodeManager uses a container executor, `LinuxContainerExecutor`, to start container processes. `LinuxContainerExecutor` uses an external binary named `container-executor` to launch containers. `Container-executor` is an executable, which has a `setuid` flag set so that it can change the ownership of the container to that of the user who submitted the application.

Since the application submitter owns container processes, the application submitter must be available on the machine running the containers. This means that all application submitters must be available on all NodeManager machines. When there are hundreds of NodeManager machines, integrating these machines with an LDAP system becomes a practical necessity.

Authorization of Applications

The ACLs can be associated with applications. For a MapReduce job, ACLs can be specified along with the job configuration. By default, the job submitter can view and modify jobs, and queue administrators can view and modify jobs. If any other user needs to view and modify jobs, then they need to be specified via `mapreduce.job.acl-view-job` and `mapreduce.job.acl-modify-job`. Just like other ACLS, these ACLs also take a comma-separated list of users and groups.

Securing Intermediate Data in a MapReduce Job

Running a MapReduce job results in the storage and transfer of intermediate data, and there are intermediate files stored on the local filesystem during merge and shuffle phases. In some cases, it is required to encrypt these intermediate files stored on the local filesystem. This can be achieved by setting the `mapreduce.job.encrypted-intermediate-data` job property to true.

When the reducers start, they pull the map outputs for shuffling. In some use cases, it is desirable to encrypt the data transfer. MapReduce supports an encrypted shuffle capability to encrypt the shuffle data using HTTPS. To enable encrypted shuffle, you must set `mapreduce.shuffle.ssl.enabled` to true in the job configuration. Note that SSL support with truststore and keystore must be enabled on all NodeManagers. It is possible to ensure client authentication by requiring certificates from the reducer side.

SUMMARY

In this chapter we covered the many types of Hadoop security features. Securing the perimeter of the Hadoop cluster using firewalls is critical to prevent unauthorized requests to Hadoop cluster. We identified the different types of machines in a Hadoop cluster and discussed the differences in securing the perimeter for these machines. The authentication of users with Kerberos was covered with a detailed overview of the Kerberos protocol. We also covered the first level of authorization available in Hadoop–Service Level Authorization. Impersonating other users securely has many use cases in intermediary services and applications, but we took a look at how to secure the HTTP channels with pluggable authentication and SSL.

Data should be secured while in motion and at rest based on the classification of data. We covered the methods and configuration to ingest data to a cluster, ensuring integrity and confidentiality using RPC and HTTP protocols. We also discussed the method to enable selective encryption to avoid performance degradation. To protect the data at rest on HDFS, we reviewed the usage of file permissions, ACLs, and HDFS transparent encryption.

Data is processed by launching applications on the cluster, so we discussed how YARN applies ACLs to authorize the submission of applications at the service and queue level. We then reviewed the role of delegation tokens used to ensure continued authentication of applications while accessing HDFS. And finally, we covered the usage of secure containers to ensure process isolation during data processing. You should now be armed with an arsenal of security techniques to implement and keep your Hadoop cluster secure.

Ecosystem at Large: Hadoop with Apache Bigtop

WHAT'S IN THIS CHAPTER?

- Understanding basic concepts of software stacks
- Reviewing specifics of open source data processing stacks
- Creating your own custom stack including Apache Hadoop
- Deploying, testing, and managing configuration

In the modern world software is becoming more and more sophisticated all of the time. The main complexity, however, lies not in the algorithms or the tricky UI experience. It is hidden from the end user and resides in the back—in the relations and communications between different parts of a software solution commonly referred to as a software stack. Why are stacks so important, and what is so special about the Apache Hadoop data processing stack?

In this chapter you will be presented with materials to help you get a better grip of data processing stacks powered by the software that forms the foundation of all modern Apache Hadoop distributions. The chapter, by no means, is a complete text book on Apache Bigtop. Instead, we will put together a quick guide on the key features of the project, and explain how it is designed. There will be a collection of available resources that help you to grow your expertise with the ecosystem.

Bigtop is an Apache Foundation project aimed to help infrastructure engineers, data scientists, and application developers to develop and advance comprehensive packaging. This requires you to test and manage the configurations of the leading open source big data components. Right now, Bigtop supports a wide range of projects, including, but not limited to, Hadoop, HBase, Ignite, and Spark. Bigtop packages RPM and DEB formats, so that you can manage and maintain your data processing cluster. Bigtop includes mechanisms, images, and recipes for deploying Hadoop stack from zero to many supported operating systems, including Debian, Ubuntu,

CentOS, Fedora, openSUSE and many others. Bigtop delivers tools and a framework for testing at various levels (packaging, platform, runtime, etc.) for both initial deployments as well as upgrade scenarios for the entire data platform, not just the individual components.

It's now time to dive into the details of this exciting project that truly spans every single corner of the modern data processing landscape.

BASICS CONCEPTS

Developers working on various applications should have a focal point where products from different teams get integrated into a final ecosystem of the software stack. In order to lower the mismatch between the storage layer and the log analysis subsystem, the APIs of the former have to be documented, supported, and stable. Developers of a log processing component can fix the version of the file system API by using Maven, Gradle, or another build and dependency management software. This approach will provide strong guarantees about compatibility at the API and binary levels.

The situation changes dramatically when both pieces of the software are deployed into a real datacenter with a configuration that is very different from one used on the developer's laptop. A lot of things will be different in the datacenter environment: kernel updates, operating system packages, disk partitioning, and more. Another variable sometimes unaccounted for is the build environment and process, tasked with producing binary artifacts for production deployment. Build servers can have stale or unclean caches. These will pollute a product's binaries with incorrect or outdated versions of the libraries, leading to different behavior in different deployment scenarios.

In many cases, software developers aren't aware about operational realities and deployment conditions where their software is being used. This leads to production releases that aren't directly consumable by the IT. My "favorite" example of this is when a large company's datacenters' operation team has a 23-step cheat-sheet on how to prepare an official release of a software application to make it deployable into a production environment.

IT professionals tasked with provisioning, deployment, and day-to-day operations of the production multi-tenant systems know how tedious and difficult it is to maintain, update, and upgrade parts of a software system including the application layer, RDBMS, web servers, and file storage. They no doubt know how non-trivial the task of changing the configuration on hundreds of computers is in one or more datacenters.

What is the "software stack" anyway? How can developers produce deployment-ready software? How can operation teams simplify configuration management and component maintenance complexities? Follow along as we explore the answers to all of these questions.

Software Stacks

A typical software stack contains a few components (usually more than two) combined together to create a complete platform so that no additional software is needed to support any applications. Applications are said to "run on" or "run on top of" the resulting platform. The most common stack examples includes Debian, LAMP, and OpenStack. In the world of data processing you should consider Hadoop-based stacks like Apache Bigtop™, as well as commercial distributions of Apache Hadoop™ based on the Bigtop: Amazon EMR. Hortonworks Data Platform is another such example.

Probably the most widely known data processing stack is Apache Hadoop™, composed of HDFS (storage layer) and MR (computation framework on top of distributed storage). This simple composition, however, is insufficient for modern day requirements. Nonetheless, Hadoop is often used as the foundation of advanced computational systems. As a result, a Hadoop-proper stack would be extended by other components such as Apache Hbase™, Apache Hive™, Apache Ambari™ (installation and management application), and so on. In the end, you might end up with something like what is shown in Table 7-1.

TABLE 7-1: Extended components make up a Hadoop proper stack

hadoop	2.7.1
hbase	0.98.12
hive	1.2.1
ignite-hadoop	1.5.0
giraph	1.1.0
kafka	0.8.1.1
zeppelin	0.5.5

The million dollar question is: How do you build, validate, deploy, and manage such a "simple" software stack? First let's talk about validation.

Test Stacks

Like the software stacks described above, you should be able to create a set of components with the sole aim of making sure that the software isn't dead on arrival and that it certainly delivers what was promised. So, by extension: A test stack contains a number of applications combined together to verify the viability of a software stack by running certain workloads, exposing components' integration points, and validating their compatibility with each other.

In the example above the test stack will include, but not be limited by, the integration testing applications, which ensures that Hbase v 0.98.16 works properly on top of Hadoop 2.7.1. It must also work with Hive 1.2.1, it must be able to use the underlying Hadoop Mapreduce, work with YARN (Hadoop resource navigator), and use Hbase 0.98.16 as the storage for external tables. Keep in mind that Zeppelin validation applications guarantee that data scientists' notebooks are properly built and configured to work with Hbase, Hive, and Ignite.

Works on My Laptop

If you aren't yet thinking "How in the world can all of these stacks be produced at all?" here's something to make you go "Hmm." A typical modern data processing stack includes anywhere between

10 and 30+ different software components. Most of them, being an independent open source project, have their own release trains, schedules, and road maps.

Don't forget that you need to add a requirement to run this stack on a CentOS7 and Ubuntu 14.04 clusters using OpenJDK8, in both development and production configurations. Oh, and what about that yesteryear stack, which right now is still used by the analytical department? It now needs to be upgraded in Q3! Given all of this, the "works on my laptop" approach is no longer viable.

DEVELOPING A CUSTOM-TAILORED STACK

How can a software developer, a data scientist, or a commercial vendor go about the development, validation, and management of a complex system that might include versions of the components not yet available on the market? Let's explore what it takes to develop a software stack that satisfies your software and operation requirements.

Apache Bigtop: The History

Apache Bigtop (`http://bigtop.apache.org`) has a history of multiple incarnations and revisions. Back in 2004-2005, the creation and delivery of Sun Microsystems Java Enterprise Stack (JES) was done with a mix of Tinderbox CI along with a build manifest describing the stack's composition: common libraries, software components such as directory server, JDK, application server versions, and so on.

Another attempt to develop the stack framework concept further was taken at Sun Microsystems, and was aimed at managing the software stacks for enterprise storage servers. The modern storage isn't simply Just a Bunch of Disks, but rather an intricate combination of the hardware, operating system, and application software on top of it. The framework was tracking a lot more things, including system drivers, different versions of the operating system, JES, and more. It was, however, very much domain-specific, had a rigid DB schema, and a very implementation aware build system.

The penultimate incarnation, and effectively the ancestor of what we know today as Apache Bigtop, was developed to manage and support the production of the Hadoop 0.20.2xx software stack at the Yahoo! Hadoop team. With the advent of security, the combinatorial complexity blew up and it became impossible to manage it with the existing time and resource constraints. It was very much specific for Yahoo's internal packaging formats and operational infrastructure, but in hindsight you could see a lot of similarities with today's open source implementation, discussed later in this chapter.

The first version of modern Apache Bigtop was initially developed by the same engineers who implemented Yahoo!'s framework. This time it introduced the correct conceptualization of software and test stacks. It was properly abstracted from component builds (they are different, because the development teams are coming from different backgrounds), it has provided the integration testing framework capable of working in a distributed environment, and it has many other improvements. An early version of the deployment recipes and packaging was contributed by developers from Cloudera. By Spring 2011 it was submitted to the Apache Software Foundation for incubation and later became a top-level project.

Today, Apache Bigtop is employed by all commercial vendors of Apache Hadoop as the base framework for their distributions. This has a number of the benefits for end users, since all of the package layouts, configuration locations, and life-cycle management routings are done in the same way across different distros. The exception to the latter rule is introduced by Apache Ambari and some closed-source cluster managers, which use their own life-cycle control circuits, circumventing the standard Linux `init.d` protocol.

Apache Bigtop: The Concept and Philosophy

Conceptually, Bigtop is a combination of four subsystems serving different purposes:

1. A stack composition manifest or Bill of Materials (BOM).
2. The Gradle build system managing artifacts creation (packages), the development environment configuration, the execution of the integration tests, and some additional functions.
3. Integration and smoke tests along with the testing framework called iTest.
4. A deployment layer providing for seamless cluster deployment using binary artifacts and the configuration management of the provisioned cluster. Deployment is implemented via Puppet recipes. It helps to quickly deploy a fully functional distributed cluster, secured or non-secured, with a properly configured components' subset. The composition of the final stack is controlled by user input.

Apache Bigtop provides the means and toolkit for stack application developers, data scientists, and commercial vendors to have a predictable and fully controllable process to iteratively design, implement, and deliver a data processing stack. Philosophically, it represents the idea of empirical bake-in, versus a rational approach in the software development. Why are all of these complications needed, and why not to use unit and functional tests, you might ask?

The complications are dictated by the nature of the environments where the stacks are designed to work. Many things can have an effect on how well the distributed system works. Permutations of kernel patch-levels and configurations could affect the stability. Versions of the runtime environment, network policies, and bandwidth allocation could directly cut into your software performance. Failures of the communication lines or services, and nuances of your own software configuration, could result in data corruption or total loss. In some situations a developer needs to do an A-B test on the stack where only a single property is getting changed, such as by applying a specific patch-set to Hbase and checking if the stack is still viable. In general, it is impossible to rationalize all of those variances: You only can guarantee that a particular composition of a software stack works in an X environment with Y configuration if you have a way to empirically validate and prove such a claim. At times an already released project has a backward incompatible change that was missed during the development, testing, and release process. This can be discovered by a full stack integration validation with Apache Bigtop (see Figure 7-1). Such findings always lead to consequent updates, thus fixing the issues for the end users.

Continuous integration tools like Jenkins and TeamCity have become a part of the day-to-day software engineering process. Naturally, using a continuous integration setup with Apache Bigtop shortens the development cycle, and improves the quality of the software by providing another tremendous benefit of the quick discovery of bugs. You can quickly glance at the current issues using information radiators like this: `https://cwiki.apache.org/confluence/display/BIGTOP/Index`.

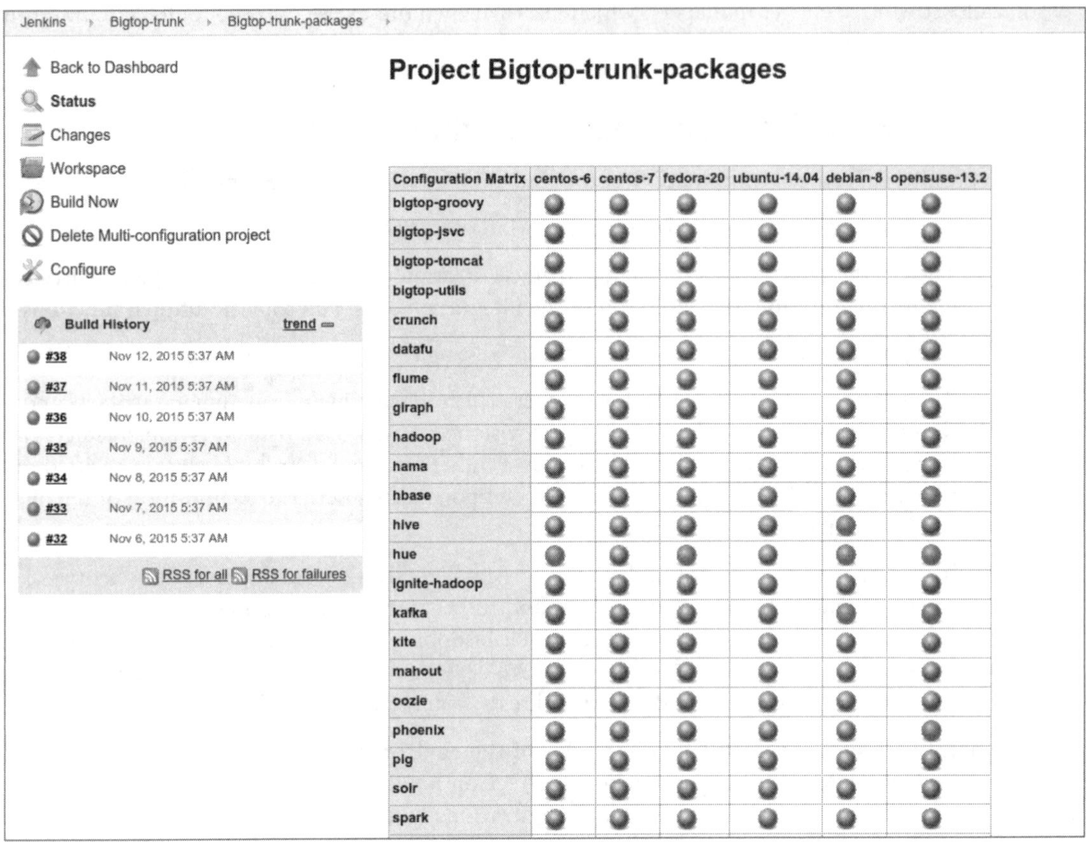

FIGURE 7-1

Now let's proceed to a hands-on exercise of creating your own Apache data processing stack. All examples in this chapter are based on the latest (at the time of writing) Apache Bigtop 1.1 release candidate.

The Structure of the Project

At the top-level, Bigtop has a few important moving parts. Let's review some of them:

- `build.gradle`: Represents the core of the build system
- `packages.gradle`: Represents the core of the build system
- `bigtop.bom`: The default stack composition manifest
- `bigtop_toolchain/`: Sets up the development environments

- `bigtop-test-framework/`: A home of iTest, the integration testing framework
- `bigtop-tests/`: Contains all the code for integration and system tests along with the Maven build to configure the environment and run the tests against a cluster
- `bigtop-deploy/`: Has all the deployment code for distributed clusters, as well as virtual and container environments
- `bigtop-packages/`: Provides all the content needed for the creation of installable binary artifacts

Let's get into some more detail about some of them.

Meet the Build System

The Apache Bigtop build system uses Gradle (`http://gradle.org/`). The Bigtop source tree includes a `gradlew` wrapper script, and in order to start working with Bigtop you need JDK7 or later, and the cloned repo of the Bigtop:

```
git clone https://git-wip-us.apache.org/repos/asf/bigtop.git
```

You can also fork this from the github.com mirror: `http://github.com/apache/bigtop.git`.

And now, to see the list of available tasks you can simply run:

```
cd bigtop
./gradlew tasks
```

Stack components can be built all at once:

```
./gradlew deb or ./gradlew rpm
```

You can also use an explicit selection:

```
./gradlew allclean hive-rpm
```

The Bigtop build is the center of most all of the activities and functionalities in the framework. It is used to create the development environment and the build binaries, to compile and run tests, to deploy project artifacts to a central repository, to build the project web-site, and to do many other things.

Bigtop has a way to specify inter-component dependencies in the stack so all upstream dependencies are automatically built first if needed. In the above example, if `-Dbuildwithdeps=true` is passed in the build time, Bigtop will first download and build Hadoop, and only then will it proceed with Hive. Hadoop, however, requires ZooKeeper, so its build will precede the creation of the Hadoop component. By default, however, Bigtop will only build the component that is explicitly specified.

Bigtop provides the functionality to generate local apt and yum repositories from existing packages. It allows a stack developer to quickly test freshly-built packages by pointing to the repo location in the local filesystem. This can be done by running:

```
./gradlew apt|yum
```

A corresponding repository will be created using all of the DEB or RPM packages found under the top-level output/ directory.

At any point, to explore all of the standard tasks available for the end user, you can execute:

```
./gradlew tasks
```

And now we are ready to check how to configure and work with the development environment, which is needed to build all of the highly complex data processing software, known as the Hadoop stack.

Toolchain and Development Environment

In order to create a stack of dozens of components, your system will need to be equipped with a lot of development tools. Keeping track of these requirements is a full-time job. Fortunately, the development needs for all of the supported platforms are readily provided by the Bigtop toolchain located under the bigtop_toolchain/ top-level directory. Bigtop is using Puppet not only for deployment, but also for its own needs, like setting up the development environment. You don't need to be a Puppet expert, however, to take advantage of it. Just make sure you have `sudo` rights and type this:

```
./gradlew toolchain
```

This will automatically install all of the packages for your system, including a correct version of the JDK needed for the stack components.

BOM Definition

Bigtop provides a Bill of Materials, or a BOM file, that expresses what components are included, their versions, the location of the source code and some other properties. The default BOM file name is `bigtop.bom`, and it describes the stack that will be created. BOM is using a simple self-documented DSL. Here's a typical component description:

```
'hbase' {
  name     = 'hbase'
  relNotes = 'Apache Hbase'
  version { base = '0.98.12'; pkg = base; release = 1 }
  tarball { destination = "${name}-${version.base}.tar.gz"
            source      = "${name}-${version.base}-src.tar.gz"}
  url   { download_path = "/$name/$name-${version.base}/"
          site =    "${apache.APACHE_MIRROR}/${download_path}"
          archive = "${apache.APACHE_ARCHIVE}/${download_path}"}
}
```

As you can see, it is possible to use the already defined variables, `pkg = base`, from the same scope, or from other sections of the BOM:

```
download_path = "/$name/$name-${version.base}.
```

The DSL processor will stop the build if any errors are detected.

The standard sources of the components are official Apache project releases. You can choose, however, to build a component from elsewhere by pointing to a different location of the source archive. The downloadable URL is automatically constructed as url.site/url.download_path/tarball.source. So, if you want to build Hbase from a GitHub repository using branch-1.2, change the definition to:

```
tarball { destination = "${name}-${version.base}.tar.gz"
          source      = "hbase-1.2.zip" }
```

```
url       { download_path = "apache/hbase/archive"
            site = "https://github.com/${download_path}"
            archive = site }
```

You can then run `./gradlew hbase-clean hbase-deb` to produce a new set of binaries for Debian.

There's also a way to create component packages directly from a Git version control system. Please refer to README.md in the top level folder of the Bigtop source tree for more information about this capability. Further in the chapter, if the location of a file isn't specified explicitly, it can be found in the top-level folder.

DEPLOYMENT

Evidently, having all of the tools to develop and validate the stack only allows you to build the packages, which has little value if there's no way to deploy it and run some workloads. Generally, software stacks come with some means to install them (or deploy them in the case of distributed environments), and to manage and control their components and state. And of course Bigtop provides a couple of ways to provision your environment. The simplest one is to use the Bigtop provisioner, which we'll cover in more detail next. More complex cases might involve editing some configuration files, and running Puppet from the command line. We cover both cases for the benefit of people who manage clusters at their day jobs, and those who just need to quickly set up an environment to verify things they are developing. Let's start with a simple case.

Bigtop Provisioner

The Bigtop provisioner is a subsystem of the framework, which provides a convenient way to spin up a fully distributed Hadoop cluster using virtual machines or Docker containers. It can be found under the bigtop-deploy/vm directory of the project source tree. The most up-to date information about this deployment method can be found at: `https://cwiki.apache.org/confluence/display/BIGTOP/Bigtop+Provisioner+User+Guide`. We will, however, explain how it works here.

Provisioner uses Vagrant and makes cluster deployment to a virtual or containerized environment quite uniform. Try the following to see how easy it is:

1. Start with `<BIGTOP_ROOT>/bigtop-deploy/vm/vagrant-puppet-docker vi vagrant config.yaml`
2. Update the docker image name from `bigtop/deploy:centos-6` or `bigtop/deploy:debian-8` and point the repository to `https://cwiki.apache.org/confluence/display/BIGTOP/Index`. Select the component you'd like to deploy: `[hadoop, yarn, hbase]`
3. And type the following: `./docker-hadoop.sh --create 3`

The standard provisioner comes with a pre-defined configuration, and if you don't need anything special you can just use it. The provisioner is integrated into the build system:

```
./gradlew -Pnum_instances=3 docker-provisioner
```

Assuming that your computer has Vagrant and Docker already installed, you will get a fully distributed cluster up and running as the result of the above command. You should be able to SSH into cluster nodes and perform the usual activities as expected. The provisioner script supports a few more commands, so refer to the top-level README.md for the most up-to-date information. To learn more about Hadoop provisioning with Docker we recommend the Evans Ye presentation on the topic available from `http://is.gd/FRP1MG`.

Master-less Puppet Deployment of a Cluster

For more complex cases of cluster provisioning, let's look into the deployment system. Bigtop Puppet recipes can be found under the bigtop-deploy/puppet directory of the project source tree. Let's see how Apache Bigtop allows you to quickly deploy a fully distributed software stack.

This is an advanced way of setting up a cluster, and unless you need to manage one on your own, you can skip the rest of this section and go directly to the "Integration Validation" section. A fully distributed deployment requires a few more steps compared to the Provisioner example above, but essentially with a few more commands so you can spin a cluster as big as you need, with optional High Availability for HDFS and/or YARN, and with or without security. Securing a Hadoop cluster includes standing and setting up your own KDC server, which isn't easy to do. As you saw in earlier chapters, Hadoop security is a difficult topic involving many variables, but combined with the security across the stack, it can quickly turn into a management nightmare. If you are interested in the topic please familiarize yourself with the presentation by Olaf Flebbe on "How to Deploy a Secure, Highly-Available Hadoop Platform." The PDF slides can be downloaded from `http://is.gd/awcCoD`.

One of the requirements we have for the deployment mechanism is to be able to work under different operation environments. The specific host names and their roles might not be known, as in the case of a company-wide deployment system. This is why the implementation is done as a master-less dynamic system where all nodes have the same set of recipes, but different nodes receive their own configuration files. Once the groundwork is done, all nodes will simultaneously be brought into their specific states, resulting in a working cluster with as many nodes as needed. The deployment system collects node information using Puppet Hiera for lookup and collection modules, and juxtaposes it with the roles definitions from Bigtop recipes. Here's a high-level example of how it works:

- Bigtop provides a default topology template file bigtop-deploy/puppet/hieradata/site.yaml defining a few key parameters of the cluster such as `bigtop::hadoop_head_node`, `hadoop::hadoop_storage_dirs`, `hadoop_cluster_node::cluster_components`, and optionally the list of `bigtop::roles`. **Important:** the head node has to be set as a fully qualified domain name (FQDN); otherwise the node identification won't work.
- By default, the roles mechanism is turned off. All nodes in the cluster are assigned a worker role, and the head node carries on the master role. So, the head node will run a NameNode process and Resource Manager process, if you deploy HDFS and YARN. The set of components is defined by `hadoop_cluster_node::cluster_components`. If the list isn't set explicitly, all available packages will be installed and configured.
- To take advantage of the roles, set `bigtop::roles_enabled: true` in the `site.yaml` and specify the roles as *per node*. This, however, might lead to a need to manage separate

configurations for different nodes, especially if your cluster topology is trivial. We will cover a possible way of handling this in the next section. The full list of roles per daemon can be found in the bigtop-deploy/puppet/manifests/cluster.pp manifest.

- The complete list of configuration parameters and their default values can be found in the bigtop-deploy/puppet/hieradata/bigtop/cluster.yaml file.

Let's now proceed to the deployment itself. First, you need a set of nodes for your cluster. It's outside of the scope of this chapter and the book to go into every single detail of the hardware provisioning. If you're reading this book, however, you're probably already aware of tools like Foreman, EC2, or others. For the simplicity of this example we won't deal with role-based deployment, and we will leave it out as an exercise for the reader.

Let's say there are five nodes up and running Ubuntu 14.04, with the `node[1-5].my.domain` as their hostnames. Nodes will be carrying their functions as follows:

- node1 through node5 will be workers.
- node1 will serve as the head node.
- node5 will be handling the gateway functions.

The deployed stack will include HDFS, the mapred-app, the ignite-hadoop, and the Hive components. The set of the component is minimalistic, yet functional, and we'll be using it in the next chapter.

Let's start working with the node1.my.domain and clone the project Git repo under /work. According to that layout, `site.yaml` will have the following content:

```
bigtop::hadoop_head_node: "node1.my.domain"
bigtop::hadoop_gateway_node: "node5.my.domain"
hadoop::hadoop_storage_dirs:
  - /data/1
  - /data/2
hadoop_cluster_node::cluster_components:
  - ignite_hadoop
  - hive
bigtop::jdk_package_name: "openjdk-7-jre-headless"
bigtop::bigtop_repo_uri: \
"http://bigtop-repos.s3.amazonaws.com/releases/1.1.0/
ubuntu/14.04/x86_64"
```

The latest versions of Bigtop have an ability to automatically detect and set the URL of the package repo for difference platforms, but I will leave it as it is here for better clarity.

Now we need to make sure that the all of the nodes have the same recipes and configurations. Because Puppet modifies the state of the system, it has to be executed under a privileged account such as root. It would be easier if you have a password-less SSH login between all of your nodes. Alternatively, you can manually enter the password when requested. To sync-up the project's content, simply `rsync` or otherwise distribute the content of the `/work` folder to all of the nodes in your cluster. In our experience, the best way to achieve this is by using `pdsh` and `rsync`. The following commands will do the trick. Be aware, though, that you need to specify the SSH user name and the path to the SSH key. Check with the `rsync` man page for more details.

```
export SSH_OPTS="ssh -p 22 -i /root/.ssh/id_dsa.pub -l root"
pdsh -w node[2-5].my.domain rsync $SSH_OPTS -avz --delete node1.my.domain:/work /
```

At this point, all of the nodes should have an identical /work folder. Puppet Hiera, however, must be able to read the configuration file and some other files from the workspace:

```
vi  bigtop-deploy/puppet/hiera.yaml
```

You can then point `datadir` to the workspace, so the line looks like this:

```
:datadir: /work/bigtop-deploy/puppet/hieradata
cp bigtop-deploy/puppet/hiera.yaml /etc/puppet/hiera
pdsh -w node[2-5].my.domain rsynch $SSH_OPTS -avz --delete
  node1.my.domain:/etc/puppet/hiera.yaml /etc/puppet/
```

The last preparation step is to make sure that all nodes have the required Puppet modules by running:

```
pdsh -w node[1-5].my.domain 'cd /work && \
puppet apply --modulepath="bigtop-deploy/puppet/modules" -e "include
  bigtop_toolchain::puppet-modules"'
```

And we are now ready for the deployment:

```
pdsh -w node[1-5].my.domain 'cd /work && \
puppet apply -d --modulepath="bigtop-deploy/puppet/modules:/etc/puppet/modules"
  bigtop-deploy/puppet/manifests/site.pp'
```

After a few minutes (your mileage might vary with different connection speeds) you should have a fully functional Hadoop cluster with a formatted HDFS. You will also have your user directories that are set with correct permissions, as well as other fully configured components with their services up and running. The node5.my.domain now has all client binaries and libraries working with cluster services. Enjoy!

Each release of Apache Bigtop comes with generated repo files for a variety of operating systems. The set for release 1.0.0 can be found at `https://cwiki.apache.org/confluence/display/BIGTOP/Index`. Similarly, release 1.1.0 will be published at `https://dist.apache.org/repos/dist/release/bigtop/bigtop-1.1.0/repos/` once the release candidate is officially accepted.

Configuration Management with Puppet

As you can see, standing up a real distributed cluster is a bit more complex than a simple provisioner, but it is still trivial enough. You might end up with nodes built from different hardware batches with different amounts of RAM and/or hard drives. The software composition of the nodes might be dissimilar to each other, and carry their own function in the pipeline. So, a subset of the nodes might only carry Apache Kafka nodes and serve the logs collection, whereas another subset may be designated to the events stream processing using Apache Flink. These node configurations and packages would have to be maintained or updated on different schedules; some of the maintenance might require service restarts and some might not. Handling these intricacies is a full time job. That's why cluster orchestration is an important topic. The orchestration is quite different from management, but both terms are often and incorrectly used interchangeably. Without getting into too many details let's consider orchestration to be composed of architecture, tools, and a process to deliver a pre-defined service. Management, on the other hand, provides tools and information radiators for automation, monitoring, and control.

Hadoop vendors do provide some tooling to help with the management routine. These tools are available as free and open source, and as proprietary commercial tools as well. You should be able to easily identify them with a quick search, but we don't recommend focusing on those tools for three main reasons:

1. They aren't compatible with the standard Linux `init.d` (or systemd) life-cycle management, and they use their own custom ways of standing up, configuring, and managing cluster services.
2. The tools are all webUI-based and interactive, which makes scripting and automation around them either impossible or considerably more difficult.
3. These tools have their custom implementations for system management, which pretty much disregards decades of operation experience put together by producers of Chef and Puppet. This is a very complex topic, and professionals are sticking to well-known frameworks, which are also well-integrated with provisional systems like Foreman.

These management tools, however, help to significantly lower the entry barrier for people not familiar with the software in question. They hide a lot of complexities and deliver a central console to observe and control system behavior. This of course has its own benefits.

So what can a professional system administrator or a DevOps engineer do? With Unix, the best result is achieved by putting together a set of smaller tools and utilities, each being responsible for a smaller piece of action. In our case, we should have a Version Control System (VCS) that is responsible for the versioning aspect of the cluster configuration, and Puppet to take care about the state management of it. It is wise to use a distributed VCS, given how all of the configuration changes must be propagated to multiple hosts. We use Git, but you can use Subversion or Mercurial if it suites you better.

The idea is pretty simple: Specific configurations have to be separated, and should be updated independently. A VCS branch mechanism fits here perfectly, with different group or role configurations living in their own branches. Now the configurations files, or their templates, as well as the versions of the software packages, can be independently managed by people with domain expertise, which are typically DevOps engineers. Once a stack update is validated in a testing environment, it can be easily pushed into production, by merging or explicitly picking certain configuration changes between branches. As soon as the change is pushed to the VCS server, all nodes can pick it up and consequently apply it in full isolation from each other. The state machine (Puppet or Chef) will automatically restart the services according to the given recipes. This process can be as fine grained as needed and can easily change without massive outages of the cluster. There's no single point of failure either, given how there isn't a single management host or service.

Here's a sketch of how it works, but please note that the installation and configuration of the Git servers is outside the scope of this chapter. This solution has essentially three parts: VCS, cron, and master-less Puppet. Each node in the cluster has a crontab entry to do the following:

```
cd /work
git pull origin/node-$ROLE-branch
puppet apply manifests/site.pp
```

The environment variable `$ROLE` might be set during the initial provisioning of the operating system or specified otherwise. The cron will execute the above set of commands as often as practical, keeping the nodes of the cluster in a coherent state per specified configurations.

INTEGRATION VALIDATION

Now that we have our desirable Hadoop-based cluster up and running, we should check if it is working as expected, and that all of the components can play nicely with each other. The best way to figure this out is by running some workloads that will not only check if separate parts of the clusters are working as expected, but will also be crossing the components' boundaries to make sure they are binary and API compatible. Bigtop has two ways to do this: via integration or smoke tests. Both kinds of tests can be written in any JVM language.

You can immediately spot how a lot of tests in the Bigtop, as well as the iTest framework, are written using the Groovy language. The main reason is because Groovy provides a unique mix of dynamic capabilities with a strong-typed language. Being a truly polyglot language, you don't have to worry much about arbitrary file extensions. Depending upon the problem at hand, you can just write your code in Java or Groovy. Groovy scripting is a very powerful tool, as you'll see in the later section discussing smoke tests. In fact, Groovy is quite deeply intertwined with the Bigtop build, the actual deployment, and the stack. Bigtop's build system, Gradle, is a type of Groovy DSL. We will use a Groovy script to format an HDFS file system and stuff the distributed cache with all of the expected libraries and files (bigtop-packages/src/common/hadoop/init-hcfs.groovy). Note how `bigtop-groovy` is a standard package of the Apache Bigtop stack.

Bigtop is currently in the almost completed transition from the Maven build system to Gradle. This proved to be more comprehensive and a better fit for the variety of the tasks needed to be managed in the Bigtop project. As a result, smoke tests are controlled by the Gradle build, whereas the old-fashioned integration tests are still relying on Maven. The latter is retrofitted into a top-level Gradle build, but full integration is not yet finished. Don't be alarmed—it is coming.

Once the transition is finished, instead of Maven modules as explained below, Bigtop will be using Gradle multi-project builds, although conceptually it won't change much for your users.

iTests and Validation Applications

All tests in Bigtop are considered to be first class citizens, similar to the production code. They aren't really tests, but rather validation applications tuned for the particular software stack. Each application has two parts to it:

- The application code can be found under test-artifacts/ along with its build environment where the target dependencies are set and particular APIs are exercised.
- Maven executors start the applications. These are simple Maven modules sitting under test-execution/ to perform the checking and setting of the environment where needed.

The Integration validation application can use the helper functionality provided by the Bigtop integration test framework (iTest). It can complement both an application and its executor. iTest is an extension to the standard JUnit v4, adding nice things like the ordered execution of tests, the ability to run tests directly from JAR files, and some other useful features. We won't, however, focus much on the iTest itself. If you are interested to learn more you can find all related information under the bigtop-test-framework/ top-level directory.

Now, tests or validation applications are much more fun. Let's first look under the hood of the development of integration application artifacts.

Stack Integration Test Development

Each validation application is represented by a Maven module. There are two parts in the development of any integration application: code changes and artifact deployment. But first, the new application has to be added to the test stack. As with any Maven project you need to create the module's structure under the bigtop-tests/test-artifacts/ folder and list it in the top-level bigtop-tests/test-artifacts/pom.xml. The module's Project Object Model (or POM in Maven-speak) will need to define all of the dependencies and resources it needs. The project's top-level POM has all of the component versions included in the stack, so in most cases modules should be able to simply list their needs in the `<dependencies>` section and versions will automatically be inherited via the parent POM.

If you look into the code of existing validation applications you will notice that they may be written as direct calls to component APIs such as Hadoop and HBase. Another possibility is to invoke command line utilities using the components that they themselves would provide. And the last, but not least, approach includes the mix of both. Some of the Hadoop or HBase tests can start calling platform APIs to bring the system into a certain state, followed up by an execution of either the Hadoop or Hbase CLI in order to check the viability of certain functionality.

Both approaches have their own merits and purposes. The validation applications working with a component API have a better chance of catching unexpected and incompatible changes. The programming interfaces tend to be finer grained yet they may not necessarily be immediately exposed in the user-facing functionality. As the result, a change at the API level might go unnoticed until the software is released to the customer. And testing aimed at the API level is especially important for publicly exposed integration layers where changes in a method semantic might not be immediately caught by the lower-level tests, yet it has all the potential to break the application contracts. Changes of this sort most likely aren't possible to test with a unit or functional test, because they might require complex setups impossible to mock or emulate. In this case, integration tests provide a valuable service for the application developers. This type of test is quite sensitive and tends to catch a lot of issues before the code hits the production clusters. On the flip side, there's a potential for a higher maintenance cost, and they might fail every now and then.

The second kind of Bigtop validation applications are most suitable for user-facing functionality involving command-line tooling like Hadoop, Hive, and Hbase. A good example of this kind is `TestDFSCLI.java` in a Hadoop module. The test uses an external definition of the Hadoop CLI command semantics and runs the Hadoop utility from the deployed cluster to validate if its functionality is as advertised. These tests tend to be more stable and carry less of a burden on the developer, but they justify the time spent on their implementation.

And now we are ready to begin with the development of a new validation application. You may need to run the new code against an existing system to make sure it performs as expected. For the applications validating APIs, all of the code needs should be satisfied by the build system, and it is easy to run and debug them in your favorite IDE. We recommend IntelliJ IDEA as the development tool of the highest caliber, but of course you can use something else.

Whenever an integration application artifact needs to be set up for the execution, you should be able to use the Maven deployment facility to install it either locally or to deploy it into a remote repository server. During the development, the local installation works for most cases. You can do it by running the following (for Hadoop tests):

```
./gradlew install-hadoop
```

Run this from the project's top-level directory. This command will also cover the installation of all additional helper modules and POM files. All artifacts JARs will be pushed into the local Maven repo, and they are used to run the integration application. Similarly, you can deploy the artifacts to a remote repo server using the not-yet-gradelized command:

```
mvn deploy -f bigtop-tests/test-artifacts/hadoop/pom.xml
```

This deployment will require you to configure your repo location and credentials using ~/.m2/settings.xml. Please refer to the Maven documentation for further instructions.

If your test code relies on the client parts of a cluster application, you might need to deploy gateway bits into your development environment. A cleverly written executor module can be very handy by enforcing particular environmental constraints and by automatically constructing the classpath. This route relies on both steps of the development process—development and artifact deployment—as well as the use of the executor modules.

Before we look at the work flow, let's quickly examine an integration application executor. They can be found under `test-execution`. One for Hadoop is located and managed by smokes/hadoop/pom.xml. Like the counterparts over in the artifacts section, executors are implemented as Maven modules. Unlike the artifact modules, these involve more complex build logic using multiple plugins and the additional `common` module. The latter defines a number of system properties commonly used across most of the executors, such as test include and exclude patterns, the dynamic creation of the test lists derived from the artifact JARs, and so on.

The complete flow of an integration application development looks as follows:

1. Develop the code of the application as in any other software development process.
2. Whenever the application artifact or its executor needs to be shared with other teammates, use the Maven install/deploy feature to deliver them to a local or shared Maven repo as explained above.
3. The application executor can be started with a command as follows:

   ```
   mvn verify -f \   bigtop-tests/test-execution/smokes/hadoop/pom.xml
   ```

4. From the project's top-level folder, by default, all tests matching `**/Test*` will be run. The executor's behavior can be controlled by supplying a few system properties:
   - `-Dorg.apache.maven-failsafe-plugin.testInclude=\`
   - `'**/IncludingTestsMask*'` to run only a subset of tests
   - `-Dorg.apache.maven-failsafe-plugin.testExclude=\`
   - `'**/ExcludingTests*'` to avoid running certain validation applications

5. Setting the log level to TRACE level is handy when you need to trace any issues with the code or the logic. This can be done by specifying `Dorg.apache.bigtop.itest.log4j .level=TRACE` in the runtime.

The up-to-date information about how to deploy and run integration and system tests can be found at the project's Wiki page.

Validating the Stack

Running the integration application in the distributed environment is quite simple once the cluster is fully deployed and you're familiar with all the tooling described earlier. As a convenience, we recommend you run your integration applications from a node that isn't a part of the worker pool, such as a gateway node. The reason is pretty simple: The worker node might be sitting behind a firewall or get fully-loaded during the validation. In both cases it might be challenging to access it if you need to debug your code. Besides, the gateway node normally would have all of the client binaries and libraries, so the integration applications will have all of the bits readily available.

Another good reason to run the tests from a designated node is to have an easier integration with the Continuous Integration infrastructure. Taking Jenkins as an example, it is quite trivial to bring up a Jenkins slave, or run a container inside of an existing slave, provision it with Hadoop stack client packages, and a clone of the Bigtop repo. Once test runs are completed, Jenkins will collect the results and present them for further processing and analysis. Trying to achieve the same results using a regular cluster node might involve additional administrative efforts, as well as ways of combining the test results back in the CI server.

Per blueprints explained in the "Development" section, `node5.my.domain` is configured as the cluster gateway. It also has the Bigtop source repo under the /work directory. Once the steps to install the validation artifacts are completed, as shown in "Stack Integration Tests Development" above, the gateway node will possess all libraries and POM files in its local Maven repo. And now you're ready to validate the integrity of the cluster stack.

```
cd /work
./gradles install-hadoop
mvn verify -f bigtop-tests/test-execution/smoke/hadoop/pom.xml
```

The above command will probably fail immediately with an angry message from Maven enforcer, telling you to set up certain environment variables. At the very least the following has to be set:

```
export HADOOP_HOME=/usr/lib/hadoop
export HADOOP_CONF_DIR=/etc/hadoop/conf
```

Once the issue is dealt with it should be smooth sailing from here. If you want to validate other components as well, you can subsequently run:

```
mvn verify -f bigtop-tests/test-execution/smoke/hive/pom.xml
mvn verify -f \    bigtop-tests/test-execution/smoke/ignite-hadoop/pom.xml
```

Or you can simply run all of the available applications in the test stack with `mvn verify`. If the deployed stack has just a few components, many tests are likely to fail. When the run is completed, the results will be available under the components' target/ folders, as is customary with Maven executed tests.

Cluster Failure Tests

The Bigtop's iTest isn't a complete distributed integration test framework if it isn't providing a facility to introduce faulty events into normal operation of the system. This is commonly called fault injection and is similar to throwing a monkey wrench into a well-working mechanism. Indeed, iTest has that monkey wrench ready. iTest currently provides three types of distributed failure:

- Service termination failure
- Service restart failure
- Network shutdown failure

The fault injection framework requires SSH password-less access to the nodes where failures will be introduced, as well as password-less sudo on these nodes. The latter is needed for the test to manipulate the system events such as network interface failures, and service start/stop. For a more detailed write-up on how to write the cluster failure tests please refer to `https://cwiki.apache.org/confluence/display/BIGTOP/Running+integration+and+system+tests#Runningintegrationandsystemtests-ClusterFailureTests`.

The current fault injection framework could be improved and extended in a variety of ways. The Bigtop community is always on the lookout for new contributions to the project, including, but not limited by the patches, bug fixes, documentation improvements, and more.

Smoke the Stack

There's a reason why integration validating applications could be deployed as Maven artifacts. A test stack represents a particular state of the software stack. Freezing and releasing the corresponding state of the test stack has numerous benefits. One such benefit is to be able to repeat the validation of the software on any new deployment from the same set of binary artifacts. Let's say you're spinning up development clusters from Apache Bigtop v1.1. On every provision, before the cluster is handled to its end user, it should be quickly verified. One way to do it is by running the integration suite v1.1 from the previously published artifacts.

In a different use case, however, it might be desirable to repeatedly validate the functionality inside of a development cycle without doing any extra steps. Recently, the Bigtop community started working toward the simplification of the test system by introducing *smoke tests*. The main difference between this and the integration tests described earlier is that smokes can be run directly from the source code. Unlike the use case with integration application artifacts, no extra preparation and deployment steps are needed.

And indeed it is quite simple. Just switch to bigtop-tests/smoke-tests/ and run:

```
./gradlew clean test -Dsmoke.tests=ignite-hadoop,hive -info
```

This will test `ignite-hadoop` and Hive deployments. A couple of things to keep in mind:

- Not all components are currently covered by the new smoke tests. There's an argument that perhaps even the existing integration validation applications should be converted into new smokes. But is hasn't been settled one way or another.

- Unless you're running smoke tests from the same branch or tag that was used to produce the components for the software stack, you might not be testing exactly what you expect. As in the case with two kinds of integration tests, the smokes could use the lower-level public APIs, or user-facing CLI tooling. The former case is more prone to failures if the targeted implementation keeps changing or is merely different. So perhaps more thorough version management discipline will have to be exercised by the user.

In general, new smoke tests are a real easy way to assess a cluster viability, verify the integration points, and stress or load the system. We certainly look forward to new development in this part of the project.

PUTTING IT ALL TOGETHER

Why should anyone be bothered with a framework to do things that anyone can perhaps build with a few keystrokes and some shell scripts? Or, what about a few lines of Python and Scala code? Let's quickly recapture what Bigtop covers and the key functionality it provides.

- Software stack composition allows a user to define a consistent presentation of a set of software components to deliver a complete platform solution or a service. This architecture increases the productivity and predictability of the software development by setting up a formal process and mechanisms at all levels of engineering organizations.
- Validation stack composition allows you to fasten together a variety of functional requirements delivered by the software stack via the provided integration test suites and feature-rich integration test framework.
- Standard Linux packaging represents an easy way to install and configure a vertical amount of software services with standard life-cycle management interfaces and configurations.
- A deployment and configuration management framework guarantees repeatable and controllable provisioning of software and validation stacks to achieve better levels of system orchestration and continuous delivery of the services.

These are four key principles of the Apache Bigtop framework. The community behind the project has invested decades of the combined experience in the system architecture and integration to deliver this top-notch industry standard facility to provide an easy way of dealing with daily data processing needs.

SUMMARY

Some people still might not be convinced that Apache Bigtop is the best thing since sliced bread. And they don't want to be burdened with all of the intricacies of a software stack development process. After all, not everybody wants to deal with system architectures and integration design. In this case, Apache Bigtop still can help you to build, manage, and improve the data processing pipeline.

The Bigtop community works very hard to regularly produce high quality releases of the Apache data processing stack, including the latest most stable releases of Apache projects. The last released version at the time of this writing is Bigtop 1.1. You can immediately start using it as was described in the "Deployment" section of this chapter.

Beyond that, you might find Bigtop's statistical modeling applications to be of a high value for data professionals. The source code and more information about it can be found in the bigtop-data-generators/ folder. The framework and the use-cases are explained in great detail in the recent presentation by RJ Nowling about "Synthetic Data Generation for Realistic Analytics" available from `http://is.gd/wQ0riv`.

MORE RESOURCES

Here are more useful resources where you can find additional information about the project, helpful hints, and best practices, as well as direct help from the development community and users. The project wiki contains the information you might find useful in solving a particular situation `https://cwiki.apache.org/confluence/display/BIGTOP/`. It delivers presentation slides, video tutorials, conference links, and more.

Bigtop blog (`https://blogs.apache.org/bigtop`) is a great way to receive announcements about new releases, interesting features, and project updates. You're also welcome to subscribe to @ASFBigtop Twitter.

Bigtop Jenkins server (`http://ci.bigtop.apache.org`) has nightly built packages for different operating systems and also reflects on the latest test runs.

8

In-Memory Computing in Hadoop Stack

WHAT'S IN THIS CHAPTER?

- Introduction to in-memory computing
- 30x faster MapReduce with Apache Ignite
- In-memory file system: HDFS caching
- Advanced use of Apache Ignite for state sharing and fast SQL

By now you are familiar with the Hadoop platform, its broader ecosystem, and some of the computation engines on top of it. You have also learned about the benefits and shortcomings of the traditional MapReduce computational framework. One benefit is linear scalability and the ability to process data in parallel, which comes with the cost of over-reliance on the underlying distributed storage. Each stage of a MapReduce job needs to be written into a filesystem that increases fault tolerance. The process of sending data from the mappers to the reducers, or so-called shuffle stage, can take a heavy toll on the network bandwidth at the time when intermediate data gets copied between the nodes.

This chapter will get into more advanced topics of data processing. In it we explore some of the alternative compute engines and computing technologies, which, unlike traditional systems, open up a great number of beneficial breakthroughs and new ways of leveraging legacy platforms.

From the beginning of Hadoop's creation there have been attempts to make the MapReduce computation engine less complex and more available for non-programmer types. The commonly available system for this is Hive, described in Chapter 4. It adds a SQL engine on top of MapReduce, providing a subset of the SQL language (HQL) for analysis of non-structured data. Evidently, although MapReduce is the engine of the system, it is still a bottleneck.

For a few years developers have been working on improvements to this model. Apache Spark, described in Chapter 3, provides an alternative computation engine, commonly dubbed as MapReduce 2.0. In this system the query plans are calculated more efficiently, and data transformations happen primarily with in-memory. As a direct result, it is possible to achieve impressive performance gains with this new model. It isn't without its own contentions though. Separate Spark jobs cannot share a state, which has to be serialized to the disk to avoid data loss. The latter limitation hits particularly hard when different data processing pipelines, or ETLs, are in need of sharing results with each other. SQL processing on Spark seems like an obvious idea, and after a few trials the community seems to be converging to use Hive HQL on top of the Spark engine. The project is relatively new, but it's already showing interesting potential.

No conversation about Hadoop databases should go without a reference to HBase, which also uses HDFS as the storage, but relies on unique data organization to achieve very impressive, sometimes close to real-time, response SLAs. This system is adopted in the solutions where short reaction time and ability to make fast updates are needed.

With a slight exception in the case of HBase, the common theme for the systems referred to above, as well as many others, is how they deal with the data storage. Because these are using computer memory only for computation and always persisting the data to a slower disk storage, we call them "disk first." But really, aren't all of the data processing systems like this? If this is the first time you are getting into the subject, you might benefit from reading some introductory materials starting with Hbase and following through with some of the links in the article. Or just simply proceed with this chapter.

INTRODUCTION TO IN-MEMORY COMPUTING

What is in-memory computing? Isn't the term overly confusing? After all, even the first generations of computers had to load the data into some sort of memory, connected to a CPU, in order to work on it. Thus, all of the computing is virtually done in memory. But the RAM is limited, making it difficult for a lot of programs trying to use it. In multi-tenant and shared operating systems, a number of processes might be competing to use RAM to keep their data objects and structures in it. Because of the physical limitations, the software usually loads and keeps in computer memory only what it needs right away, and pushes everything else to a disk system once the data isn't required anymore. However, this pattern has been a case mostly for economic reasons: The memory is quite expensive. And being a scarce resource of any computer system it is in high demand.

At the end of 1995 RAM was averaging at US$100 per Megabyte, or roughly US$100,000 for a Gigabyte. At the end of 2015, you can expect to pay about US$4–6 per Gigabyte of a consumer grade DIMM3 RAM. The price came down from US$100,000 to US$5 or so—a 20,000 times reduction. And over the same period of time the US dollar lost about 60% of its value: US$100 from 1995 could buy you $160 worth of goods today. Modern spin-drives now are going for about US$30 per Terabyte; and SSDs cost about ten times of that. What justifies the premium in the case of RAM is the performance. RAM is about 5,000 faster than a spin-drive, and it is still 2,500 times faster than an SSD.

In retrospect, paying under US$6,000 per Terabyte of RAM versus US$300 for an SSD of the same size looks like a great bargain. While it might be hard to find a single system with that much RAM, for the price of a new car you can build a multi-node computer cluster, delivering as much or even more combined memory. As with any distributed system, effectively addressing the memory shared by multiple computers is a challenge. The benefits, though, are overwhelming.

Today, more and more people are getting fixated on big data. However, "big" is subjective and isn't well defined. Leading analytical companies have done thorough research in an attempt to identify what "big" means in reality, rather than in a parallel universe of marketing white papers. The result is quite the opposite of what you might expect under the influence of big data hype. According to some surveys, in early 2015, the largest relevant dataset among nearly 800 companies was about 80TB. With a high probability, a dataset like this doesn't need to be in a cluster memory all at the same time. So, in all likelihood, an organization with a modest IT budget should even today be able to afford in-memory processing.

Apparently, there is a demand for these types of computation nodes. Amazon has just announced new high-performing X1 instances—virtual slices of physical servers—carrying up to 2TB of RAM. X1 instances will be also equipped with more than 100 vCPUs. While the pricing information isn't available yet, it is not so difficult to imagine where it will go in a year, considering the high stakes and creative competition in this space.

Modern computer architecture put forward by von Neumann and Alan Turing in 1945 is what we are likely to have for a while, unless quantum technology makes a leap. Until then, RAM seems to be the most promising medium of storage as both prices come down and non-volatile designs spring to life.

On the other hand, the development of the technologies that let you "connect" the RAM across multiple computers is extremely challenging. A quick look into the modern commercial market of these solutions reveals that less than a dozen companies have the expertise and are innovative to the point where they can embark on this path.

The vertical markets for the technology are huge and growing rapidly. Among typical uses of in-memory computing across different industries are:

- Investment and retail banking
- Medical imaging processing
- Natural language processing and cognitive computing
- Real-time sentiment analysis
- Insurance claim processing and modeling
- Real-time ad platforms
- Merchant platform for online games
- Hyper-local advertising
- Geospatial/GIS processing
- Real-time machine learning
- Complex event processing of streaming sensor data

So, how can in-memory computing be beneficial for the processing of massive amounts of data? Is it practical or even possible to deal with modern volumes of data in memory? Over the rest of this chapter we will dive deeper into a very interesting Apache Software Foundation top-level project called Apache Ignite™.

APACHE IGNITE: MEMORY FIRST

Here's what we consider to be a correct definition of in-memory computing: the middleware software that stores data in RAM, across a cluster of computers, and processes it in parallel. As it will immediately become evident, "stores data in RAM" is the key factor that puts IMC systems apart from what was referred to as "disk first." In these systems RAM is considered to be the primary storage, not only for the software code, but also for the data the code is written to work with. The data of course needs to be somehow transferred into RAM, unless it is directly generated by the software. And this can be achieved by different means, starting with good old loading from disk storage, to streaming it over the network from external sources. However, once the data is in memory, it isn't off-loaded to the external storage to preserve the updates or changes in a state. Instead, it is retained there and it's immediately available to the software applications that might need it. Clearly, at some point, the data might not fit into the RAM anymore. In this case, part of it needs to be evicted from RAM to the secondary storage. As we'll see later in this chapter, Apache Ignite has some clever ways of dealing with this.

Wait, some might say, but how is this different from JVM memory management where the garbage collection deals with old and unused objects? First of all, the garbage collection is quite expensive for large heap sizes. For production systems configured with 128+ GB of JVM heap, it is indeed very tricky to make it work without long pauses where the memory needs to be swept from the stale data structures. Second, garbage collection (GC) lacks the fine granularity of eviction: If an object isn't referenced by anything, it gets collected. But what can you do in the case when a large collection fills the node's RAM completely? How do you automatically get rid of just some elements in it? GC won't address this use case because every element of the collection is at least referenced by the collection itself.

Let's consider a more elaborate example where a collection is spanning the memory of more than just one node. In this example, the collection is partitioned in a way that some elements are replicated on the first two nodes. Some other elements are replicated on the other two, and so on. In this particular case, GC will be completely helpless. Perhaps you can resort to a distributed garbage collection, but this is pretty much guaranteed to grind your system to a halt.

A more common solution is to provide a cache implementation as a way of loading/off-loading data between persistent storage and RAM. A commonly used API standard today is described in JSR107 or JCache, and is implemented by many vendors. JCache standardizes (among other things):

- In-memory key-value store
- Basic cache operations
- ConcurrentMap APIs
- Pluggable persistence

So, let's see how Apache Ignite deals with all of these complexities and what you can do better by adding an Ignite cluster into your data stack. But first, let's quickly revisit Ignite's architecture: what components it consists of and what functionality they have.

System Architecture of Apache Ignite

Apache Ignite has started as a data grid platform (see Figure 8-1). Data grids were a widely popular idea in the early 2000s. But it took a massive change in the economics of the computer industry, including the vast improvements in network hardware, as well as the dramatic drop in the prices of RAM, to make a data grid platform affordable. Modern Apache Ignite has overgrown its own crib and became a data fabric, combining together a data storage layer, computing and service layers, and many more.

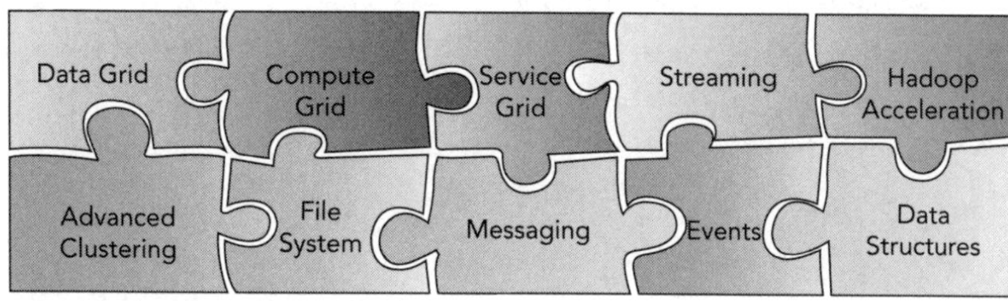

FIGURE 8-1

Each piece in the puzzle plays a different role. Some of them are convenience adapters allowing other applications and tools to be plugged into the core and take advantage of effective in-memory cache. Others, like data grid, provide the functionality core to the platform itself. Using a cluster RAM as the primary storage allows all of the components in the stack to collaboratively use it without expensive roundtrips to a filesystem.

Data Grid

The Ignite in-memory data grid is a key value in-memory store, which enables caching data within a distributed cluster memory (see Figure 8-2). It has been built from the ground up to linearly scale to hundreds of nodes with strong semantics of data locality and affinity data routing, thus reducing redundant data noise.

Generally speaking, this layer provides the storage facility with clever replication techniques and the ability to plug secondary storage systems for data persistence. And as you will see later in this chapter, this is the foundation for the rest of the platform. Ignite operates with essentially a cache or, more precisely, a distributed partitioned hash map. Every cluster node owns a portion of the data, thus supporting the linear scalability of the storage.

Users can create as many caches as needed. A cache can be created as `PARTITIONED`, `REPLICATED`, or `LOCAL`. As the name suggests, a `PARTITIONED` cache allows you to divide the data into partitions, and all partitions get equally split between participating nodes (see Figure 8-3). This allows you to store and work with multi-terabyte datasets across all cluster nodes. This type of cache fits well the situations with large datasets that need to be frequently updated.

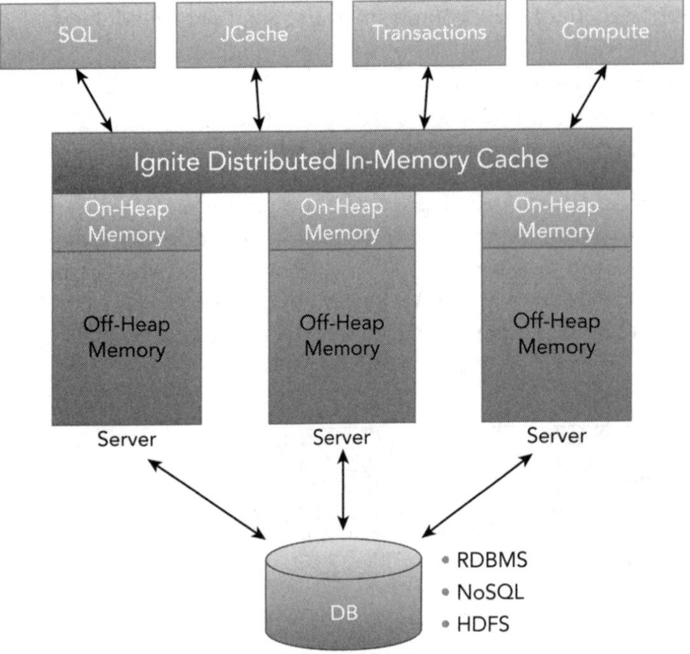

FIGURE 8-2

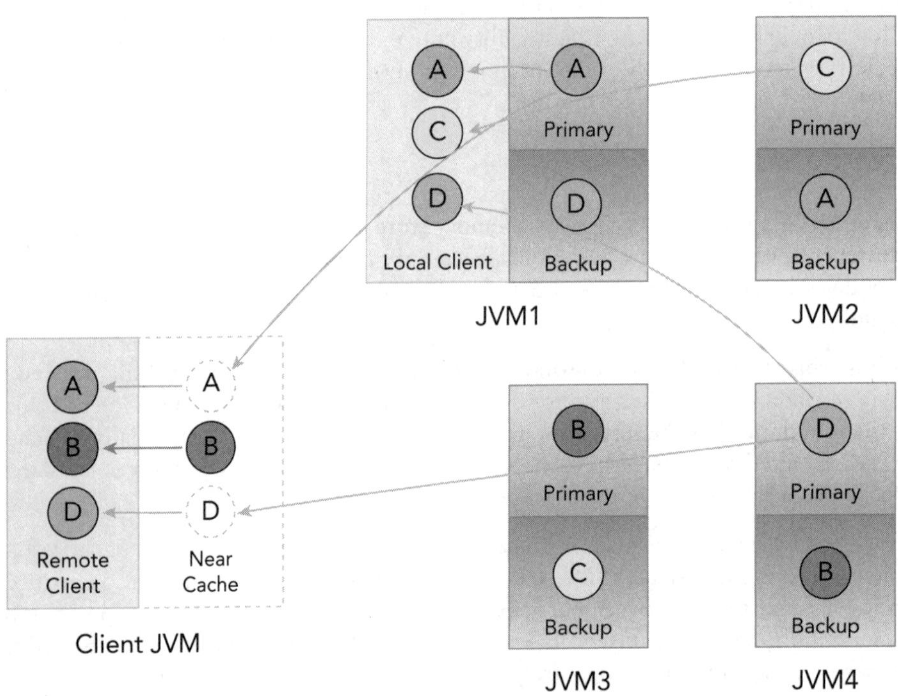

FIGURE 8-3

The REPLICATED cache (see Figure 8-4) makes a copy of the data on every node in the cluster, so it provides the highest level of data availability. Clearly, such redundancy sacrifices performance and scalability. Under the hood, a replicated cache is a special variation of a partitioned cache, where every key has a primary copy and backups on all other cluster nodes.

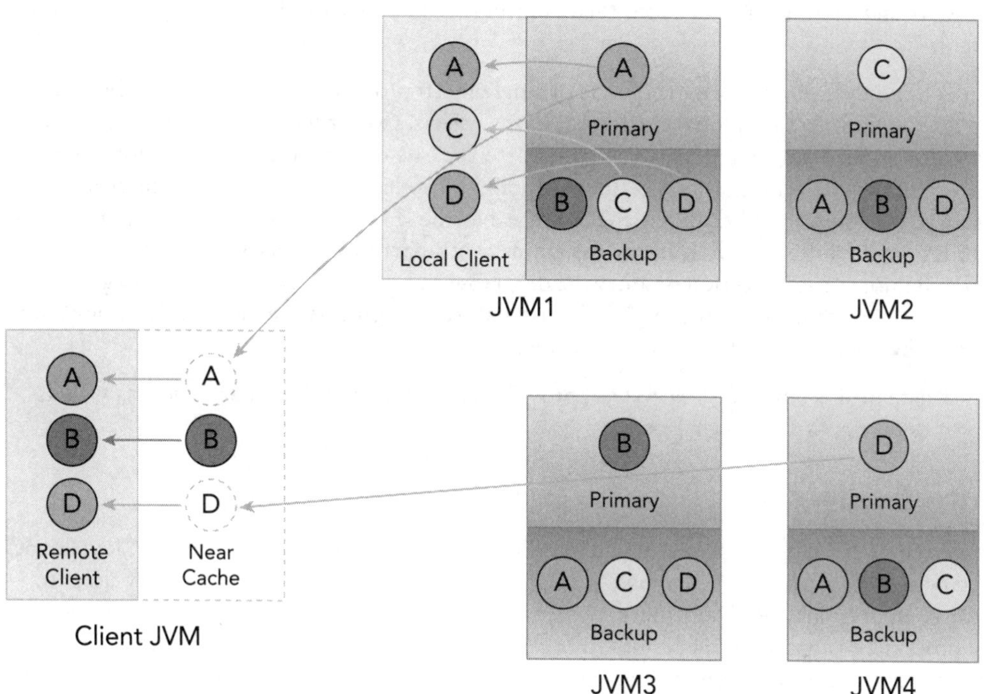

FIGURE 8-4

And finally, the caches created in LOCAL mode have no data distribution property. As such, these are ideal for the situations where the data is read-only, or where data needs to be refreshed at intervals. Cluster singletons are discussed later, which can benefit from LOCAL caches.

A Discourse on High Availability

Like other key-value stores, Ignite operates with the notion of data locality or affinity. Unlike others, this hashing mechanism is pluggable. Every client can determine which node a key belongs to by plugging it into a hashing function, without a need for any special mapping servers or nodes serving and managing the metadata. This is quite important for a number of reasons. Let's review some of them.

The master-less property automatically removes the Single Point Of Failure (SPOF) scenarios, increasing the availability as well as the scalability of the fabric. SPOF is one of the common issues with HDFS. If a NameNode cannot be reached because of a network or hardware failure, or just over a long GC pause, the whole HDFS cluster becomes non-responsive. To deal with this Hadoop provides a special HA framework. In essence, it uses Apache Zookeeper for a leader reelection based on the ZAB protocol. When configured with HA support, HDFS runs active and standby NameNodes, which are kept in sync via the Zookeeper apparatus: Once the active master is down, the clients are forced to use a standby master that becomes active. The algorithm works well for the primary-backup use case. This is a very common problem for single-master distributed systems. The HDFS NameNode is a SPOF, so its high-availability framework is quite elaborate. It involves many moving parts and significantly increases the operational complexity and overall footprint of the file system.

Another common yet often overlooked issue of single master (or single-active master) distributed systems is their unfitness for global clustering. In the case of two or more clusters working over a WAN connection, a single master isolation leads to the loss of the service of the whole global system. The leader-reelection protocols like ZAB might also lead to a pretty bad complication called split-brain. Let's define split-brain: Say the clusterA has the leader node at the moment, and clusterB's nodes are the followers of it. In the case of network partitioning between the two clusters, clusterB will initiate the reelection of a new leader. However, clusterA still has a running master. Now, two parts of what earlier was a global cluster start diverging as the data modifications are not coordinated by one, but now two isolated masters.

The Ignite data grid is a master-less system, providing better availability guarantees, as well as protection against split-brain situations.

Compute Grid

Distributed computations are performed in parallel fashion to gain high performance, low latency, and linear scalability. The Ignite compute grid provides a set of simple APIs that allow users to distribute computations and data processing across multiple computers in the cluster. Distributed parallel processing is based on the ability to take any computation and execute it on any set of cluster nodes and return the results back. This layer of the fabric has properties for load balancing, fault tolerance, data and compute collocation, and many others.

The compute grid is what allows an application to take advantage of multiple computation nodes in the cluster, so the execution isn't hindered by resource contentions. Ignite lacks job scheduler in the traditional sense of the word. There is not one designated component that tracks the cluster resource utilization, job resources demands, and so on. All jobs are mapped to cluster nodes during the initial tasks split or client side closure execution. Once jobs arrive at the designated nodes, they are submitted to a thread pool, and are then executed at random. There are, however, mechanisms allowing you to change the execution order if necessary. We will talk about the efficiency of this approach in the section on in-memory MapReduce.

With jobs sent directly to compute nodes and getting executed in a thread pool, a need in a centralized job manager disappears. This once again improves the overall availability of the system. However, compute nodes still might get shut down or crashed or start running slow. For cases like this, Ignite supports automatic job failover. In case of a crash, jobs are automatically transferred to other available nodes and get re-executed. As a result, Ignite provides at least one guarantee, and until there's at least one running node, no job will be lost.

Please refer to the Ignite documentation for in-depth details on the topic.

Service Grid

The Service Grid allows for the deployment of arbitrary user-defined services on the cluster. You can implement and deploy any service, such as custom counters, ID generators, hierarchical maps, and more. This layer allows you to control the life-cycle and cardinality of the deployed services, and provides guarantees of continuous availability in the event of failures or topology changes. Singleton services are an especially interesting case of cardinality control. A user can deploy three types of singletons including:

- Node singletons
- Cluster singletons
- Key-affinity singletons, when a service is run depending on the presence of a key

Together with the advanced clustering layer, this functionality creates a very potent system to deploy and manage non-trivial topologies of distributed services in a cluster. Fundamentally, there are no practical obstacles to implementing a resource allocator similar to YARN using Ignite service grid, if anyone indeed needs yet another resource negotiator.

Memory Management

While memory management and the model used by Ignite should be discussed as a part of the Data grid layer, let's examine it a bit further here. As mentioned earlier, Apache Ignite provides an implementation of the JSR107 specification. It goes beyond JCache, however, and provides the facilities for data loading, querying, asynchronous mode, and many more. In order to achieve the best performance and low-latency results, the system needs to go outside of the traditional JVM-heap and disk storage ecosystem. We have briefly touched on the existing issues of GC pausing with larger heap sizes. For this particular reason the data grid adds the support for off-heap memory.

Ignite implements a multi-tiered memory management model. Generally, the following three types of memory are supported:

- On-heap memory (JVM heap with GC)
- Off-heap memory (not managed by JVM, no garbage collection)
- Swap memory

Each tier has a higher capacity with the payoff of a higher latency than the next. Depending on the data size and performance considerations, a user can create a cache in one of the tiers. Optionally, the data from lower tiers can be evicted to a higher tier. Table 8-1 described the modes of creating a cache.

TABLE 8-1: Cache creating modes

MEMORY MODE	DESCRIPTION
`ONHEAP_TIERED`	Store entries on-heap and evict to off-heap and optionally to swap.
`OFFHEAP_TIERED`	Store entries off-heap, bypassing on-heap and optionally evicting to swap.
`OFFHEAP_VALUES`	Store keys on-heap and values off-heap.

The following code snippet provides a quick look into the action:

```
CacheConfiguration cacheCfg = new CacheConfiguration();
cacheCfg.setMemoryMode(CacheMemoryMode.ONHEAP_TIERED);
// Set off-heap memory to 10GB (0 for unlimited)
cacheCfg.setOffHeapMaxMemory(10 * 1024L * 1024L * 1024L);
CacheFifoEvictionPolicy evctPolicy = new   CacheFifoEvictionPolicy();
// Store only 100,000 entries on-heap.
evctPolicy.setMaxSize(100000);
cacheCfg.setEvictionPolicy(evctPolicy);
IgniteConfiguration cfg = new IgniteConfiguration();
cfg.setCacheConfiguration(cacheCfg);
```

Eviction policies are pluggable. Ignite has a ready implementation for a number of policies like LRU, FIFO, sorted, and some others. Custom eviction policies also can be provided by the user.

The seamless up and down transitions between different memory tiers is beneficial for application developers. This complex logic is now available for *any* component via simple APIs, and better yet, the in-memory data can be shared between the applications via simple abstractions like a filesystem.

Persistence Store

This feature allows for data read/write through, from, and to a persistent storage. Persistent storage could be a relational database server like PostgreSQL, or a NOSQL system like Cassandra, or a distributed filesystem like HDFS. As an added benefit, the Ignite CacheStore interface that simplifies the work with JCache CacheLoader and CacheWriter is fully transactional. Ignite offers an option of asynchronous persistence, or *write-behind* for situations with a high rate of cache updates. The latter is likely to negatively impact the performance of the storage system with a high operational load. Write-behind is a fancy term for a batch operation, where updates are accumulated for a while and then asynchronously flushed into the persistent store.

Ignite also has a facility of automatic persistence to be used to retrieve and write-through domain models from and to a relational database. Ignite comes with its own DB schema mapping wizard supporting automatic integration with persistent stores. The utility automatically connects to an underlying database and generates all required OR-mapping configurations and POJO domain model classes. As the schema-less data formats gain more and more popularity, a similar functionality might soon be provided for data-interchange formats like JSON.

LEGACY HADOOP ACCELERATION WITH IGNITE

As demonstrated above, all parts of Apache Ignite are useful and have a huge value-add for application developers, both in the traditional enterprise environment, as well as for schema-on read and streaming architectures. What might be particularly interesting for the Hadoop audience, however, is an in-memory acceleration layer. Generally, it includes two parts:

- The in-memory filesystem, or the Ignite File System (IGFS), has a pluggable secondary filesystem for effective caching into a persistent storage.
- The in-memory high-performance MapReduce implementation that fully and transparently replaces one in Hadoop. With Ignite MapReduce you don't need JobTracker or ResourceManager, because all of the scheduling is done via Compute Grid.

Benefits of In-Memory Storage

Ever since the early days of computing, disk storage was considered to be slow. If a program had to work with a diskstore then it was viewed as a performance penalty. RAM disk was one of the earlies technologies providing an interface to store files in memory. It was introduced in 1980 for the CP/M operating system. Interestingly enough, even today this technology is available on pretty much any Linux distribution as a standard tool. Ubuntu, for example, creates a special `tmpfs` limited to half of the physical computer memory. The `tmpfs` can be mounted to the user space and used by anyone. Quick unscientific microbenchmarking shows that writing a 1GB file to ramdisk happens at the rate of 2.8 GB/s. Doing the same into a decent SSD drive is a way lengthier process averaging at 2.8 MB/s, or three orders of magnitude slower. But this is nothing new. We know that RAM is way faster than any secondary storage, as previously discussed.

RAM disk only provides a filesystem abstraction. The applications that need to share the data would have to resort to reading and writing files and directories, even if the data is represented by different structures. Eventually, the data would need to be serialized into something suitable for files, and then de-serialized when it's needed. Also, advanced processing-like transactions become tricky if possible at all in the frame of a pure file paradigm. And in a distributed environment, where the data needs to be replicated and shared across multiple actors, the block-level abstraction of a file system only adds to the complexity for the software system.

Evidently, while glorious, the RAM disk concept has its design limits, yet it serves its original goals and use cases pretty well. There were, mostly academic and without any notable industry adoption, attempts to find a solution for distributed RAM disk, or to devise an implementation of network RAM. The latter perhaps is least interesting considering its potentials for network congestions caused by over-the-LAN swaps.

With that in mind, we can pause for a moment and reminisce on what we know about Apache Ignite's distributed cache and its properties. It is a distributed key-value store, with strong consistency guarantees, and simple APIs allowing plug-in to a variety of adapters. Being essentially a distributed object store, it is well suited for block storage if needed. And this leads to an idea of using Ignite Data Grid to provide filesystem caching. We have already discussed the strong persistence support in Apache Ignite. The filesystem adapter discussed below is just one of the possible implementations.

Memory Filesystem: HDFS Caching

HDFS and other Hadoop Compatible File Systems (HCFS) seem to be a pretty common way of implementing a scalable distributed storage. But like any disk-based storage it will be a constant disadvantage compared to the RAM. We have covered the difficulties for attempting to cache distributed content using memory technologies that are only suitable for locally stored data. With this we will stop exploring any further the possibilities of speeding up local access via RAM caching, while facing performance and implementation challenges working with distributed content. Instead we will look into how the filesystem can be implemented as a side-property of distributed object storage.

Ignite File System (IGFS) is an in-memory filesystem allowing working with files and directories over existing cache infrastructure. IGFS can either work as a purely in-memory file system, or delegate to another filesystem (e.g., various Hadoop-like filesystem implementations) acting as a caching layer. In addition, IGFS provides an API to execute MapReduce tasks over the filesystem data. IGFS supports regular file and directory operations. And being a part of the middleware platform it could be configured and accessed directly from Java application code.

Apache Ignite is shipped with HCFS, like the IGFS subsystem called `IgniteHadoopFileSystem`. Any client capable of working with HCFS APIs will be able to take advantage of this implementation in plug-n-play fashion, and significantly reduce I/O and improve both latency and throughput. Figure 8-5 illustrates this architecture.

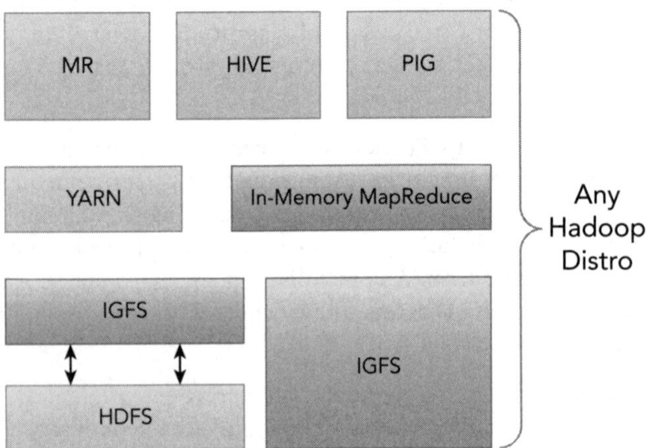

FIGURE 8-5

The configuration of the IGFS is quite simple, and if you're provisioning a cluster using Apache Bigtop deployment it will be readily done for you. From the operational standpoint, the Ignite process needs to have access to some of the Hadoop JAR files; a client needs to have a couple of Ignite JARs to be added in its classpath. A common way to do it is by adding them into the `HADOOP_CLASSPATH` environment variable. The IGFS can be accessed via its own filesystem URL. Here are some examples:

```
igfs://igfs@node2.my.domain/
igfs://igfs@localhost/
```

When IGFS is configured to front an HCFS instance, a user can still access the latter. In this case all benefits of the in-memory caching won't be accessible.

In-Memory MapReduce

Ignite in-Memory MapReduce allows you to effectively parallelize the processing of the data stored in any HDFS-compatible filesystem. It eliminates the overhead associated with job tracker and task trackers in a standard Hadoop architecture, while providing low-latency, HPC-style distributed processing. The diagram in Figure 8-6 illustrates the difference between the two implementations.

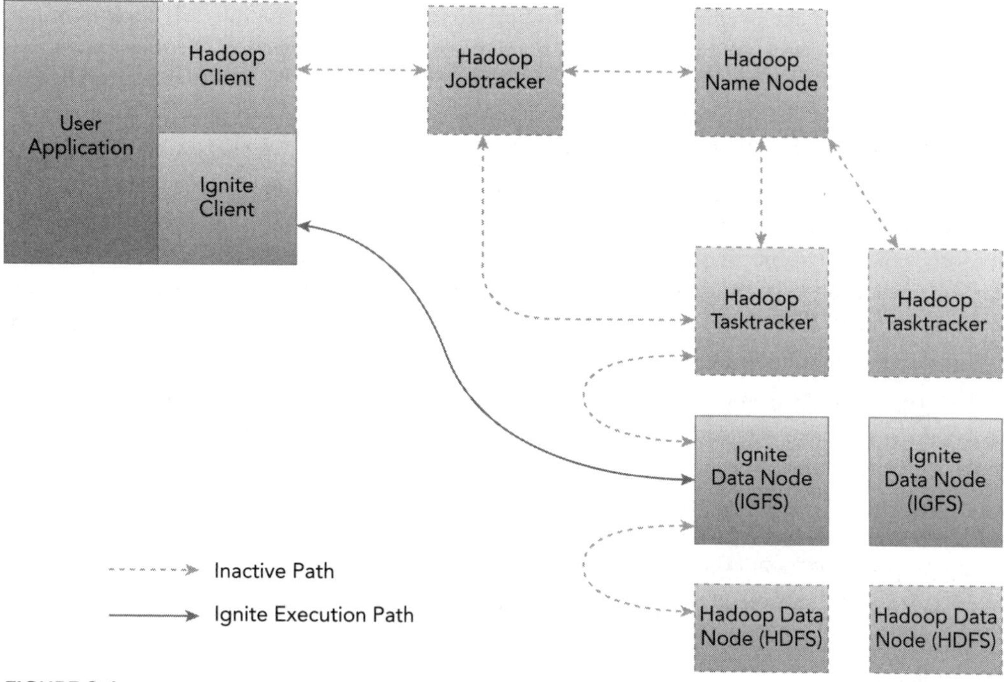

FIGURE 8-6

While there are other alternatives to MapReduce (most notably Apache Spark), Ignite's component is:

- **Non-intrusive:** No changes need to be made in the Hadoop layer.
- **Completely transparent and fully compatible with the existing MapReduce protocol:** User applications don't need to be recompiled, redeployed, or changed in any way. A simple environment variable setting is enough to start using the new engine.
- **Preserving legacy code:** No development time needs to be spent on rewiring an application to a different library or API. Better yet—there's no need to learn a new programming language.

If you still have the cluster we've built and deployed in the last chapter, now is the time to dust it off, because we're going to use it. The way the cluster has been deployed was to include a distributed disk storage layer (HDFS), Hive, and Apache Ignite accelerator components. There's no trace of either JobTracker (MR1) or YARN (MR2) software bits in our cluster. We have done this for a more dramatic effect, because no MapReduce application would work without either of their components in place. This includes Hive with its reliance on the MapReduce computation engine. The stack, however, has mapred-app deployed, but it doesn't include anything beyond MapReduce application code examples.

Let's see how Apache Ignite helps. During the deployment exercise in Chapter 7, Bigtop orchestration provided a few client side configuration files allowing *any* Hadoop client to take advantage of Ignite accelerator. By default these are set under /etc/hadoop/ignite.client.conf/ on every node of the cluster where Ignite is deployed. There, you can find three files that should already look familiar to you: `core-site.xml`, `mapred-site.xml`, and `hive-site.xml`. But surprise! The files are way simpler than you might remember from the Hadoop documentation. For the first two essentially just set new values for `fs.defaultFS` and `mapreduce.jobtracker.address` locations. And the last one is even more trivial, so we won't bother talking about it.

If you look into core and mapred site files you'll notice that both NameNode and JobTracker addresses are set to a localhost, instead of some arbitrary hostname. We have already touched upon the reason in the "A Discourse on High-Availability section. Any of the nodes in a cluster can disappear for one reason or another. However, in the master-less environment (or rather in the multi-master environment) this should be of a little concern for a client application, because the request will simply go elsewhere and be served.

Okay, let's run a standard MapReduce job. There's no need to go a find some MapReduce code, because we already have some example archives from the mapred-app component. First, let's point clients to the accelerator layer instead of base Hadoop:

```
export HADOOP_CONF_DIR=/etc/hadoop/ignite.client.conf/
export HADOOP_CLASSPATH=/usr/lib/ignite-hadoop/libs/ignite-core-1.5.jar:\/usr/↵
  lib/ignite-hadoop/libs/ignite-hadoop/ignite-hadoop-1.5.jar
```

The last export is required if your cluster is configured to use HDFS as a secondary filesystem. Our Bigtop cluster is. And that's it. You're all set to run legacy MapReduce code with the in-memory computation engine!

Let's run some PI estimations. Who likes to type if they don't have to, so we will set a variable to point to our example JAR, followed by a standard Hadoop command:

```
export \
   MR_JAR=/usr/lib/hadoop-mapreduce/hadoop-mapreduce-examples.jar
hadoop jar $MR_JAR pi 20 20
```

How was it? Pretty fast? How about wordcount—a traditional Hello, World for MapReduce? We'll grab *The Adventures of Tom Sawyer* by Mark Twain and count the words in it:

```
wget -O - https://www.gutenberg.org/ebooks/76.txt.utf-8 | \
     hadoop fs -put - 76.txt
hadoop jar $MR_JAR wordcount 76.txt w-count
```

And to check the results, run:

```
hadoop fs -cat w-count/part-r-00000
```

You have probably noticed how the output of the jobs is different from what you would expect to see with Hadoop MapReduce. But this is perhaps the only difference in the user experience. However, performance and availability-wise, it works way faster and better without changing anything in the application.

You can experiment a little to measure the time differences that can be achieved with different jobs. By now you have an experience with the toolset, and using Bigtop deployment it is very easy to add, configure, and start YARN with MR2 on your cluster. Refer to Chapter 7 to see how it is done. Once ready, simply unset the `HADOOP_CONF_DIR` variable and re-run jobs with the Hadoop MapReduce framework. My own experiments show as much as 30 times performance improvements when switching to Apache Ignite in-Memory MapReduce.

Similarly, it is possible to dramatically speed up Hive queries without making any changes to the Hive or queries themselves. We will simply refer you to an article about doing this here: `http://drcos.boudnik.org/2015/10/lets-speed-up-apache-hive-with-apache.html`. It includes detailed instructions and explanations.

ADVANCED USE OF APACHE IGNITE

By now you have learned how to run existing MapReduce code with no changes or even recompilation while getting a huge performance boost. The MapReduce paradigm isn't the most sexy thing in the computing world. After all, only so many problems can be solved with massive parallel processing, which isn't the most common approach anymore, even in the Hadoop ecosystem.

With all of the free time you now have due to MapReduce acceleration, you're ready to go further. This section covers a few advanced topics, but before that we want to provide a clear demarcation between Apache Spark, a popular machine learning and computation engine, and Apache Ignite.

Spark and Ignite

On multiple occasions we've witnessed people being confused about alleged similarities between Apache Ignite and Apache Spark. While these two share some commonalities being distributed systems with computation capabilities and additional benefits like streaming, they are actually completely different. Initially, we called this section "Spark vs Ignite," but then we realized that this was a false dichotomy. These systems aren't competing, but rather somewhat complementing each other. Let's review these differences in depth.

- Ignite is an in-memory computing system, e.g., the one that treats RAM as primary storage facility. Spark only uses RAM for processing. A memory-first approach is faster, because the system can do indexing, reduce the fetch time, and avoid (de)serializations.
- Ignite's MapReduce is fully compatible with Hadoop MR APIs, which let everyone simply reuse existing legacy MR code, yet run it with a greater than 30x performance improvement.
- The streaming in Ignite isn't quantified by the size of an RDD. In other words, you don't need to fill an RDD first before processing it; you can actually do the real streaming and CEP. This means there are no delays in a stream content processing in the case of Ignite.
- Spill-overs are a common issue for in-memory computing systems: After all, the RAM is limited. In Spark where RDDs are immutable, if an RDD was created with its size more than 1/2 node's RAM, then a transformation and generation of the consequent RDD is likely to fill all the node's memory, which will cause the spill-over, unless the new RDD is created on a different node. This will eat into network bandwidth. Ignite doesn't have this issue with data spill-overs, because its caches can be updated in an atomic or transactional manner. Spill-overs are still possible: The strategies to deal with it are explained in the off-heap memory chapter of Ignite documentation.
- As one of its components, Ignite provides the first-class citizen filesystem caching layer.
- Ignite uses off-heap memory to avoid GC pauses, and does it highly efficiently.
- Ignite guarantees a strong consistency.

- Ignite fully supports SQL99 as one of the ways to process the data with full support for ACID transactions.
- Ignite provides in-memory SQL indexes functionality, which lets you avoid full scans of datasets, directly leading to very significant performance improvements.
- Spark focuses on advanced use-cases of machine learning (ML) and analytical data processing. While training ML models, you might get into the situation where certain part of the training is incorrect. With Spark it should be trivial to quickly retrace all of the steps up to the point of divergence, as all inter-RDD transitions are already recorded for better fault tolerance.

While the potential use cases for both technologies don't seem to overlap at all, there are a few places where Ignite can help to significantly improve Spark work-flows.

Sharing the State

Apache Spark provides a strong property of data isolation. The prevalent design pattern around Spark is that SparkContext is only used inside of one process (or job). While there are legitimate reasons for it, a number of important cases exist where different jobs might need to share the context and/or state. The only way to do it in Spark is to use the secondary storage, either directly or via some sort of RAM disk layer. The former, obviously, is no good for the system performance. The latter doesn't help with sharing a state or context across node boundaries, and is also bound to a filesystem API.

Naturally, an efficient distributed cache could be the answer we are looking for. And fortunately, there's one right there. Apache Ignite provides an implementation of `SparkRDD` abstraction, which allows easily sharing a state in memory across Spark jobs. The main difference between native `SparkRDD` and `IgniteRDD` is that the latter provides a shared in-memory view on data across different Spark jobs, workers, or applications, while native `SparkRDD` cannot be seen by other Spark jobs or applications.

`IgniteRDD` is implemented as a live view over a distributed Ignite cache, which may be deployed either within the Spark job executing process, or on a worker, or in its own cluster (see Figure 8-7). Depending on the chosen deployment mode, either the shared state may exist only during the lifespan of a Spark application (embedded mode), or it may out-survive the Spark application (standalone mode), in which case the state can be shared across multiple Spark applications.

`IgniteRDD` isn't immutable, and all changes in the cache will be immediately visible to RDD users. Here's the best part: The cache content can be changed via another RDD or could come from other external sources, like different applications in the cluster. This is a very important characteristic, because it enables Spark to be deeply integrated with tools like Hive, BI front-ends, and many more without a smallest change to the Spark or tools in question. This is a real data collaboration made possible by in-memory computing platform.

`IgniteRDD` uses the partitioned nature of underlying caches, and provides partition information to a Spark executor. Affinity (or locality) of the data is also available. Reading and writing is easy with this new structure. Because `IgniteRDD` is a live view into a cache, the Spark application doesn't need to explicitly load the data, and all usual RDD API calls can be used immediately once the object is created.

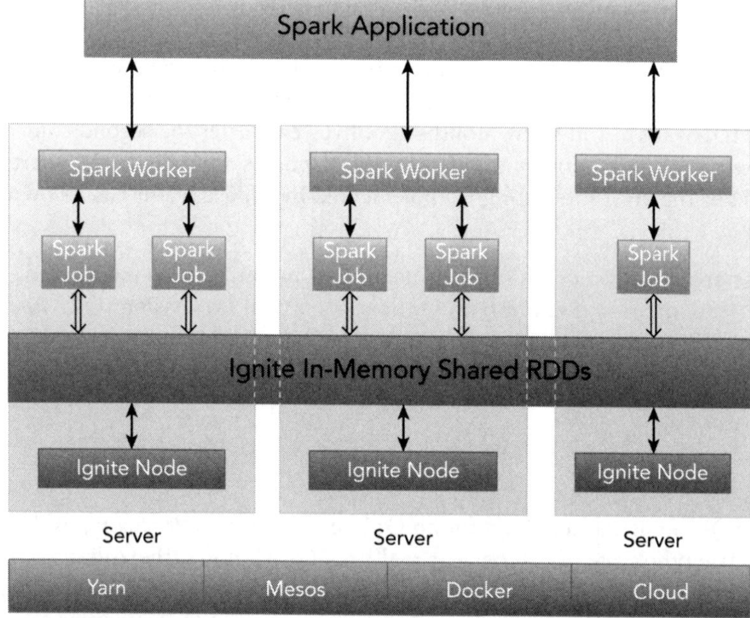

FIGURE 8-7

The following code fragment shows these benefits in action. If you want to try it yourself, please add and deploy the `spark` component to the Apache Bigtop cluster from the last exercise. Then simply follow Section 8 from the training script that we have up on the Apache Bigtop wiki.

Because `IgniteRDD` is mutable, it is now possible to build and rebuild its indexes. Having an index speeds up the lookup and searches, because an application can avoid constant full scans of the data sets. This leads us to the next advanced use case for Apache Ignite.

In-Memory SQL on Hadoop

Traditionally, SQL is perhaps the most often used language for data processing. A lot of data professionals are very familiar with it. This book, and this very chapter, have already touched on Apache Hive. A very different approach and a good example of advanced SQL on Hadoop is a new Apache Incubator project called HAWQ. In essence, it is a variation of the PostgreSQL server using HDFS for the storage. It provides both SQL for Hadoop and the analytics MPP database. Postgres clustering has been around for a while, and now with linear scalability of HDFS storage it definitely has its time in the spotlight.

Perhaps a majority of the SQL-on-Hadoop difficulties are coming from the storage system. HDFS has been designed and built first and foremost with scalability and redundancy in mind. Data loss or corruption is a very serious issue for distributed storage, and it has been the main design goal for the development team. For this particular reason, the files are split into blocks. Multiple copies of the blocks, or replicas, then send to different data nodes. Two logically sequential blocks of the same file most likely won't end up on the same data node, assuming you have more than a single data node in the cluster. Query planning, especially an optimal one, becomes a real engineering and scientific hassle.

Another underwater stone waiting to be hit by Hadoop SQL engines is the lack of decent updates for HDFS files. HDFS initially was a write-once system. And if a file needs to get updated, a user has to simply write a new file. This would contain the content of the old one plus whatever had to be updated. Imagine how well it worked for big files. On a second try, HDFS was extended with a working append operation (HDFS-265). And a few months ago, five years after the second coming of append, a nice truncated implementation was added as well. Updates are still tough. There a few strategies for it, and perhaps the most interesting is implemented by HBase, yet it has its own inefficiencies.

But neither HDFS nor HBase are main topics, as fascinating as they might be. The mentioned limitations are jamming the Hadoop ecosystem into an Online Analytical Processing (OLAP) bucket, with the exception of HBase. There's also a couple of attempts to build transactional support using HDFS snapshots and HDFS truncate, but it isn't clear how much legs those have. Time will tell.

SQL with Ignite

Updates are important for a SQL engine, and critical for an Online Transaction Processing (OLTP) engine. As businesses start getting the taste of fast or near real-time OLAP flows, they often want to tap into the speed that OLTP provides. And that is where in-memory systems are coming to play with their unparalleled performance, ACID transaction support, and fast distributed queries. And Apache Ignite shines here.

To start with, the querying of the data is one of the fundamental functionalities of `IgniteCache`. A cache could be indexed to speed up the data lookups. If a cache sits in off-heap memory, the index will reside in off-heap as well, improving the performance even further. Several querying methods are provided including scan queries, SQL queries, and text-based queries based on Lucine indexing.

By now you might have noticed that most of the cool functionalities available from Ignite are merely clever crafted views into `IgniteCache`. But the data itself is managed by the same key-value distributed store without costly transformations or transitions between the format. SQL queries are no different. Ignite supports free-form SQL queries virtually without any limitations. SQL syntax is ANSI-99 compliant. You can use any SQL function, any aggregation, and any grouping, and Ignite will figure out where to fetch the results from. Ignite also supports distributed SQL joins. Moreover, if data resides in different caches, Ignite allows for cross-cache queries and joins as well.

There are two main ways that query is executed in Ignite:

- If you execute the query against the `REPLICATED` cache, then Ignite assumes that all data is available locally, and you can run a simple local SQL query in an H2 database engine. The same will happen for `LOCAL` caches.
- If you execute the query against the `PARTITIONED` cache, it works like this: The query is first parsed and split into multiple map queries and a single reduce query. Then all of the map queries are executed on all data nodes of participating caches, providing results to the reduce node, which will in turn run the reduce query over the intermediate results.

Running a SQL query on a cache is as trivial as:

```
IgniteCache<Long, Person> cache = ignite.cache("mycache");
SqlQuery sql = new SqlQuery(Person.class, "salary > ?");
// Find only persons earning more than 1,000.
try (QueryCursor<Entry<Long, Person>> cursor = cache.query(sql.setArgs(1000))) {
  for (Entry<Long, Person> e : cursor)
    System.out.println(e.getValue().toString());
}
```

While we cannot think of a place or occupation paying less than $1,000 as an example, the code is pretty clean and self-explanatory.

The data stored in a cache is an object, with its own structure. At some level, an object structure could be looked upon as a table schema in the relational world. But what if the object in question has an elaborate structure with complex rules about what fields can be exposed and what fields can't be exposed? Apache Ignite provides transparent access to object fields, further reducing the network overhead and traffic. In order to make the fields visible to SQL queries, they have to be annotated with `@QuerySqlField`. This adds an additional control for the data security. Building upon the example above, let's change it slightly:

```
// Select with join between Person and Organization.
SqlFieldsQuery sql = new SqlFieldsQuery(
  "select concat(firstName, ' ', lastName), Organization.name "
  + "from Person, Organization where "
  + "Person.orgId = Organization.id and "
  + "Person.salary > ?");
// Only find persons with salary > 1000.
try (QueryCursor<List<?>> cursor = cache.query(sql.setArgs(1000))) {
  for (List<?> row : cursor)
    System.out.println("personName=" + row.get(0) +
      ", orgName=" + row.get(1));
}
```

As we alluded to earlier, indexing the data is important if fast queries are required. Ignite has a few ways of creating the indexes for a single column, or a group index via annotations or API calls. The class `Person` we used above might look like this:

```
public class Person implements Serializable {
  /** Indexed in a group index with "salary". */
  @QuerySqlField(orderedGroups={@QuerySqlField.Group(
    name = "age_salary_idx", order = 0, descending = true)})
  private int age;
  /** Indexed separately and in a group index with "age". */
  @QuerySqlField(index = true,
    orderedGroups={@QuerySqlField.Group(
    name = "age_salary_idx", order = 3)})
  private double salary;
}
```

Running SQL from Java or any other language is a lot of fun, as we know. But sometimes it makes sense to be boring and simply use a good old SQL client. This is why Ignite has a way to run the H2 debug console out of the box. This powerful tool allows you to have a great introspection into the data structure, as well as to run SQL queries interactively right from the browser. To enable this, simply start a local Ignite node with the `IGNITE_H2_DEBUG_CONSOLE` system property.

If you have another favorite SQL client, you can use it directly via a standard JDBC connection. The Ignite JDBC driver is based on the Ignite Java client. As a result, all client specific configuration parameters, like SSL-security and others, can be used on a JDBC connection. To get connected specify the JDBC URL:

```
jdbc:ignite://<hostname>:<port>/<cache_name>
```

Port numbers, as well as the cache name, could be omitted, in which case the defaults will be used. Everything we discussed above about exposing the object fields for querying and other topics is still relevant in the case of the JDBC connection to the Ignite caches.

Apache Bigtop adds out of the box integration between Apache Zeppelin (incubating) and Apache Ignite. Zeppelin is a project providing web-based notebooks for interactive data analytics.

Streaming with Apache Ignite

The last topic we want to touch on is streaming, which is very important for near- and real-time platforms to be able to work with streamed content. Because of the transient nature of a data stream, it is vital to be able to process the data as it goes through. There are a few very interesting open source systems in this field. As with in-memory, some of them are capable of conducting streams on the back of their fundamental data organization (like Spark); and some of them were made with streaming as the primary design goal (Apache Flink).

Ignite has its own streaming processing framework, and like everything else in this platform it's a clever layer on top of the Data Grid. A simple diagram is shown in Figure 8-8.

- Client nodes inject finite or continuous streams of data into Ignite caches using Ignite Data Streamers. Data streamers are fault tolerant and provide at-least-once semantic. Streamers are going hand-in-hand with `StreamReceiver`, which could be used to introduce custom logic before adding new data. `StreamTransformer` allows you to perform data transformation and updates, and `StreamVisor` allows you to scan the tuples in stream and optionally execute a custom logic based on their values.
- Data is automatically partitioned between Ignite data nodes, and each node receives an equal amount of it.
- Streamed data can be concurrently processed directly on the Ignite data nodes in a co-located fashion.
- Clients can also perform concurrent SQL queries on the streamed data. Ignite supports the full set of data indexing capabilities, together with Ignite SQL, TEXT, and Predicate based cache queries to query the streaming content.

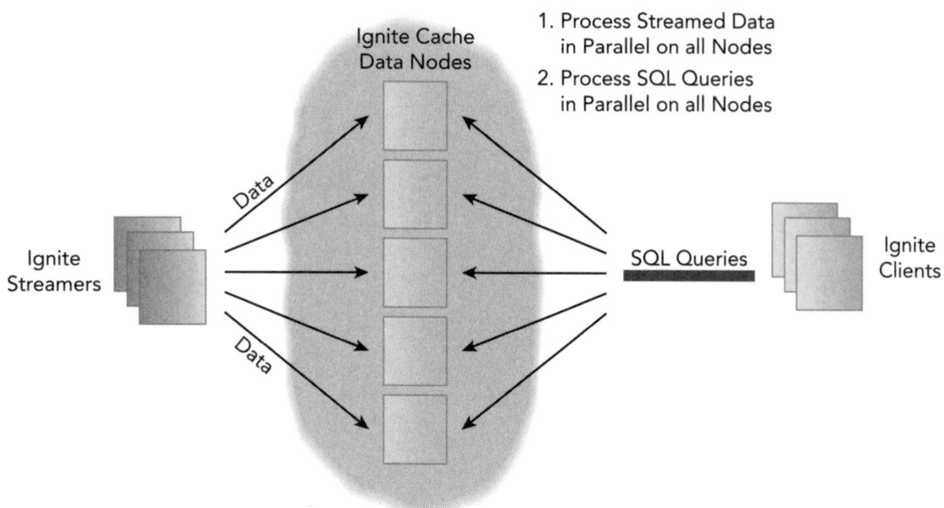

FIGURE 8-8

Streamed data can be queried via sliding windows. A stream can literally be infinite, and trying to query the data from the beginning of time seems to be quite impractical. Instead, you might want to figure out certain properties of the dataset over a period of time. Something like "Which songs were listened to the most in the last 12 hours?" For this, a sliding data window works perfectly. Sliding windows are configured as Ignite cache eviction policies, and can be time-based, size-based, or batch-based. You can configure one sliding-window per cache. However, you can easily define more than one cache if you need different sliding windows for the same data.

SUMMARY

As has been demonstrated in this chapter, Apache Ignite is a very powerful data-processing platform providing a high-performance memory-first storage system as its foundation. The distrusted key-value store makes it extremely easy to have a variety of logic and functional live views into the data. And the efficient computation engine paradigm makes programmatic or SQL-based data processing a breeze. A computation layer can be used for the acceleration of legacy Hadoop MapReduce and tools like Hive, which uses it as the engine.

The Apache Ignite cluster can be easily scaled up and down and can seamlessly span heterogeneous hardware environments including on-premise datacenters, both virtual and hardware, as well as cloud deployments. This makes it ideal for quick expansion of the Ignite applications from a developer's laptop to a cloud data center without an interruption. Built-in a high degree of fault-tolerance and master-less architecture also makes the platform a great candidate for production systems in mission critical environments.

Full SQL99 capabilities effectively remove the learning barrier for business analysts and business intelligence professionals. Unlike other systems in the Hadoop ecosystem today, Apache Ignite fully supports data indexing, and high-performance ACID transaction.

GLOSSARY

activities A logical grouping or classification of one or more jobs running on a cluster.

balancer A service ensuring that all nodes in the cluster store contain about the same amount of data within a set range. Data is balanced over the nodes in the cluster, not over the disks in a node.

cluster (Hadoop) A set of nodes configured to work together based on a common Hadoop component stack, with HDFS and MapReduce as the foundation.

components (Hadoop architecture) The individual installed software products composing a complete Hadoop cluster. Some components are active and include servers, such as HDFS, and some are passive libraries. The servers of active components provide a service.

Components consist of roles that represent the different configurations required by the component. They have a role on each host server. For example, HDFS roles include NameNode, secondary NameNode, and DataNode.

DataNode A server and component role of HDFS that stores data. A DataNode performs filesystem operations assigned by the NameNode. The DataNode stores the data within a Hadoop cluster. It is a slave node to the NameNode, which submits requests to all of the nodes within a cluster for filesystems operations.

distributed metadata Distributed metadata means that the NameNode is eliminated by storing the metadata throughout the DataNodes in the cluster. This type of Hadoop architecture was developed to resolve the problem of a single point of failure within a Hadoop system, the NameNode.

Hadoop A batch processing infrastructure that stores files and distributes work across a group of servers. The infrastructure is composed of HDFS and MapReduce components. Hadoop is an open source software platform designed to store and process quantities of data that are too large for just one particular device or server. Hadoop's strength lies in its ability to scale across thousands of commodity servers that don't share memory or disk space.

Hadoop assigns tasks across servers (called "worker nodes" or "slave nodes"), essentially simultaneously running them together. This gives it the ability to analyze large quantities of data. By balancing tasks across different location it allows bigger jobs to be completed faster.

Hadoop can be thought of as an ecosystem—it's composed of many different components that all work together to create a single platform. There are two key functional components within this ecosystem: the storage of data (Hadoop Distributed File System, or HDFS) and the framework for running parallel computations on this data (MapReduce).

Hadoop Common Usually only referred to by programmers, Hadoop Common is a common utilities library that contains code to support some of the other modules within the

Hadoop ecosystem. When Hive and HBase want to access HDFS, for example, they do so using JARs (Java archives), which are libraries of Java code stored in Hadoop Common.

HBase HBase is a columnar database management system that is built on top of Hadoop and runs on HDFS. Like MapReduce, HBase applications are written in Java, as well as other languages via their Thrift database, which is a framework that allows cross-language services development. The key difference between MapReduce and HBase is that HBase is intended to work with random workloads.

Hcatalog Table and storage management service for Hadoop data that presents a table abstraction so that you do not need to know where or how your data is stored.

HDFS An open source filesystem designed to store extremely large (megabytes to petabytes) data files with streaming data access patterns. HDFS splits these files into data blocks and distributes the blocks across hosts (datanodes) in a cluster. HDFS enables Hadoop to store huge files. It's a scalable filesystem that distributes and stores data across all machines in a Hadoop cluster. Each HDFS cluster contains the following:

- **NameNode:** Runs on a "master node" that tracks and directs the storage of the cluster.
- **DataNode:** Runs on "slave nodes," which make up the majority of the machines within a cluster. The NameNode instructs data files to be split into blocks, each of which are replicated three times and stored on machines across the cluster. These replicas ensure the entire system won't go down if one server fails or is taken offline—known as "fault tolerance."
- **Client:** Client machines have Hadoop installed on them. They're responsible for loading data into the cluster, submitting MapReduce jobs and viewing the results of the job once complete.

Hive A data warehouse built on top of Hadoop providing data summarization, query, and analysis. A SQL-like syntax called Hive Query Language (HiveQL) is part of Hive. HiveQL is used to create programs that run just as MapReduce would on a cluster. In a very general sense, Hive is used for complex, long-running tasks and analyses on large sets of data. Hive provides a mechanism to project structure onto this data and query the data using a SQL-like language called HiveQL. At the same time this language also allows traditional map/reduce programmers to plug in their custom mappers and reducers when it is inconvenient or inefficient to express this logic in HiveQL.

HiveQL A SQL-like programming language used with Hive.

Impala Like Hive, Impala also uses SQL syntax instead of Java to access data. The difference between Hive and Impala is speed: A query using Hive may take minutes, hours, or longer, yet a query using Impala usually take seconds (or less).

Impala is used for analysis that you want to run and return quickly on a small subset of your data, e.g. analyzing the sales of a large warehouse company for a single product. Impala is used as an analytic tool on top of prepared, more structured data.

hosts Devices, such as a computer or a switch, attached to a computer or telecommunications network, or a point in a network topology where lines intersect or branch.

job A mapper or reducer execution across a dataset. A job may split data to be processed across mapper tasks for parallel processing, with a master (JobTracker) scheduling and monitoring jobs across slaves (TaskTracker).

JobTracker A service that assigns MapReduce tasks to specific nodes in the cluster, preferably those nodes functioning as a DataNode. JobTracker schedules mapper and reducer jobs among TaskTrackers, with an awareness of data location.

MapReduce A process of distributing work across a cluster used by the MapReduce engine. It processes input dataset records, mapping input key-value pairs to a set of intermediate key-value pairs. Reducers merge a set of processed values, which share a key to smaller set of values, and combiners perform local (on the same host) aggregation of intermediate output, reducing the amount of data transferred from Mapper to Reducer.

MapReduce is the process used to process the large amount of data Hadoop stores in HDFS. Originally created by Google, its strength lies in the ability to divide a single large data processing job into smaller tasks.

Once the tasks have been created, they're spread across multiple nodes and run simultaneously. The "reduce" phase combines the results together. The following nodes are used in this process:

- **JobTracker:** The JobTracker oversees how MapReduce jobs are split up into tasks and divided among nodes within the cluster.
- **TaskTracker:** The TaskTracker accepts tasks from the JobTracker, and performs the work and alerts the JobTracker once it's done. TaskTrackers and DataNodes are located on the same nodes to improve performance.
- **Data locality:** Map executing code on the node where the data resides. All clusters should have the appropriate topology. Hadoop map code must have the ability to read data locally. Hadoop must be aware of the topology of the nodes where tasks are executed. Tasktracker nodes are used to execute map tasks, and so the Hadoop scheduler needs information about node topology for proper task assignment. In other words, whenever you use a MapReduce program on a particular part of HDFS data, you always want to run that program on the node, or machine, that actually stores this data in HDFS. Doing so allows processes to be run much faster, since it prevents you from having to move large amounts of data around.

  When a MapReduce job is executed, part of what the JobTracker does is look to see which machines the information required for the task is located on. Once it is located, the NameNode splits data files into blocks, each one replicated three times: The first is stored on the same machine as the block, while the second and third are each stored on separate machines. This is part of Hadoop's distributive process.

  Storing the data across three machines thus gives you a much higher chance of achieving data locality, since it's likely that at least one of the machines will be freed up enough to process the data stored at that particular location.

NameNode A service that maintains a directory of all files in HDFS and tracks where data is stored in the cluster. Maintaining master-to-slave data nodes.

nodes An abstract unit that composes a cluster; a vertex in a graph.

Pig (Apache Pig) A programming language designed to handle any type of data. Pig helps users to focus more on analyzing large datasets and less time writing map programs and reduce programs.

Like Hive and Impala, Pig is a high-level platform used for creating MapReduce programs more easily. The programming language Pig uses is called Pig Latin, and it allows you to extract, transform, and load (ETL) data at a very high level. This greatly reduces the effort if this was written in JAVA code; PIG is only a fraction of that.

While Hive and Impala require data to be more structured in order to be analyzed, Pig allows you to work with unstructured data. In other words, while Hive and Impala are essentially query engines used for more straightforward analysis, Pig's ETL capability means it can work on unstructured data, cleaning it up and organizing it so that queries can be run against it.

slot A map or reduce computation unit on a node. Each active map or reduce task occupies one slot, which could be a map or a reduce slot. A TaskTracker has a configured number of slots available, and JobTracker allocates work to the TaskTracker with available slots nearest to the data.

Stack (Hadoop) Hadoop software layers; applications that interact directly with Hadoop.

- Data processing layer; encapsulates the MapReduce framework
- Data storage layer; the file system (HDFS)

Sqoop ETL tool to support transfer of data between Hadoop and structured data sources. A connection and transfer mechanism that moves data between Hadoop and relational databases.

task A mapper or reducer instance operating on a slice of data. Tasks are executed by the Hadoop TaskTracker, which assigns tasks to nodes with resources available for executing the task. Each active map or reduce task occupies one slot.

TaskAttempt An instance of a map or reduce task, which is identified by a task ID. The JobTracker may run a task on more than one node, either if it fails or to enable getting faster results from another node; this adds to the number of attempts.

TaskWaiting A task state of waiting to be launched.

YARN YARN is a resource manager that was created by separating the processing engine and resource management capabilities of MapReduce. It is an updated way of handling the delegation of resources for MapReduce jobs. It takes the place of the JobTracker and TaskTracker. YARN supports multiple processing models in addition to MapReduce. It is responsible for managing and monitoring workloads, maintaining a multi-tenant environment, implementing security controls, and managing high availability features of Hadoop.

INDEX

Symbols and Numerals

A

B

C

D

H

I

J

K

L

M

N

O

P

Q

R

S

T

U

V

W

X

Y

Z